2305

Sixth

D1394014

STRIKE

Peter Wilsher is fifty-seven, and has worked for the past twenty-five years with *The Sunday Times*, as Editor of Business News, Foreign Editor and now as Associate Editor, Special Projects. He wrote *The Pound in Your Pocket* and was co-author of *Exploding Cities*.

Donald Macintyre is thirty-eight. He has been Labour Editor of *The Sunday Times* since February 1983, and before that Labour Correspondent of *The Times* and the *Daily Express*, covering industrial relations for national newspapers throughout the past decade. Since the strike he has left *The Sunday Times* to take up a similar position on *The Times*. He is the author of *Talking About Trade Unions*.

Michael Jones is forty-eight. After a varied journalistic career as industrial writer, lobby correspondent and News Editor and Assistant Editor to *The Times Business News*, he has been Political Editor of *The Sunday Times* since early 1984.

STRIKE

Thatcher, Scargill and the Miners

Written and edited by Peter Wilsher, Donald
Macintyre and Michael Jones

With the Sunday Times Insight Team

ANDRE DEUTSCH

First published September 1985 by
André Deutsch Limited
105 Great Russell Street
London WC1B 3LJ

Published simultaneously in paperback by
Coronet Books Limited

Photoset by Rowland Phototypesetting Limited
Bury St Edmunds, Suffolk
Printed in Great Britain by
Ebenezer Baylis & Son
Worcester

ISBN 0 233 97825 9

Written and edited by Peter Wilsher, Donald Macintyre and Michael Jones.

Contributors:
Roger Ratcliffe, Sheffield, who covered the development of the strike in Nottinghamshire, South Yorkshire and the East Midlands.
George Rosie, Edinburgh, reporting on Scotland.
Chris Tighe, Newcastle, embracing Yorkshire and the North East.
James Tucker, Cardiff, following events in South Wales.
Brian Morris, Manchester, for Lancashire and the North West.
John Huxley, Industrial Editor, Business News.
Martin Kettle, Home Affairs Correspondent.

Researchers: Parin Jan Mohamed and Ros Franey.

Picture design and cover: David Gibbons.

CONTENTS

ILLUSTRATIONS

Top: The strike's first martyr. Yorkshire miner David Jones who died at Ollerton on 14 April 1984.
Bottom: Arthur Scargill emerges into an adoring crowd after conference on 19 April rejects a ballot. (Neville Payne)

The Alamo. The miners' own name for their picketing redoubt at Cortonwood. (Duncan Baxter)

Police charge in the battle of Orgreave, the South Yorkshire coke works which Scargill failed to close by mass picketing. (John Sturrock)

Lorry driver and TGWU docker square up during ports strike which opened up a second front in the government's confrontation with the miners. (Colin Davey)

NUM delegation joins the vote of overwhelming support for the union at the TUC in Brighton's conference centre in September. (Jeremy Nicholl)

Top Left: Ian MacGregor arrives at Edinburgh peace talks in September shielding his head from cameramen with a plastic bag. (Jim Gallaway)
Top Right: Roger Windsor and the Libyan connection. (Duncan Baxter)
Bottom: Dick Bryan (left) and Ken Cross, pit deputies at Ollerton colliery on the brink of what would have been their union's first ever national strike. (Duncan Baxter)

Police escort for miners returning to work at Whittle colliery. (Simon Wilson)

Top Left: Herbert Brewer, Derbyshire solicitor, the first receiver appointed by the high court to control NUM funds handed over within a week to insolvency expert Michael Arnold (right). (Press Association)

Bottom: Peter Walker, post-strike. (Sally Soames)

Sid Vincent, Lancashire area secretary, with companion Joan Hodkinson, discovered on his winter holiday in Tenerife ten months into the strike. (Derek Ive)

Devoted picket in Derbyshire audience in November, as support for the strike begins to crumble. (Steve Taylor)

Top: The taxi in which Cardiff cab driver David Wilkie was killed while bringing a working miner to Merthyr Vale colliery on 30 November 1984. (Howard Hill)
Bottom: David Wilkie. (Denis Stephens)

The men at Merthyr Vale colliery return to work. (Jeremy Nicholl)

Introduction

The great miners' strike of 1984–5 was one of the most significant events in Britain's postwar history. Although ostensibly about no more than the further slimming down of an industry which had already been in decline for over three decades it was, in fact, about much, much more.

Union power grew inexorably in the 1960s and 1970s and became strong enough to resist the will of elected governments, Tory and Labour. When Harold Wilson's first government tried to master it in 1969 the unions forced him to think again. When Edward Heath attempted to control it, first within a new legal framework and then with pay controls, he was rewarded with electoral defeat. When James Callaghan tried to make the unions a partner in running the country he was rewarded with a winter of discontent which led to his government going the way of Heath's. It was only a matter of time before another government faced the same challenge.

The fourth great struggle between union power and elected government, however, took on an added dimension because it matched a Marxist revolutionary, Arthur Scargill, against the apostle of market forces, Margaret Thatcher. Never before had the battle lines been so starkly drawn. Scargill believed his mass pickets were in the vanguard of the socialist revolution, Thatcher believed she had a parliamentary majority for the market economy. Scargill thought that the coal industry should be run largely for the benefit of his members, Thatcher that it should conform to the dictates of the marketplace. Scargill saw union power as the key to building a society fit for the working man, Thatcher saw union power as the single most important reason for Britain's postwar economic decline. Above all, Scargill thought that, although the government had just won a famous election victory, it could still be defeated by direct action. Thatcher, though she had gone out of her way to avoid a head-on clash with the unions in her first term, knew that the recent history of the country made some sort of confrontation inevitable.

From the start, *The Sunday Times* took a firm editorial line: for the sake of liberal democracy, economic recovery and the rolling back of union power, and for the sake of the sensible voices in the Labour party and the TUC, Scargill and his forces had to be defeated, and would be. It was a position from which we never wavered throughout this long, brutal dispute. Our views, however, were kept to where they belong in a quality newspaper: the editorial column. For us the miners' strike was above all a massive reporting and analysing task to give our readers an impartial and well-informed picture of what was really happening.

Our journalists acquitted themselves superbly. While other papers predicted power cuts by the late autumn of 1984 or reported breakaway unions in Nottinghamshire, *The Sunday Times* stuck to the facts. We reported accurately on the true coal stocks position. We revealed divisions in the National Coal Board as deep as those on the executive of the National Union of Mineworkers. We polled miners and discovered that, at one stage, there may indeed have been a majority for a strike if a ballot had been called. We exposed Scargill's Libyan connection in the scoop of the year, maybe even the decade. Indeed, our reports were accurate enough for Scargill, at one stage, to accuse our labour staff of bugging his executive (we hadn't).

This book is a product of that extensive reporting, and of exhaustive investigations carried out in the aftermath of the strike. It is the first complete account of the most important industrial dispute since the 1926 General Strike and, though future research is bound to reveal more as the strike fades into history, the basic elements of the story are here for all to read.

The book has not been written to grind any axes, justify any editorial position or to tell the tale from any particular angle. In classic Insight style it merely relates, dispassionately and impartially, the inside story of a cataclysmic battle whose outcome will affect this country for years to come. Under the painstaking guidance of senior editorial writer Peter Wilsher, the Insight team has done a superb job in producing a classic of contemporary history.

Andrew Neil, Editor, *The Sunday Times*, July 1985

Chapter 1

Countdown to Cortonwood

On Saturday, 3 December 1983, Arthur Scargill took a day out to travel to the tiny cathedral city of Wells, in Somerset. The first stage of the miners' campaign to halt pit closures, taking the form of a national ban of all overtime working, was already five weeks under way, and the forty-five-year-old NUM president was energetically crisscrossing the country to organise and plan for the larger struggles ahead. Somerset, in the normal way, would scarcely have figured in such preparations. The last of its modest coalmines had closed a decade before. But this was a special occasion. A hundred years previously, in the nearby village of Wookey, one of the legendary figures of twentieth-century trade unionism had been born. And although Arthur James Cook, as general secretary of the NUM's forerunner, the Miners' Federation of Great Britain, had led his members (then numbering almost 900,000, against today's dwindling 185,000) to defeat in the 1926 General Strike and subsequent seven-month lockout, a reverse which broke the pitmen's power for a generation, Scargill had always admired him as an heroic example. The Cook centenary celebration, held at the Blue School, Wells, with colliery band, free crèche and two-tier entrance fee (£2.50 waged, £1 unwaged), was a fitting occasion for rededication and resolve.

1

In many ways the two men were extraordinarily alike – fiery, charismatic radicals, just into their forties when they reached their top union jobs, capable of rousing audiences to hysteria and opponents to near-apoplexy. Both also presided over a bitter, damaging split in their members' ranks as deep divisions over policy smashed the unity that constituted their major strength. When Cook died, worn out and broken, in 1931, one obituarist wrote that there had never been a leader like him: 'never one so hated by the government, so obnoxious to the mine-owners, so much a thorn in the flesh of other general secretaries of unions; never one who . . . had so much unfeigned reverence and enthusiastic support from his fellow-miners'. The words, with the possible exception of 'reverence', would fit Scargill like a 'Coal Not Dole' tee-shirt. As Lord Shinwell, the veteran Labour politician who presided over the birth of the NCB, told an interviewer on his hundredth birthday in 1984: 'There is always an Arthur Scargill. In my day he was called Arthur Cook.'

On that centenary Saturday, however, it was the difference not the similarity which set off the most telling resonance. Cook, though loyal and tireless, to the point of wrecking his health, in support of his national executive's decisions, always saw the dangers inherent in blind, unwavering defiance of the rest of society. Scargill admits no such doubts. In his fifteen-minute tribute he struck all the expected notes – solidarity, justice of the cause, the inevitability of victory – and repeated some of Cook's own words, uttered in the bleak aftermath of 1926 as he watched his starving, beaten followers go back to longer hours, victimisation, lower pay and less bargaining power. 'No public man of our generation,' the older leader had written, 'has been attacked so bitterly and so repeatedly by politicians and public alike. What is the reason for this amazing unpopularity? What's wrong with Cook?' And then the older leader gave his own answer: 'I have decided to stand by the mass of the workers, knowing full well that the machine of the trade union movement and the labour party must destroy me, in order to serve capitalism. Very well, I shall be prepared to suffer even death in the cause of the workers.' It was heady stuff. But in the end, realism took over from rhetoric, as Cook in a later passage was forced to admit: 'We have lost ground . . . But we shall regain it in a very short time.'

Scargill, too, had seen much ground lost as Britain's coal market shrank during most of the postwar period, and he was determined to regain it. But in the light of later events, he might profitably have pondered on the warnings embedded in the A. J. Cook memorial pamphlet which was on sale at the rally. In particular there was Cook's anguished heartcry, uttered during the autumn of 1926 as he watched hungry, desperate men in their thousands join the drift back to work: 'I never believed that the miners could win on their own.' Equally relevant is his prophetic question, as his colleagues voted to reject yet another conciliation move (by the Church of England bishops, as it happens, just to underline further the 1926/1984 parallels): 'Is it leadership to sit still and drift, drift to disaster? That is not leadership.'

Some of those present at the Cook meetings would come to appreciate the full force of those warnings, even if their significance did not sink in at the time. Kim Howells, for instance, the articulate and far from moderate research officer for the South Wales NUM, who was there representing the region that had been Cook's main power base, later emerged as one of the most forthright critics of Scargill's intransigence and his counter-productive picketing tactics. Others remained convinced Scargill supporters to the end. They included Dennis Skinner, the militant leftwing MP for Bolsover in Derbyshire, who was several times suspended from attendance at the House of Commons for the un-parliamentary methods he chose to express that support.

But these, apart from Scargill himself, were relatively minor characters in the developing drama. The leading actors were otherwise engaged that weekend. Only Ian MacGregor, the seventy-year-old Scottish-American who had taken over the chairmanship of the National Coal Board just two months earlier, was actually addressing himself to the problems of the industry that had been put into his charge – and then merely to suggest, mildly, during a relaxed Saturday morning chat with industrial correspondents, that the miners might care to drop their overtime ban for a few weeks so as to earn some extra money for Christmas, before resuming their action in the New Year. It was hardly the attitude of a man bracing himself for the toughest conflict in Britain's long industrial history.

Mrs Margaret Thatcher's mind was on quite different matters as she prepared to fly to Athens for yet another angry tussle over Britain's contributions to Common Market finance. And although the energy secretary, Peter Walker, in his Worcester constituency, was attacking the Labour party leader, Neil Kinnock, as 'the toady of the big union bosses' for his failure to condemn an outbreak of violent mass-picketing – and Kinnock himself, at a national women's conference in London, was lambasting the government for not acting decisively 'in circumstances of industrial break-down' – the subject of their scorn was nothing to do with coal but the night-long pitched battle that had raged earlier that week round the beleaguered offices of a giveaway newspaper called the *Stockport Messenger*. Only the fact that several busloads of Scottish miners had joined the 4,000-strong army of print workers, London dockers and miscellaneous activists confronting the 1,500 police outside Eddie Shah's print works provided even a tenuous link with the countrywide explosions to come. The important point, though, was that even with the numerical odds so heavily against them, the Cheshire police won. The newspaper staffs got in to work and the delivery lorries ran, just as a large minority of unintimidated miners and an endless tide of unimpeded coal trucks and trains would keep the lights from flickering right through 1984 and into one of the coldest Januarys in the records of the Central Electricity Generating Board.

Coal is a very ancient industry – in Britain the more obvious outcrops were exploited in Roman times – but the period of its true greatness was more or less bounded by the reigns of Queen Victoria and Edward VII. In 1913, at the end of a century characterised by the advance of steam power, there were 3,000 working pits in Britain, which had built a world-wide empire on the strength of the growth, and the profits, they had helped to produce. Between them they delivered almost 300m. tonnes a year: anthracite to heat the homes and factory boilers, bunkering fuel to drive the ocean ships and continental railway trains, coking coal to make possible an international avalanche of iron and steel. A burgeoning export trade supplied more than 10 per cent of the entire world market at that time, and Cardiff, as the main shipping point, throbbed like the Gulf oil ports in the past couple of decades. In the great Edwardian boom years, 126,000 immigrants walked, cycled or rode to South Wales to meet the insatiable demand – not only, like the young Arthur Cook, from nearby England, but from Scotland, Ireland and all over Europe.

There are still Spanish Rows and Espagna Avenues in the Cynon Valley (not to mention a whole underground section called Italy *fach* at the last remaining mine in the Rhondda) to recall that heady time; and when the Great War ended the expectation was that the growth would simply start up again. It was in 1923 that employment in the British coalfields reached its all-time peak, at 1,250,000. But by then, though few recognised the turning point, the trade was already on the slide. Since then coal, at least in these islands, has entered into an uninterrupted cycle of decline.

In 1947, when the 958 largest surviving pits were taken into public ownership (another 400 tiny ones continued to operate privately under licence), over 90 per cent of the nation's primary energy requirements were still being dug out of the ground. But annual output had already dropped to 200m. tonnes, while manpower, though recently boosted by an urgent postwar recruiting drive, barely topped the 700,000 mark. Even that precarious dominance quickly came under multiple attack. To start with, coal could not cope with demand, even before any serious rivals appeared. The first Plan for Coal (the one to which Scargill constantly referred during the dispute was the fourth) was drawn up in 1950 and set a target of 240m. tonnes a year, to be realised through an investment of £520m. It was never met. The best

NCB year, 1955–6, produced 228m. tonnes, from all sources, and imports had to be rushed in, to the tune of 17m. tonnes. The plan was revised upwards, with a new forecast of 250m. tonnes by 1970, and a more than doubled investment commitment.

By now the competition was well set, and getting tougher by the year. Oil, largely from the Middle East, which had previously been used mainly for road transport, started to take off in 1957. Not only was it cheaper but also much more convenient and clean. British Rail rebuffed the nostalgia lobby and started to phase out steam in favour of diesel. Householders, even outside the smokeless zones, blocked up their grates, installed unsightly tanks in their gardens and switched to oil-fired central heating. Nuclear power made its first but steadily growing contribution to the electricity grid. As natural gas, pumped from the North Sea, began to flow through the nationwide pipe network in the late 1960s, another massive group of coal customers, the municipal and state-operated gasworks, closed down in scores.

In 1969, for the last time, coal still outstripped all other sources combined to provide 50.4 per cent of the nation's primary fuel intake. The 1967 white paper on fuel policy recognised reality to some extent and scaled back the 1970 coal forecast to 152m. tonnes, which was just about in line with current consumption forecasts. But the slither was far from over. Oil beat coal into clear second place in 1971, and by 1974, the year of the three-day week, Edward Heath's electoral defeat and the first impact of the Yom Kippur oil-price increases, coal's share of the total British fuel market had dropped to barely one-third.

The National Union of Mineworkers was then thirty years old. Its wartime birth, in 1944, replacing the old, loose federation of county associations which had been a source of weakness, rivalry and disunity for the best part of a century, realised one of the miners' longest-standing aspirations. When the second soon followed, with the passing of the 1946 Coal Nationalisation Act, the combination created a general atmosphere of euphoria among both officials and men. Arthur Horner, the NUM's first general secretary, had expressed some reservations on both counts – he thought the constitution that the union finally agreed for itself had 'emasculated' its strength by allowing too much autonomy to the individual areas (including a chastened Nottingham, readmitted after eleven years in the wilderness, following the agonies of 1926); and as a good Communist he doubted the new Board's real ability, or indeed willingness, to resist the 'pervasive erosion' of market forces. But even he supported a policy of full cooperation in order that the Labour party's great nationalisation experiment should be given the maximum chance to succeed.

The honeymoon lasted just about ten years. In the general climate of postwar optimism some 150 of the older, smaller pits were eliminated without protest, and virtually without loss of manpower. But then harsher realities intervened. As coal's share of energy demand started its precipitate fall, and simultaneously the first effects of large-scale underground mechanisation made themselves felt, mines began to shut down at a rate approaching one a week – 264 closed between 1957 and 1963, and many were very far from antique. Rothes, a showplace colliery in Fife, opened five years earlier by the Queen herself and planned to employ 2,500 men and raise 5,000 tonnes a day, was abandoned forever in 1962 before even reaching its full production target; and the advent of a new Labour government in 1964 barely hindered the scythe. By 1970, when Edward Heath led the Conservatives once again back to power, the number of active mines had dropped below 300 – a two-thirds shrinkage in less than twenty-five years. Meanwhile working conditions below ground had dramatically changed. The powered hydraulic roof support, the rotary cutter and the armoured conveyor belt came in, as one commentator said, 'like an avalanche'. Where, as recently as 1955, only 9.2 per cent of production had been power-loaded, by the end of the 1960s the figure had already reached 92.2 per cent.

The beginnings of the transformation of the NUM, from a predominantly moderate and compliant partner in this process to the spearhead of leftwing opposition it has become under the presidency of Arthur Scargill, can be dated most plausibly to 1968, the year of the campaign to elect Lawrence Daly as general secretary to succeed the veteran Will Paynter. Both Paynter and his own predecessor, Arthur Horner, had been committed Welsh Communists, with a background in the dark depression years; but they saw their overriding responsibility as loyally serving a succession of rightwing presidents and national executives whose basic policy had always been to go along with such powerful NCB chairmen as Lord Robens (majestically making his transition from Labour Cabinet minister to corporate tycoon) and Sir James Bowman (who had actually been drafted to the job from the vice-presidency of the union). Up to the moment of Paynter's retirement (he finally died during 1984) the contraction of the industry had proceeded with relative smoothness. There were plenty of alternative jobs – 346,000 miners left voluntarily in the eight years prior to 1968 – and there was plenty of work, too, for those who chose to stay. The rich central coalfields in Yorkshire, Nottingham and the Midlands saw an influx of displaced Scots, Welshmen, Lancastrians and North-Easterners on a scale unequalled since the late Victorian growth years, and the character (and accent) of whole villages and districts were transformed by the newcomers. But gradually, as economic horizons darkened and men who had often uprooted their families two or three times already became reluctant to face further change, a new spirit of resistance stirred.

The year before, 1967, had seen the number of forced redundancies rocket, to 12,900 – more than six times the highest previous annual figure – as the Board realised that it could no longer absorb all the men displaced by closures who still wanted to stay in mining. As part of his election campaign, Daly (a former Scottish communist, who had quit the party in 1956 over the Soviet invasion of Hungary) wrote a scorching pamphlet called *The Miners and the Nation*. This openly advocated industrial action to 'secure a change in fuel policy', to 'protect our mining communities from the worst effects of redundancy', and to 'win conditions and rewards that would hold young, skillful and intelligent men in our modern coal industry'. After years of relative peace and quiescence in the coalfields (almost all stoppages had been concerned with purely local disputes) the warning was largely ignored in the higher reaches of government ant the NCB. But it was vigorously discussed among the rank–and–file. Many new groups sprang up, looking for ways to harry the official leadership, which was increasingly seen as passive and supine. One of the most active was the Barnsley Miners' Forum, set up by one Arthur Scargill, a twenty-nine-year-old face worker, hitherto scarcely known outside his own Woolley Colliery just north of the ancient Yorkshire mining town. The Forum, meeting every Friday in the local Co-op Hall, attracted hundreds of young miners and pit-engineers to hear Daly, Mick McGahey, Jack Dunn from Kent, Emlyn Williams from South Wales, and other noted activists, outlining their strategy for a more aggressive future. In the run-off Daly took 52.3 per cent of the national vote, comfortably beating his only opponent, the pragmatically cautious Joe Gormley from Lancashire. And although Gormley was far from a write-off – he soon became national president and strongly influenced NUM policy throughout the 1970s – there was little question that the militants had made an important advance.

The first manifestation of the new spirit came in 1969. An improvement in surface workers' hours had been agreed union policy for years but nothing ever seemed to happen. Starting in South Wales, where there had been particular impatience over the issue, a brushfire trail of unofficial strikes spread across the country. For a fortnight 130,000 miners at 140 pits defied their leaders (Sam Bullough, the Yorkshire area chairman and national vice-president, was unceremoniously voted out of the chair when he refused to accept an abrasive Scargill motion) and although the organisation was chaotic and the immediate results meagre, it was a significant rehearsal. Young miners, with no postwar experience of serious industrial action, found not only that there were ways

9

to exert pressure in high places, but that they could bulldoze, and if necessary bypass, their own elected executives. In 1972, the whole industry agreed to put these discoveries to the test.

Although Gormley's election to the presidency in 1971 represented a small setback for the militant left – their candidate, Mick McGahey, had lost by 92,883 votes to 117,663 – their policies, and a growing truculence in pursuing them, had taken firm hold. When the time came to negotiate the annual pay claim, the stage was set for confrontation. The pitmen, with a sense of grievance fuelled by more closures and a sharply diminished ranking in the national pay league (from first to seventeenth, their statisticians reckoned, over the two-and-a-half postwar decades) were spoiling for a fight. The NCB negotiators were palpably insensitive to this change of mood; and the Heath government, which had been in office then for two years, was committed to both a far-reaching programme of trade union law reform and to an incomes policy which sought to impose an 8 per cent limit on all pay awards. The NUM, briskly ignoring this, was looking for 17 per cent for face-workers, 47 per cent elsewhere underground, and 44 per cent on the surface. Late in November a poll produced a 58.8 per cent majority in favour of strike action, and after some further abortive negotiations notice was given that a national withdrawal of labour – the first since 1926 – would take place on 9 January 1972.

This was the dispute that first projected Scargill to general recognition, although he was not even a full-time union official at the time. Born on 11 January 1938, the only son of Harold and Alice Scargill, in the pit village of Worsborough, south of Barnsley, he had been brought up in the mainstream of leftwing trade unionism, coal-mining version. His father had worked in the industry all his life, always active in his Federation, and later NUM branch, and a convinced and undeviating member of the Communist party. But his own early political experience was less clearcut. He went to work, aged fifteen, at Woolley, several miles from his home, on the grounds that it was much bigger than the village pit in Worsborough and offered more scope for advancement. He worked on the surface there for two-and-a-half years before being promoted underground as a pit-pony driver. At sixteen he tried to join the Barnsley Labour party, which showed no interest, and in frustration wrote an angry letter to the *Daily Worker*, the predecessor of today's *Morning Star*, which has supported him so wholeheartedly in more recent times. Within twenty-four hours a Communist party organiser was round to his home with an application form, and on 11 March 1955, the minutes of the Barnsley Young Communist League record that they collectively visited Billy Smart's Circus – all nine of them at that time – and acquired two new members, including the youthful Scargill. His rise in the League was rapid – branch secretary within months, speaking on the same platform as the CP general secretary, the veteran Harry Pollitt, national youth committee member at the 1956 party congress, and the next year off for the first of many visits to Moscow (where he met the Soviet leaders Kruschev and Bulganin) for the World Youth Festival. But although it was his fellow-pitmen at Woolley who voted him on to that trip, he was having an uphill struggle to achieve recognition in his own union. He was even expelled once from his branch, when he flouted his seniors and organised other young miners to strike over inadequate training, and it took the personal intervention of the Yorkshire area president to get him reinstated. In 1960, just before he stood, and comprehensively lost, as Communist candidate for the Worsborough urban district council (his only known attempt to win a non-union post), he even organised a strike against his own branch officials, in an attempt to get them to change the day of their regular weekly meeting. He won his point, and soon after was elected himself to the branch committee. Tentatively, and against much opposition, he was on his way.

That year he met his future wife, Anne, then the eighteen-year-old daughter of another local miners' union official. He taught her to drive, they had their first date at a Young Communist League debate, and they married in September 1961. By then he was attending a part-time day release course at Leeds University, arranged so that selected young miners could study social history and industrial relations. During his three years on that course he first came into contact with Professor Vic Allen (author of many radical works, including *The Militancy of British Miners*) who has ever since been one of his main political and intellectual mentors. In 1962 or 1963, for reasons and in circumstances that have never become wholly clear (Scargill himself has given widely varying accounts) he finally left the Young Communists. Ever since he has vehemently insisted that he is not and never has been an actual card-carrying member of the Communist party – even suing successfully one or two people who have suggested otherwise. After that, his sense of both political and career direction appears to have briefly faltered – he first joined the Co-operative Party then switched to Labour and on one or two occasions thought seriously both of leaving mining altogether and of seeking a management job with the Coal Board. But by 1972 his doubts had settled and he was clearly a rising star, even though his reputation barely extended beyond Barnsley and the more percipient talent-spotters in the NUM hierarchy. That was now to change; and the events which projected Scargill to national notoriety that year were still exercising a powerful, and perhaps even crucial influence during the climactic conflicts of 1984–5.

The 1972 coal strike lasted seven weeks and won the miners more than two-thirds of their massive pay demand. By 15 February, when the government's hastily-convened Court of Enquiry under Lord Wilberforce produced its rush report, electricity was barely trickling through to the nation's factories and offices, twelve major generating stations were shut down. 1.4m workers were idle and ministers were talking about calling in the troops to avoid a total industrial shutdown, expected within a fortnight. It was a comprehensive defeat for the government, imposed by two main means – the wholesale deployment of 'flying pickets' and a systematic, well-planned strangulation of the nation's power supplies. And although every NUM area, and almost the whole of the union's 200,000-strong membership took part, it was the previously unknown Scargill, dramatically identifying himself with both these winning strategies, who reaped most of the publicity rewards. First, as the man who arranged and executed the effective blacking-out of East Anglia, and then as the 'Hero of Saltley Gate', the vast West Midlands gas works which 1,000 police tried for a week to keep open, only to fail when 12,000 assorted trade union demonstrators converged on the plant, he was rarely off the television screens; and he has been a prime focus of media attention ever since.

In the longer run he may well have been too successful for his own good. There is evidence that both the police and the Central Electricity Generating Board, in their different ways, determined that they would never let themselves be made fools of on that scale again. The contingency plans sketched out in the aftermath of those 1972 débâcles played a large part in containing the pickets and keeping the lights burning during the replay twelve years later. But for the moment, Scargill was on his way. Later that year he won, almost unopposed, the important post of Compensation Agent for the Yorkshire NUM; shortly afterwards, thanks to the first of a series of opportune retirements, he inherited a place on the union's national executive. In 1973, following a brilliant forensic performance at the enquiry into the Lofthouse colliery disaster, he won hands down the succession to the Yorkshire presidency, polling more than his two opponents combined. When the NUM annual conference came round that autumn, marked by growing pressure for another very substantial wage claim, the combination of Communists like McGahey and Labour radicals like Scargill brought the left, for the first time in the union's history, to within touching distance of an absolute majority – something they finally achieved, with even more far-reaching consequences, soon after Scargill won the national presidency for himself in 1981.

Even though Gormley retained nominal control his room for manoeuvre was now tightly constrained. An overtime ban, called in support of the pay claim, hardened into full-scale strike action – against the president's advice – in February 1974. That was just as the Middle East oil powers started to curtail supplies and push up prices in the wake of the recent Arab–Israeli war. The Prime Minister, Edward Heath, put the country on a three-day week, called a general election on the emotive question 'who governs Britain?', and went down to narrow defeat, allowing a minority Labour administration to resume office. Almost their first action, after settling with the miners on extremely favourable terms, was to publish, with tripartite agreement from the NCB, the NUM and the Department of Energy, the glowingly ambitious 1974 Plan for Coal, which has ever since remained Scargill's personal bible and ark of the covenant. Unhappily, it has turned out, in almost every economic, industrial and political respect, an unattainable dream. And the 'successes' of 1974, with the bitter resentment they engendered at every level of the Conservative party, could hardly fail to boomerang once the electoral roundabout made its next full turn. The higher Scargill rose during the 1970s, the more aggressive his pronouncements on the obscenity of capitalism and the inevitability of the class war, the firmer the hold established by the left within the NUM, and the more clearly the miners emerged as the shock-troops of an increasingly debilitated trade union movement, the more inescapably they identified themselves as the target for an ultimate showdown. In 1979, when Margaret Thatcher moved into No. 10 Downing Street, the battle lines were already broadly drawn.

At the end of their study of the 1974 strike and its political consequences (*The Fall of Heath*, 1976), Stephen Fay and Hugo Young concluded: 'Neither Gormley, nor McGahey, nor the miners beat Heath. Ted Heath beat himself.' That was not the way those apocalyptic events were incorporated into Tory thinking, particularly among the party's present leaders. To Sir Geoffrey Howe and Lord Whitelaw, both members of the inner group formed to deal with the emergency (as it was officially designated, in contrast to 1984, within hours of the miners even declaring an overtime ban), to Margaret Thatcher, Peter Walker and Sir Keith Joseph, all members of the Heath Cabinet, and to Patrick Jenkin, brought in as energy minister just in time to advise the nation to clean its teeth in the dark, the episode constituted a flagrant abuse of industrial power. When a second general election, that same autumn, confirmed Heath's defeat and gave Labour a slender but still absolute majority, the party's tougher-minded strategists embarked on a far-reaching re-appraisal of the policies that had so comprehensively failed. This came to embrace elements as diverse as the financial framework of the state industries, the enforcement of public order and a much stricter limitation of welfare benefits for anyone who chose to go on strike. Many of these explorations were fully justified in their own right: nationalised industry finances have long been in a parlous mess, and street violence, as seen in the 1981 urban riots, can extend far beyond picket lines. But all these topics were also linked to the prime objective of ensuring that the extra-parliamentary flouting of government decisions by the deployment of union muscle could never happen again.

The first soundings were not encouraging. Soon after Mrs Thatcher took over the Tory leadership in February 1975, she invited Lord Carrington, who as Heath's energy secretary had been in the thick of the battle, to identify the key lessons that needed to be learned. He spent almost eighteen months holding highly confidential hearings, mainly with senior businessmen and civil servants, and at the end of 1977 delivered a daunting document. Its main message, as revealed when it finally leaked out in the spring of 1978, was that strong unions, with command over sophisticated new technologies, were now virtually unassailable by the old means of 'sending in the troops' and that there had therefore been an irrevocable shift in the balance of shop floor forces. This applied particularly to the fuel and power sector, where groups like the miners and the electricity workers now had ample ability to throttle the political and economic life of the country.

The Carrington verdict, with its undertones of appeasement and compromise, was not accepted as the last word. Even while its investigations were proceeding, a parallel inquiry under the rightwing MP Nicholas Ridley (now minister of transport) was taking a hard look at the nationalised industries; and this, though concerned with much of the same subject matter, was reaching toward some very different conclusions. Most of these would have been either meaningless or unattainable if British trade unions did indeed possess the effective veto that Carrington claimed over any serious proposals for radical change.

Basically Ridley sought to cut the state corporations free from the ever more costly safety harness of subsidies and Treasury subventions they enjoyed and force them to stand on their own feet. This would be done in the first instance by setting 'totally inflexible' targets for the return required on the billions of pounds worth of capital employed, and firmly replacing those managers who could not stand the heat when the policy led, inevitably, to large-scale layoffs and the closure of uneconomic plants. The government, in its turn, would stand clear of any direct involvement in the control of prices and wages in these industries, and gradually taper off its commitment to finance their investment programmes – from 100 per cent in the first year down to maybe 50 per cent in the sixth, and self-support by the start of the second decade. Management should be better paid, more highly motivated and freed from ministerial involvement in day-to-day affairs. Main boards should be stripped down to mainly supervisory functions with predominantly part-time membership, while executives redirected their energies to running the smaller, leaner, profit-centred companies into which these monolithic structures should be progressively split (a pattern Ridley then preferred, in most cases, to outright privatisation). Subsidies would only be acceptable when ministers were prepared to cost them out and argue persuasively with a sceptical Treasury on behalf of the 'uneconomic activities' they sought to preserve from the rigours of the competitive market.

Ridley's analysis, which then went off for further refinement by the powerful economic reconstruction group set up under Howe and Joseph, did not shirk the opposition which such proposals could hardly fail to ignite. Industries, he argued, fell into three categories, classified in ascending order of trouble they might cause. Buses, air transport, education, steel, ports and telephones would be the easiest to handle; railways, docks, coal and garbage collection fell into an intermediate category; and water, sewers, gas, electricity and the health service had to be recognised as areas where any government would provoke trouble at its peril.

Following up on this, Ridley and his co-authors then added an appendix, suggesting ways to counter any political threat that might be conjured up by 'enemies of the next Tory government' in response to an attempt to implement these or similar ideas. Many miners' pickets in 1984 were reported to be carrying dog-eared cuttings from *The Economist* of 27 May 1978, in which this annex was summarised. In the light of later events, it is worth quoting the five-part Ridley strategy at some length.

Before any major challenge had to be faced, either over a wage claim or a prospect of large redundancies – especially when one of the 'vulnerable industries' was affected, and there was a likelihood of support from 'the full force of communist disrupters' – the following steps should be put in train:

● Return on capital figures should be rigged so that an above-average wage claim could be paid to the 'vulnerable' industries.

● The eventual battle should be on ground chosen by the Tories, in a field they thought could be won (Ridley at that time suggested railways, British Leyland, the civil service or steel).

● Every precaution should be taken against a challenge in electricity or gas. Anyway, redundancies in these industries were unlikely to be required. The group believed that the most likely battleground would be the coal industry. They wanted a Thatcher government to: (a) build up maximum coal stocks, particularly at the power stations; (b) make contingency plans for the import of coal; (c) encourage the recruitment of non-union lorry drivers by haulage companies to help move coal where necessary; (d) introduce dual coal/oil firing at all power stations as quickly as possible.

● The group believed that the greatest deterrent to any strike would be 'to cut off the money supply to the strikers, and make the union finance them'. Strikers in

17

nationalised industries should not be treated differently from strikers in other industries.

● There should be a large, mobile squad of police equipped and prepared to uphold the law against violent picketing. 'Good non-union drivers' should be recruited to cross picket lines with police protection.

Whether or not 'the eventual battle' took place on ground deliberately chosen and prepared by Mrs Thatcher's government is still a matter of controversy, and we shall examine the evidence at a later stage. But undoubtedly the Ridley team was expressing a robust and reasoned confidence that such a conflict, whatever the conventional wisdom, could be won; and it gave an eerily prescient sketch of the tactics that might be, and to a large extent actually were, employed. The notice was duly filed away in various trade union archives, and even before its publication clear-sighted realists like Lawrence Daly took care to remind the miners that they might not have things all their own way for ever (at the 1976 annual conference, for example, he was pleading with delegates to moderate their increasingly bitter criticism of Labour ministers on the grounds that the NUM 'must avoid a situation in which the people we will be facing across the negotiating table are the Michael Heseltines of the Conservative party'). Few of those in a position to act, though, took Ridley really seriously, and hardly any preparations were made, either then or later, to counter his clearly stated warnings.

The events of 1974 left the miners doubly euphoric: conscious of their new, post-OPEC place in the sun and well aware of their enhanced industrial power. Convinced Tories like Sir Keith Joseph were admitting, publicly, that they had their hands 'on the nation's jugular vein', and initially, at any rate, there was wide recognition of their election-winning role. The Lord Mayor's Show in London that year featured a float full of coal, piled as high as a double-decker bus, escorted by burly colliers. On 5 March, five days after the poll, Michael Foot, secretary for employment, authorised the NCB to negotiate a wage settlement 'unfettered by previous government dictates' and guaranteed that the Treasury would foot any bill necessary to purchase an immediate return to work. Within weeks the union, the Board and the department of energy were cooperating on an urgent tripartite review of the future, and by July, on the eve of the NUM conference, every delegate received a copy of *The Coal Industry Examination: Interim Report* which embodied, in all essentials, what has become Arthur Scargill's equivalent of Holy Writ, the famous 1974 Plan for Coal.

In broad terms, this committed the government to a massive programme of investment in new and existing pits. The stated objectives included the underpinning of long-term job security, financing better disability payments and pensions, and the development of new markets, both for their own sake and to reduce dependence on the industry's one remaining big customer, the Central Electricity Generating Board. The document, rushed out at high speed to placate and reassure the miners, received a warm welcome, but disappointment soon set in. The fourfold rise in oil prices may have given coal a new lease of life; but the resulting world recession, plus a keen new interest in energy-saving, made this hard to translate into extra sales and enhanced pay-packets. After two years of 'maximum restraint' the miners' political loyalties quickly frayed. When Harold Wilson, then Prime Minister, appealed for patience and support of his 'social contract', Scargill, as Yorkshire president, responded by demanding £100 a week for face-workers and scornfully attacked 'the social con-trick'.

Gormley continued to advocate moderation, and the NUM played a very restrained part during the 'winter of discontent', 1978–9, which returned Labour once more – and perhaps permanently – to the electoral wilderness. But the increasingly disenchanted miners were withdrawing their backing in other, more immediate ways. At the Ashfield by-election in 1977, where pitmen made up a substantial slice of the local vote, Labour lost a previously rock-safe seat to the Tories. More and more NUM members opted out of paying the political levy, the major source of Labour party funds. The Plan for Coal forecasts (made, as one authority, Professor Derek Spooner, puts it, 'in the hysterical climate' of

1974) had already been sharply pruned. Britain's total energy requirements, which were 'bound to increase' according to the earlier version, had in fact dropped by nearly 10 per cent in just three years (and indeed have not yet fully recovered). The confident projections that coal sales would top 150 million tonnes by 1985 had been briskly lopped to 135 million tonnes when the new energy secretary, Tony Benn, published his 1977 revision *Coal for the Future*.

The general mood of discontent triggered one particularly important development within the NUM itself. Traditionally coalmining wages had been calculated on a piecework basis, with the pay for particular tasks and 'stints' being the subject of intense local bargaining and much variation. This was a key factor in preserving the fierce regional autonomy that characterised the old prewar Federation, and has to a large extent been carried over into the quasi-independent area rulebooks of today. In 1966, however, the advent of widespread mechanisation and the resultant changes in work patterns had brought, via the National Power Loading Agreement, a standard wage structure throughout the industry, which gave it a unity and a singleness of interest that it had never previously enjoyed. This unity had been one of the prime objectives, never realised in their day, of the earlier miners' leaders, and its achievement helped to ensure the resounding victories of 1972 and 1974.

But in 1978 the nationwide cohesion broke down once more. Under the tight forms of incomes policy forced on Wilson and his successor, James Callaghan, by inflation and the weakness of sterling, 'productivity agreements' were almost the only way for a group of workers to win extra pay rewards. From the coalfields, particularly the high-profit areas like Nottinghamshire, came a swelling demand for the reintroduction of 'incentive payments', which the NCB was happy to encourage for reasons of its own. Seeing the dangers, the more militant members of the NUM executive, with Scargill as a particularly vehement voice, fought hard to discourage this divisive move. In December 1977, when there was a nationwide pithead ballot on the issue, a majority of 110,634 to 87,901 against the change seemed to indicate that they had won. The victory was short-lived, though. The national decision, properly sought and achieved in just the way that Scargill and the executive were so strongly criticised for refusing to allow in 1984, was swiftly overturned in a series of local insurrections. In January 1978, as area vote followed area vote, the men indicated, pretty unequivocally, that for them the choice was money first and unity a poor, rather theoretical, second. It was to prove a critical decision when 1984 came round.

For the rest of 1978, however, the decision brought a measure of tranquillity to the industry, as the men strove to earn the new, often enticing bonuses now available. A general election was clearly imminent, and by early 1979, when it was actually called, the miners had agreed to close ranks in a determination not to make life more difficult than necessary for the party which they still saw, despite its backslidings and failures, as the best support for their cause. Mrs Thatcher, as widely noted at the time, had recently come out in open condemnation of union power. 'Some fear flying pickets more than they fear the law,' she told the Bow Group in April 1978, and the miners, who had pioneered and perfected that technique, were clearly in her sights. When the May votes were counted, sixteen of the eighteen candidates sponsored by the NUM were safely returned. But as Joe Gormley said tartly in his national executive report that summer: 'this pattern was not followed in the rest of the country, and it resulted in the return of a Conservative government.'

Mrs Thatcher's final ascent to supreme office began with a small joke. At the launch of her election manifesto on 11 April 1979 she was asked: 'Do you think you have enough policemen, soldiers, whatever it takes, to have a confrontation with extremists?' To general laughter led by her deputy, William Whitelaw, she replied: 'I don't think we are quite on the same wavelength.' But almost her first action three weeks later, when she moved into No. 10, Downing St, was to give Whitelaw, as home secretary, responsibility

21

for the Civil Contingencies Unit, whose sole task is to foresee and prepare for such confrontations. Known throughout Whitehall as 'Cuckoo' (from its initials), this is the most recent in a long line of shadowy organisations set up, usually within the framework of the Cabinet Office, to handle those domestic problems, like a stoppage in one or more of the essential industries, which have the potential to escalate into a national emergency.

The current version was formed by Edward Heath after his first, 1972, encounter with the miners (its earliest job, that same August, was to defuse a dock strike that was threatening widespread food shortages). Its head, from April 1979 to 1982, was Robert Wade-Gery, at present British high commissioner in New Delhi, and in the autumn of 1979, when the Cabinet first pondered the possibility of another major coal strike, he was asked to update the relevant CCU files. News of the government's concern surfaced publicly in October, when a Cabinet memo was leaked, intimating that 'a nuclear programme would have the advantage of removing a substantial portion of electricity production from the dangers of industrial action by coalminers or transport workers'. The decision to site a large new light-water reactor at Sizewell, on the Suffolk coast, followed within a year; and many of the dispositions that determined the outcome in 1984–5 were probably initiated around that time.

For the miners themselves, though, the early signals were ambiguous. A 'special case' pay rise, amounting to a substantial 20 per cent, was offered by the National Coal Board in November 1979, despite ministerial objections that it was too high, and reluctantly accepted by the NUM after the executive failed to win enough votes to support rejection and a strike. But 1980, which found even moderates like the chancellor, Sir Geoffrey Howe, advocating measures to 'stop the militants running wild', brought a number of important policy moves. There was the new Employment Act, introduced by James Prior, which stripped all legal immunity from pickets except those engaged at their own place of work (or at most with their employers' 'first supplier or first customer'); the social security rules were amended so that any claimant on strike was 'deemed' to be receiving support from his union, even when no actual payment was available, so that the overall level of benefit would be sharply reduced; and a revised Coal Industry Act laid down that the NCB must break even, without any operating subsidy, by at latest the financial year 1983–4. It was clear to all concerned that this last could never be achieved merely by abandoning those pits that were unsafe or physically exhausted: the programme would have to start looking hard, for the first time since the drastic rundown of the 1960s, at the realities of 'economic performance'.

Scargill's response, after a round of denunciatory speeches, was to call for a ballot among his 66,000 Yorkshire members, on the resolution: 'Are you in favour of giving the NUM Yorkshire Area authority to take various forms of industrial action (including strike action, if necessary) to stop the closure of any pit, unless on the grounds of exhaustion?' The result, declared in January 1981, was a resounding 86 per cent approval. Little noticed at the time, except by the union archivists, it was a decision with a very long fuse: its exact force and relevance became a prime legal issue three years later during the tumultuous court arguments that then beset and largely hamstrung the NUM. Both the national and Yorkshire executives claimed it as an open mandate for future action; those opposed argued that it referred purely to the threatened closure of one colliery, Orgreave, and effectively lapsed when that threat was withdrawn. Various courts are still wrestling over which side is in the right.

In 1981, however, the issue was swiftly submerged by more immediate events. Within days the NCB chairman, Sir Derek Ezra, called in Joe Gormley and his executive to outline his plans for responding to the government's recent imposition of strict cash limits on state industry spending, including his own. Provokingly he declined to discuss how these would affect the future of any particular collieries, saying that the detailed announcements would have to come from the areas concerned. The meeting left the miners' leaders angrily (and as it turned out exaggeratedly) convinced that he was talking about the elimination of at least thirty pits and 30,000 jobs.

23

Strike

In a then unprecedented display of unity, militants and moderates unanimously agreed on an ultimatum to Mrs Thatcher: either bail out the coal industry within seven days and shelve the shutdown proposals; or face the near certainty of a solid, ballot-backed, national strike.

Many areas did not bother to wait. Hundreds of men walked off the job in Durham, Yorkshire and South Wales, ignoring all Gormley's impassioned warnings that such precipitate action might be putting themselves and the union at risk. In sharp contrast to 1984, there were immediate, unsolicited pledges of massive support, from the seamen, from the transport workers, and most notably from Bill Sirs of the steelworkers and Sid Weighell of the railwaymen, who both said they could not rule out the possibility of a general strike unless the Cabinet quickly forced the Board to back down. Before the seven-day countdown expired, Ezra and Gormley were locked in talks with David Howell, the then energy secretary, to negotiate the government's surrender. The miners' president emerged to announce that 'a hell of a lot' of money had been made available to the industry, and that strike action could be safely abandoned. Not all the participants agreed; in several districts men said they would only go back with 'copper-bottomed guarantees', and Scargill himself, who at one point was jeeringly heckled for his lack of activity, voted against the executive and tried to keep Yorkshire out. But it was already over. John Biffen, a senior minister, went on television to admit that he and his colleagues had given in to 'industrial muscle' and that all the threatened mines had been reprieved.

It remains unclear to this day who was really responsible for the débâcle. One intriguing theory is that Ezra, knowing that the government was still unprepared to face a major dispute, unilaterally triggered the confrontation in order to 'bounce' the Treasury and the industry department into releasing additional funding to support the Board's massive investment plans. But whatever the mechanics and the motives, many of the miners' leaders even at the time were sure that the inevitable showdown had only been postponed. Scargill told *Marxism Today* that he doubted whether the

24

occasion could qualify as 'a total victory'; and Mick McGahey, the NUM vice-president, more tersely described the Downing Street response as 'not so much a U-turn, more a body-swerve'.

Gormley's first idea of 'a hell of a lot of money' had been £500 million in additional subsidies; in the end, though, the miners reluctantly accepted – as a 'first instalment' – a rather smaller placatory package. This included £50 million worth of grants for industrialists willing to convert factories and plant back to coal, and a jump of up to £10,000 (making a total of nearly £36,000) in the compensation offered to pit-workers taking early retirement. But the main item was a £200 million cash injection. This, as Howell explained to the Commons, essentially covered the cost of withdrawing the closure programme (which had actually been for twenty-three pits and 13,000 jobs) and compensating those customers who had gone abroad in search of cheap coal and were now, as part of the truce arrangements, forbidden to bring it in. This particularly affected the Central Electricity Generating Board, which had signed a large, irrevocable contract with Australia, and was now forced to let the deliveries pile up in Rotterdam, ultimately to the tune of some 3m. tonnes. That deal cost the taxpayers about £30 million a year, and persuaded at least one senior British manager that coal had finally succumbed to 'the finances of the madhouse'.

The second instalment never really materialised in monetary terms, and Gormley, who that summer had announced his intention to retire the following spring, did not press for payment. Instead Mrs Thatcher announced a major government reshuffle. In the course of this Howell found himself demoted to junior minister for transport, and the energy portfolio, with its attendant seat in the Cabinet, went to the monetarist, former financial journalist and now chancellor of the exchequer, Nigel Lawson, the man who later said that, from the Treasury's point of view, whatever it cost to resist the miners was an excellent investment.

During his two years on the job, coal appeared to be almost the least of Lawson's worries. Engaged as he was in furious rows over the privatisation of state assets like Britoil,

British Nuclear Fuels and the Wytch Farm gas field, Hansard records few significant exchanges on the NCB and its affairs. But those that can be found are all significant, and there is little doubt among informed Conservatives that many of the key weapons available to Peter Walker in the 1984–5 affray – particularly the leeway to guarantee that the country would suffer no power cuts – were those that Lawson had forged. He strongly approved the tactics outlined in the Ridley analysis, and he systematically set about assembling the means to make them work.

The first important hint of what was happening came in July 1982. Gormley, by deliberately delaying his departure until after Mick McGahey, long his obvious successor, reached fifty-five and was therefore no longer constitutionally able to stand, had effectively ensured that Scargill would step into his shoes; and the Yorkshire leader, effortlessly outflanking a trio of rather lack-lustre 'moderates', duly sailed through on 8 December 1981, with a convincing 70.3 per cent of the total vote. He could hardly be described as all-powerful – he suffered the first of several rebuffs, even before taking office, when a national ballot rejected his call for strike action over a 23 per cent pay claim – but equally he was quite clearly the miners' firm choice. Six months later, when Lawson was urged in the Commons 'to put it to Mr Scargill that there was no point in producing coal merely to stockpile it', he was cheerfully able to decline, on the grounds that the new NUM president was on holiday in Cuba and not expected back for several weeks. But he did let drop, without elaboration or comment, the information that the CEGB was currently holding reserves of 22 million tonnes at its various generating stations, and that the NCB had as much again at the pitheads. When one fire-eating backbencher urged an even larger build-up 'in case threats from Mr Scargill should regrettably materialise', the energy secretary loftily announced that that was a matter for the two boards. But he was sure they were aware of 'the factor mentioned'.

In fact the NCB was being openly encouraged to over-produce at that time. Managers, whose performance is still (subject to any post-strike reforms) rated not on profit but on their ability to meet and exceed volume targets, were paying both hefty overtime and large production bonuses to fill the overflowing pityards – just as the NUM had short-sightedly insisted they should, in the negotiations that ended the 1981 struggles – and the CEGB was asking, and getting, a premium to make even more storage space available. By February 1983, that phase in the preparations was essentially complete, with over 50 million tonnes, or half a year's output, stacked up, if needed, to keep the home fires burning. Now Lawson was ready to set the next vital piece on the table. Chatting casually to journalists in his Leicestershire constituency, Blaby, he warmly agreed, in response to rumours that Ian MacGregor, the man who had halved British Steel's workforce in the previous three years, might be taking over the NCB, that he was 'just the calibre of man we need to head this great industry'. A month later he announced that MacGregor was indeed ready to take the job, as from 1 September; and the miners' executive, already braced for trouble after an abortive and divisive attempt to save the threatened Welsh pit, Tymawr Lewis Merthyr (another Scargill ballot defeat), took this as a certain sign that they would soon have a real fight on their hands.

Later memorably excoriated by the bishop of Durham as 'an elderly imported American', Ian Kinloch MacGregor was, and is, the epitome of the transnational meritocrat. Born in a temporary wooden cabin outside the perimeter fence at the British Aluminium plant at Kinlochleven, Argyllshire, where his father worked as an accountant, he went to school in Edinburgh, took a first in metallurgy at Glasgow University, and then, deciding he did not much fancy laboratory work, deliberately chose a job at William Beardmore's Clydeside steelworks. There, in the harsh recession years of the 1930s, he quickly grasped the virtues of hard work, long hours and no nonsense from the workforce, and built himself a big enough reputation, while still in his twenties, to be recruited in 1940 by Lord Beaverbrook, Churchill's favourite troubleshooter, as part of the élite team sent to Washington to buy, borrow and cajole essential war supplies. In 1945, when Britain returned a Labour govern-

27

ment, he elected to make his career in the United States, where he became a naturalised citizen, a Florida Republican voter, chairman of the billion-dollar Amax Corporation (formed from a merger between American Metal Climax and his own former employer, International Molybdenum), a multi-millionaire in his own right, and, as several British governments have now acknowledged, one of the most expensive and sought-after business brains of his time.

The efforts to tempt him home began as early as 1975, when Eric Varley, then Labour's industry secretary, tried to interest him in the task of revivifying British Leyland (he settled for part-time, non-executive chairman). He was approached for British Steel virtually every time the top job fell vacant during the 1970s, and finally agreed in 1980 to sign a three-year contract, at which point an unbelieving Parliament first heard what his services would cost: £1.8 million, on top of a normal state industry chairman's salary, to be paid in the form of a combined 'transfer fee' and 'performance bond', to the partners in the New York investment house of Lazard Frères, to which he had attached himself after reaching Amax's statutory retiring age. When Lawson made his formal announcement of the Coal Board appointment, he roundly defended his candidate's record. At steel, he said, he had raised the industry's productivity level from abysmal to near the best in Europe; and although the £1.5 million that Lazards would receive for the loan of his services (unconditionally this time) was indeed a great deal of money, 'it is only the amount that the NCB is losing every day'.

MacGregor's actual achievement at BSC, on which the 'performance' payment will be assessed, is still technically under adjudication; but on one aspect at least there is no argument: between 1980, when he arrived, and 1983, when he departed, the Corporation's payroll was cut from 166,000 to 85,000; and the main iron and steel union, which fought for fifteen weeks to halt the process, was comprehensively outmanoeuvred. Scargill could hardly fail to draw the obvious conclusion: 'We have constantly warned that this man's mission is to savagely butcher the British coal industry.' But

Lawson dismissed such imputations. 'I was not seeking a hatchet man,' he said. 'Hatchet men come much cheaper than this.' And MacGregor, on Scottish television, described himself more as 'a plastic surgeon, trying to redeem the features of aged properties that need some kind of face-lift'. Coal, in his view, offered better recovery chances than most of Britain's industrial relics; and he assured a House of Lords energy committee that his first priority would be to have samplers made for the bedrooms of all NCB executives, reading 'Petrochemicals came from coal at the beginning of this century, and will return there at the end of it.' Lady Llewelyn-Davies of Hastoe promised to turn her needle urgently to the task.

It was a deceptively cosy note. MacGregor, already well over seventy, might allow himself the momentary luxury of looking forward to the coal markets of the twenty-first century, but a more immediate remit went with his new job. He was to take over an industry that was technically and endemically insolvent, free it from its dependence on an endless succession of government grants, and put it into a state of clear financial balance by 1987–8. Although the original 1980 break-even target had been postponed by four years, it was still a daunting task. And from the NUM's point of view there could be little doubt about the way it would be tackled. In the United States the new NCB chairman had built his reputation as a successful coal man on two things: massive exploitation of the eighty-foot-thick open-cast deposits which lie just twenty-five feet beneath the surface of Wyoming, and unyielding opposition to the activities, or even presence, of trade unions. The vast Belle Ayr mine, capable of producing a third as much as all the pits in Britain put together, was closed by strike action for the first three months of 1975, and picketed on a major scale for another two years. But at the end of the day the United Mineworkers of America had to admit defeat, and effectively since then they have ceased to exist as a serious force in the rich, nearly inexhaustible coal-measures of the Middle West. During the early period of his own strike, Arthur Scargill almost always wore the baseball cap presented to him by a visiting UMWA delegation, as a reminder of what he was up against. But after the large-scale drift back to work began in autumn 1984 it disappeared from the photographs. Either it was lost, or it had become too poignant a symbol.

British coal, which MacGregor had agreed to take over on 1 September, was a very different affair from his Wyoming triumph. By then the NCB would be in the middle of a financial year in which it would record a loss of £410m., before paying interest charges of £467m., and require an £875m. deficit grant from the government in order to keep in the black. Its assets consisted essentially of 170 deep mines, plus some open-cast mainly operated by other people under licence. Of these pits, only twenty-two had consistently covered their operating costs, and a bare fifty or sixty had done better than break even, on average, over the six-year period 1976–81 which had been intensively studied by the Monopolies Commission. Geographically they spread across large parts of industrial Britain. But the regularly profitable were increasingly concentrated in the eastern–central part of the country represented by the counties of Yorkshire, Derbyshire and Nottinghamshire. Elsewhere, especially in Scotland, South Wales and the North-East, once the proud giants of the trade, there was little but red ink. Yet each unit tended to be the heart and focus of its own long-established community, whose main purpose in life, and sometimes the sole source of jobs and income, was the production of coal. Any abrupt attempt to impose regular business standards – and MacGregor, whose age alone made him a man in a hurry, had only three years to play with – was bound, in these circumstances, to meet resistance of the most radical and far-reaching kind.

That is getting too far ahead of the story, though. Soon after MacGregor's appointment was officially confirmed, Mrs Thatcher announced that a general election would be held in June 1983. The Conservative Campaign Guide contented itself with some fairly neutral references to the coal industry, to whose problems the government claimed to have 'maintained an understanding and flexible approach'. There had been a disappointingly slow growth in productivity, it noted

– a full 20 per cent below the levels promised in the 1974 Plan for Coal. Much of that shortfall arose because 'old and inefficient capacity' had not been phased out at the 3–4 million tonnes a year rate envisaged in the Plan, as a result of which the least profitable slice of deep-mined capacity had managed to notch up losses totalling £250 million in the year 1981–2. But there were signs that the need for better performance was being grasped – notably, the Guide implied, in the triple rejection of Mr Scargill's most recent strike calls, two over pay, and one over the recent South Wales pit closure proposal.

In the event the Tories were reaffirmed in office with an almost landslide majority of 141 seats, and the miners were revealed, by psephological analysis, to have played a not inconsiderable part in the triumph. Two mining constituencies, Cannock and Burntwood and Sherwood (containing more pits than any other in the country), both returned Conservative MPs; two others, Normanton and Blyth Valley, shifted from rock-solid Labour to marginal; and in not one of the twelve polling districts held to be most dominated by pitmen did Michael Foot's candidates get even as much as 60 per cent of the vote. Eight days after the results were declared, the Prime Minister reshuffled her Cabinet, promoted Nigel Lawson to chancellor, and offered a new job to Peter Walker, a former Edward Heath protégé, widely regarded as one of the more liberal and socially aware members of the party, who had been working his return passage to the inner councils by way of the department of agriculture and endless late-night farm price negotiations in Brussels. 'Peter,' she said, 'I want you to go to Energy. We are going to have a miners' strike.'

Scargill and his supporters on the left, who were now about to become, for the first time in NUM history, an absolute majority among the twenty-four voting members on the executive, had in turn been reconsidering their own strategy. For over a year the president had been claiming the existence of an NCB 'hit-list' of pits scheduled for shutdown. He had documents, he said, leaked to him from sources deep within the Board, showing that no fewer than seventy-five were

31

slated to disappear. Soon after, the union's newspaper, *The Miner,* printed fifty-five of the alleged names, and a special session of the House of Commons Energy Committee was called to get at the facts. Both sides presented their case, and in the end the NCB conceded that the papers were genuine but argued that they did not mean what Mr Scargill claimed. They were merely working summaries showing various measures of economic performance, and were not intended in any way as the basis for actual decisions. Scargill expressed much scepticism, but had to agree, in light of the plentiful evidence, that his members were not yet ready to accept the reality of the threat.

For a time in early 1983 he toyed with the idea of a 'big hitter' approach, where the thirty most profitable pits in the country – headed by Thoresby in Nottinghamshire and Daw Mill in the South Midlands – should be brought out on strike and a levy raised on the rest of the membership to pay their wages. As between them the thirty in normal times produce a full third of the industry's annual output (34 million tonnes), while employing barely a fifth of its labour (42,000 men), and contribute profits aggregating almost £200 million, this might have been forged into quite an effective weapon – especially as, without them, the Board's losses could have rocketed to beyond the £600 million mark. But the notion was not pursued. Instead, at the annual NUM conference held in Perth that July an emergency resolution was unanimously passed instructing the executive 'to immediately embark on a campaign to win the whole-hearted support of miners not only to oppose pit and works closures, but all reductions in manpower'. It also empowered the executive to hold a national ballot on the subject 'at a time deemed most apropriate', and Jack Taylor, who had succeeded Scargill as Yorkshire president, underlined one of the crucial issues to come. 'NEC must run this battle,' he said. 'We cannot have areas on their own . . . because when we are divided they will beat us.' But in the approaching turmoil his prescient advice was forgotten, not least as it turned out by Taylor himself. Ironically a motion from Kent demanding a delegate conference rather than a ballot was dropped when the executive

32

firmly indicated that they would recommend its rejection.
Taylor's battle, however, was some way ahead: indeed,
many competent and well-placed observers were still arguing,
with varying degrees of conviction, that it might be avoided.
The NCB announced its last pre-MacGregor results – an
outright loss of £111 million, after receiving £374 million
in grants and paying £366 million in interest charges. The
Monopolies and Mergers Commission, which had been asked
by the energy department to assess the Board's performance,
produced two immensely detailed volumes of evidence to
support its generally unflattering conclusions – that too much
investment had gone into projects 'which are either unprofit-
able or of doubtful profitability' and that overall aims in
regard to output and demand seemed 'undesirably vague'.
The NUM agreed, with reluctance, to accept the closure of
Cardowan in Scotland and Brynlliw in South Wales, both
well up the Commission's list of 'high-cost' pits, and also the
merger of Lynemouth in Northumberland with its large
modern neighbour, Ellington. Norman Siddall, retiring after
an illness-wracked year as caretaker chairman to the NCB,
discounted the prospect of an early confrontation. 'There
has got to be quite a combination of factors put together to
get an all-out strike in the coal industry,' he said.

Scargill had already met the new energy secretary, Peter
Walker ('The tea was nice, but the conversation was hor-
rible'), and commiserated with the police ('our friends on
the other side of the picket line') over the 'very low' pay
rise they had been offered under the government's latest,
post-election public sector pay restraint formula – a mere 8
per cent. Now he had the opportunity to shake hands with
MacGregor, who had moved into his new office on 1 September. The NCB chairman laconically reported: 'We had a
very civilised meeting' and pointed out to inquiring journalists that, in order to become independent of the taxpayers,
he would need to improve results by around £600 million a
year. During a whirlwind tour of the coalfields, the 'butcher',
in relatively affable mood, told the men at Bilston Glen
(which later became the first Scottish pit to produce coal
during the strike): 'Perform, and you have a future; don't,

and you have no future; it's as simple as that.' When he departed he left orders that each of the twenty-four miners he had talked to should be served with a pint of beer. Ten days later, on 30 September, he responded to the NUM's almost ritual demand for a 'substantial' pay rise by making a 'first and final' offer of 5.2 per cent and indicating that there could be no slowdown in the closure programme. Cronton in Lancashire, Monckton Hall in Scotland, Britannia in South Wales and Newstead and Moor Green in Nottinghamshire were now added to the list. The fuse was lit, and gently fizzing.

Initially, though, it was a very slow burn. Scargill, with uncharacteristic self-effacement, said he would leave the response to a delegates' meeting called for 21 October in the unlikely surroundings of London's City University. For the moment he contented himself with some rude remarks about NCB accounting methods ('Fanny Cradock's Cookbook') which he said had eliminated £200 million worth of profit by undervaluing the towering, unsaleable stocks. MacGregor went to Wales and mused aloud that the offer could always be reduced ('circumstances may change my generosity'). Gerald Kaufman, the Labour party's shadow home affairs spokesman, developed an elaborate sociological argument to prove that the affluent miners no longer had the stomach for a real fight. 'More and more they are joining other well-paid workers in owner-occupied, semi-detached houses, and if they live in council houses they quite often want to buy them,' he informed the readers of *The Times*. 'In the early 1970s the coalminers were manifestly underprivileged. Then, they were eager to lead their fellow-workers to the barricades; now they seem conspicuously unwilling to die in any ditches.' To illustrate his point Scargill unexpectedly reverred an earlier veto, and offered to meet the NCB and the government in December for tripartite talks on the future of the industry, despite MacGregor's insistence that the agenda must centre on the vexed question of excess capacity.

The meeting did in fact take place, with the NCB revealing a broad outline of its plans and Scargill dismissing them as 'a recipe for disaster'. But by then the plot had moved on.

34

At the City University, branch and lodge representatives, gathered from all over the British Isles, voted with impressive unanimity to call an all-out ban on overtime working to take effect from 31 October. This was in protest at both the size of the pay offer and MacGregor's unabated intention to slim down the loss-making end of the industry. The Board quietly instituted a crash maintenance programme to make maximum use of the few days' grace on offer, and MacGregor, that weekend, took the opportunity to tell colliery clerical staff, meeting in Wallsend-on-Tyne, that they and their colleagues had better brace themselves 'to get out of the hopeless places' that could never contribute to coal's prosperity, or even survival. The fuse was well and truly ablaze.

For all the unanimity of the vote, the overtime ban was not without its critics. Some, like Jack Collins, from the small but always ultra-radical Kent coalfields, deplored the delay and moved for immediate action. Others, like Roy Ottey, the leader of the much more moderate power workers, representing most of the engineers and technicians in the union (he later resigned from the national executive in protest at Scargill's high-handed defiance of the law), argued, without much effect, that some consultation with the Board should logically precede all-out confrontation. But the president rejected both views. A week was needed, he insisted, to make all the necessary preparations; but on the other hand there was, at that stage, absolutely no useful room for talks. 'Make no mistake,' he told both hotheads and doubters, 'our view is that this action will escalate, because MacGregor will take some form of action against our members, as he did at British Steel. But at this stage, for God's sake, let us have total unity of purpose.'

That unity was indeed achieved: so successfully in fact that the ban was maintained throughout the strike, even in those working pits that never stopped production for a single day, and was still being widely observed weeks after all the men finally went back to their jobs. But the promised escalation was slow to come. Two months later, in mid-January, Mac-

Gregor was cheerfully assuring television viewers that the industry could operate for twenty years without overtime, and no customer would even notice. Instead it was in the NUM's ranks that tempers started to fray. The significance of overtime in coalmining is that repair work and mechanical preparation is normally done at weekends, so that production can start with the first shift on Monday morning and continue without interruption through the week. Suspending this activity at first hits only the pay packets of a relatively small group of craftsmen and specialists, but it soon works through to the rest of the workforce (which is why similar action in support of the previous year's pay round had petered out in under a month).

By Christmas large numbers of men found themselves laid off and losing wages – in January 19,000 men were sent home on a single day – and dissension started to mount. It particularly affected the winding engine operators in North Staffordshire, who reckoned that their Sunday work was not overtime but a contractual sixth shift, and that they were being unfairly penalised without having the chance to take part in a proper democratic ballot on the ban. Ten other branches in Ottey's power group supported them. The row quickly snowballed, along lines that presented an extraordinarily accurate preview of larger events to come. Scargill rejected any idea of putting the issue to a vote, and later flatly denied that there had ever been such a request. The Staffordshire winders threatened to defy the ban and go into work as usual. Pickets, in ugly mood, prevented them getting through the colliery gates; and then, as they had promised, the winders withdrew their labour for twenty-four hours and thus made work impossible that day for all the 5,000 pitmen in the West Midlands area. Trying to limit the damage, the power group, despite its basic sympathy, suspended the dissidents from membership and disbanded their branch; but they in turn sought and obtained legal opinion that the union's action had been 'against the principles of natural justice' and got themselves promptly reinstated. After that they dropped their efforts to defy the ban and followed the wishes of the majority; but from then on the winders, who at one point had seriously considered setting up their own independent union, were always in the forefront of the 'give us a ballot' movement that so seriously diluted the NUM's otherwise formidable fighting power.

For the moment, though, the winders episode took second place to a much more immediate event: the election of a new NUM general secretary to fill the post vacated by Lawrence Daly, now ready to retire after several years of intermittent illness. The sole leftwing candidate and strong starting favourite was Peter Heathfield, the Derbyshire area secretary, later to emerge, with Scargill and McGahey, as one of the three key leadership figures in the developing dispute. But as polling day, 20 January, neared, a significant dark horse started catching up fast on the rails. John Walsh, the NUM's North Yorkshire agent and a former rugby league amateur international, had been campaigning vigorously on the union's lack of tangible success to match its class-war rhetoric. 'We want less aggro and more results,' he said, and claimed that under Scargill miners' real wages had virtually stood still. But the real cutting edge of his challenge was his insistence that there should have been a ballot on the current pay offer before taking any serious industrial steps.

In the event Heathfield scraped home by 3,516 votes (in an electorate of 191,000 members) and chose to interpret the result as a clear endorsement of the executive's policies. Commenting on a MORI opinion poll commissioned by *The Sunday Times*, he said: 'It shows clear support for the overtime ban, and I am identified as a supporter of the ban.' Afterwards the narrowness of his victory was advanced as one of the factors persuading Scargill to avoid putting the strike decision itself to a national vote. But Walsh's large and unexpected support should have carried a clear warning: that even at that early stage the NUM was deeply divided, so that any strategy dependent on total solidarity must carry a high degree of risk. One important source of division was the overtime ban itself. Several of the more militant union branches passed motions deploring the way 'the media' had concentrated only on the pay claim, and excluded any refer-

ence to the question of closures. But others, notably Manton
in South Yorkshire, were 'confused' and 'unhappy' at the
linkage, and consistently voted down resolutions seeking to
escalate the action.

Meanwhile the pressure was tightening, for both sides.
Local disputes flared in half a dozen coalfields, putting the
future of several more pits in increased doubt. In January
the NCB's Scottish area director, Albert Wheeler, announced
that Polmaise, near Stirling, which had been out of production for three years pending completion of an ambitious
£15 million development programme (during which period
it had suffered an endless assortment of arguments, lockouts
and legal actions), was now to be permanently abandoned.
Shortly after, closure notice was given for another Scots pit,
Bogside, where it was said – and bitterly disputed – that
withdrawal of safety cover thanks to the overtime ban had
resulted in irreversible flooding. The Polmaise men stopped
work in protest (thus becoming the earliest group to go on
full strike) but the Scottish area, after an acrimonious vote,
stopped short of coming out in support. Many NUM officials,
both militant and moderate, saw this failure as a warning –
that even under heavy provocation it might be difficult to
fan discontent into a real flame.

At Bullcliffe Wood, a small mine north of Barnsley, there
was a unique incident when men routinely transferred to the
next-door Denby Grange colliery, after exhaustion of the
face they had been working on, were halted and turned back
by an underground picket line – after which Bullcliffe Wood,
with its thirty jobs, was peremptorily added to the Board's
'death row' list. At Manvers Main, in South Yorkshire, there
was the makings of an area-wide strike over 'snap time' when
an impatient management jumped the gun by imposing a
minor change in mealtimes which the union had agreed,
but only for implementation after the end of the overtime
prohibition. Fights, slanging matches and sackings erupted
everywhere as managers tried to keep up discipline and
output among frustrated men who were finding themselves
up to £40 a week out of pocket, and had as yet no inkling
of how much worse there was to come. MacGregor himself

was knocked to the ground, though probably by accident, during a February visit to Ellington colliery in Northumberland, where angry miners also scratched his car and let the tyres down to express their displeasure over his plan to shed 600 jobs at the older Bates pit just down the road.

The Board too had its troubles. MacGregor's January insouciance had contained a strong infusion of bravado. The overtime ban, by reducing the amount of excess production (output was down by about 6.5m. tonnes), was having a beneficial effect on cash-flow; but it was beginning to inflict serious damage on the highly vulnerable profit-and-loss account. The reasons for this were abstruse, and Peter Walker and Ian MacGregor spent most of 28 February trying, not very successfully, to explain them to the House of Commons Energy Committee (which also had much difficulty in understanding how the NCB could suddenly find itself faced with an unanticipated £128 million bill for subsidence, mostly in the Mansfield area, where it threatened to destroy the profitability of some of the richest pits in the country). But the upshot was clear enough: at a time of the acutest financial stringency, affecting every department of state from education to public health, coal found it necessary to seek an emergency subvention of some £289 million, with at least £100 million directly attributable to the overtime problem, just to keep itself technically out of the red.

It could not go on. And although neither Walker nor MacGregor gave any hint to the MPs, the decision had already been made to raise the ante. As MacGregor confirmed in a private interview two months later, the Board's view was that Scargill had been spoiling for a fight from the minute he took over as NUM president. His strategy, once the gloves were off, was to let the overtime ban grind on through the summer, gradually eroding stocks and tightening the financial screws, 'and then go for the grand slam in the autumn'. This had to be pre-empted. And pre-empted it was to be.

Chapter 2

The Strike Begins

MacGregor, with the full backing of the government, had primed his own detonator to go off on 6 March when he and his deputy, Jimmy Cowan, were due to meet the assembled national executives of the three main mining unions and unveil their plans to start streamlining the industry and cutting its losses. But for two quite separate sets of reasons, the explosion that actually resulted was of a very different order, in kind and in magnitude, to the one that had been planned. The underlying strategy was to offer Scargill and the NUM executive a challenge which they could not refuse, but to which they could only respond by calling a national strike ballot, in circumstances and on terms which had been carefully tailored to ensure that they must inevitably lose. The Thatcher government thought that some kind of confrontation with the miners was probably inevitable, hence the systematic build-up of stocks and many other precautionary preparations. But it was not envisaged that the spring of 1984 would see the start of the conflict. That it did so can be explained first by the premature announcement of a pit closure in Yorkshire, of which Whitehall at any rate had absolutely no prior warning; and second by the fact that nobody in the government or Coal Board had foreseen the amount of room that Scargill, under pressure, would be able to find for constitutional acrobatics. Together these factors ensured that an engagement intended to be quick, cheap and decisive turned into the longest, costliest dispute in the country's industrial history.

In London, preparations went forward for the 6 March presentation without any real appreciation that the war was already five days old. It had begun on 1 March in the little South Yorkshire mining town of Wath-upon-Dearne with the revelation by the local NCB area director that he planned to shut down, at the earliest possible date, a pit called Cortonwood. Barely a handful of people in Britain can ever have heard of the name. But without that decision the whole protracted strike would have taken a very different course, maybe never started at all. Even if it had got going, several of the most critical elements – the avoidance of a ballot, the mob picketing of Nottinghamshire, the swift mobilisation of a massive police presence, the proliferation of legal entanglements – could have worked themselves out in very different ways.

It is worth unravelling in some detail the events of those first days as a guide to understanding the inner mechanics of the struggle: not least because the people most intimately concerned – the families and communities that lost savings and friends, courted arrest and permanent unemployment, and in some cases probably hastened the destruction of what they were supposed to be fighting for – often understood little or nothing of the manoeuvring that was going on behind the scenes.

The closing of Cortonwood had been a strong possibility for months – it had first been discussed by the NCB managers the previous November – but in the third week of February it moved to the top of the South Yorkshire betting. That was when the area director, George Hayes, like his colleagues from the other eleven coalfields, was summoned to Hobart House to be given his output target for 1984–5. Previously such budgets had just been sent out by letter, but this time they were the subject of a fifteen-minute personal interview with MacGregor and Cowan. As one NCB executive said: 'It was a touch of sheer theatre.' Though Hayes was disappointed with his allotted objective, a cut of 500,000 tonnes, bringing his area's effective capacity down to 7.1m. tonnes, he was not particularly surprised. But it did face him with some tight decisions. If he did not move quickly he might have to close two pits to meet the target. If however he was able to shut Cortonwood by the end of April and at the same time coax better performances from his other two big lossmakers, Manvers and Kilnhurst, he should just be able to get into the black without further surgery.

Hayes and his colleagues nevertheless hesitated before the announcement. First they discussed the dispute at Manvers. Attempts were being made to spread it, but the area managers doubted if the militants involved would succeed: 'Some of the NUM left had been running round with a lighted match looking for a blue fuse paper,' said one. 'But Manvers was pretty damp.' Second, and more important, they considered the timing. Hayes planned to make his Cortonwood announcement, which he realised must have a dramatic impact, at one of the regular colliery review meetings, at which directors like himself go through the prospects for each pit in their area with officials from the industry's three unions, representing miners, supervisors and managers. Hayes had fixed the next such meeting for 1 March, which was deliberately chosen to come after the national consultative meeting where MacGregor, as everyone concerned knew, intended to unveil his overall cutback plans. But that event, originally set for February, had now been pushed back to 6 March. Hayes had to decide whether to defer his own arrangements or press on regardless. As he had already changed his date once he was reluctant 'to bugger the NUM about again' in the words of one of his managers. He decided, in the event, to go ahead. It was a fateful choice.

Senior ministers said after the strike that they had known nothing of the Cortonwood announcement until it became headline news. Indeed a letter listing all the redundancy benefits and job guarantees on offer which was sent out some weeks later to all the 830 Cortonwood pitmen, in a belated attempt to repair the damage, was unquestionably written at the government's behest. The NCB have always insisted, for public consumption, that the closure decision was Hayes's alone. There is however a widespread belief within the NCB that in the final days before 1 March he did seek advice at Board level on whether to proceed and was simply told: 'You have your instructions.'

Whatever had been happening behind the scenes, officials from the three mining unions assembled on Thursday 1 March to hear Hayes give his regular review of plans and prospects for South Yorkshire's fifteen surviving pits. In his headquarters office at Wath-upon-Dearne, lined with sombre paintings of old mine workings and shadowed by the winding-gear of the already strikebound Manvers Main, Hayes told them that he would take the collieries in alphabetical order, with the exception of Cortonwood, about which he had something special to say. When he finally came to it, the message was simple and stark. Cortonwood had lost £10m. between 1977 and 1983, with another £4m. debit already accumulated in the current year. Its coal, which cost £64 a tonne to bring to the surface, could not, even in the most favourable circumstances, command more than £47 a tonne. In fact, with the general rundown of the steel industry, its sole customer, and its changing technical requirements, Cortonwood coal was now almost unsaleable. Half a year's output was already eating its head off in the pityard (with financing costs of £7 a tonne) and even if the remaining 1.2m. tonnes of reserves were mined to the last cobble they would only last until 1989. The economics of the pit were already 'very bad', but once production was cut back, as it must be, to the last two remaining faces, it would become 'catastrophic'. The Board's intention, therefore, taking everything into account, was to close it as soon as possible, and in any case to cease production by mid-April.

At this point, as the NUM's official meeting notes record, 'there was an outcry from the union representatives present'. Ken Homer, the area finance secretary, exploded that they were 'completely dismayed' to find themselves subject to such a *fait accompli*, and Jack Taylor, the Yorkshire president, underlined what he saw as the inner significance of Hayes's announcement. 'For the very first time, in very clear words, and in very clear terms,' he said, Yorkshire miners were being asked to accept a purely economic closure in their area, 'and there was no dancing round that position'. Hayes reiterated tersely that there was 'absolutely no market' for Cortonwood coal, and that the only solution was to close it 'very quickly indeed'.

George Hayes is a blunt Yorkshire mining engineer of the old school, with a patent dislike for dissembling. He said at the time, and has frequently repeated since, that this was in no way planned as a unilateral *coup de main*. The intention was always to go through the normal, long-established review procedure (even if the unions had lately found it increasingly unsatisfactory) so that all those concerned could have their say. That assurance was accepted by the managers and the pit deputies who agreed to attend a further meeting. But the NUM, claiming that the procedure had been flouted, refused even to consult their diaries. They stormed out and prepared for battle.

Their complaint was not without substance. The form of Hayes's announcement was indeed a technical breach of the procedure. Strictly speaking he should merely have expressed the Board's concern about Cortonwood and asked for a reconvened meeting with the branch representatives present to discuss the proposals more fully. In his impatience to get improved area performance, mainly to avert the serious consequences he foresaw would flow from any delay, he had jumped the gun. In fact, he even surprised his own staff. They had discussed among themselves the urgent desirability of halting Cortonwood's production and had identified the end of April as the optimum cut-off date. But they had not expected Hayes to give an actual date at this first meeting, still less to advance it by a fortnight, to mid-April. Inadvertently, he had handed the miners a basis for claiming that the board was riding roughshod over cherished and long-established rights.

The first group to take up this theme was the NUM branch committee at Cortonwood itself. Alerted by Arnie Young, the South Yorkshire area agent, who drove straight to the threatened pit from Hayes's office, they hastily called an emergency meeting that weekend. Five hundred people packed themselves into the small parish hall at Brampton Bierlow, the village where Cortonwood is sited, and where the largest group of its pitmen live. It was the biggest branch gathering anyone there could ever remember, and Jack Wake, the branch secretary, spoke in stark and sombre terms. He warned his audience, old men and young men alike, that Cortonwood could well have turned its last bucket of coal already, when the late shift came up on Friday afternoon, and that the pit which had represented their livelihood for the past 111 years, was 'on the operating table', and very probably headed towards the morgue.

In an angry and unanimous vote it was agreed to fight the closure (although Cortonwood, traditionally moderate, had previously opposed such proposals elsewhere, including the ballot of 1981) and ask the rest of Yorkshire to take action in support. On Sunday evening, 4 March, the dignitaries of the NUM and the Labour party in Yorkshire gathered, as they do every year, in Sheffield City Hall for the annual colliery brass band festival. Roy Mason, the NUM-sponsored MP for Barnsley (and himself both an ex-miner and former minister of fuel and power), was asked by a local miners' leader if he would be attending the hastily organised area council meeting which Owen Briscoe, the Yorkshire secretary, had spent a hectic weekend arranging. Mason said he would be there. 'Good,' the official replied. 'It will be historic.'

Throughout the winter, a number of branches in the county had been spoiling to intensify the fight, but until Cortonwood they remained in the minority. Back in February, Silverwood, near Rotherham, had tried and failed to escalate the overtime ban into a full strike. That same weekend, 3–4 March, eight of the fifteen South Yorkshire pits – justifying the Board's sceptical predictions – had declined to come out in support of the Manvers protesters. So when the Yorkshire area council met, on Monday, 5 March, to decide what to do in response to Hayes's ultimatum, the outcome was by no means cut-and-dried. In recognition of this the motion rejecting the Cortonwood closure was beefed up with a reference to Bullcliffe Wood, the much smaller Barnsley pit, which also happened to be under threat.

It was Kellingley, the huge North Yorkshire pit, which pinpointed the central dilemma. For months, said its delegate, 'the NUM as a whole has been awaiting a situation where a branch wishes to fight for its continued existence'. Yet when Polmaise and Bogside presented just such an opportunity, Scotland turned its back. However, Yorkshire was made of sterner, or perhaps less cautious, stuff. The decisive speech was made by Mick Carter, the Cortonwood delegate. Carter, bearded, bespectacled and forceful, eloquently outlined the pit's recent history. He described how it had been promised a life of at least five years, how the men from neighbouring Elsecar, recently closed, had been transferred there within the last few weeks with a promise of continuing jobs, and how more than £1m. had just been invested in new underground roadways, modernising the power plant and even renovating the pithead baths. In response, the meeting overwhelmingly defeated a motion that branches should have the chance to pause for more thought and voted to stop work 'as from last shift Friday 9th March to stop the action of the NCB to butcher our pits and jobs', and to call on all other areas – and other unions – for immediate support.

Half the local pits joined in with a will, and the other half, whatever their inclinations, were almost immediately faced with the choice of crossing picket lines or submitting to the common cause. One of the most determined rejectionists was a face-worker at Manton, Robert Taylor, who later inflicted much damage on the union with his successful claims that its March decisions had been seriously in breach of both the common law and its own rulebook. On Monday, 5 March, as he later told the High Court, he went to work as usual. But on the Tuesday evening, after four hours underground, he was 'withdrawn' and escorted by police out of the colliery. Only three days earlier his 1,250 workmates had overwhelmingly voted to have nothing to do with strikes. But now there were 200 pickets swarming inside the gates, many of them barricading the cage doors to prevent anyone going below. 'The following day,' Taylor recalls, 'I was advised not to work as my safety could not be guaranteed. I have not worked since.'

By the time Taylor made his final 1984 trip down the Manton main shaft, events elsewhere had already moved into decisively higher gear. That morning in Room 16 at Hobart House, the NCB's London head office, MacGregor and Cowan had been matter-of-factly outlining, for the benefit of the senior leaders in the three mining unions, their plans for restructuring coal into a 'high-volume, low-cost industry'. Although these were couched throughout in low-key and ostensibly non-provocative terms (the meeting began with cordial greetings for the NUM's new general secretary, Peter Heathfield, and included a reaffirmation of the government's willingness to invest another £800m. in pit development over the coming year), the central message was sufficient to send Scargill and his companions into a cold fury. The Board's proposals – to take out 4m. tonnes of capacity, broadly involving the elimination of twenty mines and around 20,000 jobs – amounted to 'savage butchery', the tight-lipped NUM president told a succession of press conferences, radio news programmes and television reporters in the course of the next few hectic hours. Without question they would 'call forth all action to defend our members' interests: make no mistake about that'.

At first sight it is not at all self-evident just why the reaction should have been so belligerent. The scale of the cuts, though substantial, was no greater than had been achieved, almost without opposition, under Norman Siddall's patient and diplomatic guidance in 1983 (which saw a total of twenty-one pits phased out, and the agreement of 20,000 men, mostly over fifty-five, to take early retirement). Nor did it differ much from the closure targets agreed, though never actually achieved, under the famous 1974 Plan for Coal. The tone of the presentation was almost exaggeratedly unemphatic. Cowan did most of the talking, much of it illustrated with lantern slides, while MacGregor sat impassively in the background. The key information was extracted only when Scargill asked whether the 4m. tonne capacity reduction referred to would mean 'a similar programme of rundown' to that experienced in the previous year. Cowan, with a poker face, agreed that the manpower reduction would be 'of broadly the same order' and the countdown was on. Scargill, through-out the strike, always used the Plan to define the un-acceptability of these proposals. The document, he claimed, never envisaged the closure of a pit on 'economic grounds', only when it became unsafe or exhausted. In the sense that the phrases 'pit closure' and 'economic grounds' are nowhere explicitly linked, this is strictly true. But it is clear from the text that the concept of 'exhaustion' is closely based on whether or not a particular mine's reserves could be economi-cally developed or its output profitably sold. While the indus-try was still, on balance, expanding as it had been up to the Siddall period, there was no real opposition even by the NUM to closing down superannuated, high-cost collieries to make way for investment in new low-cost replacements. But what MacGregor now sought was a net reduction in capacity for the whole industry on the grounds that there was no longer a market for all the coal it could produce. In translation that became 'the closure of uneconomic pits' and the subject of total resistance.

It is common ground among those present that the general atmosphere was a great deal more tense than the cold print of (still confidential) minutes would suggest. Room 16, known unaffectionately as 'the Mausoleum', is a formidably oppres-sive setting for any occasion, never mind one where a Thatcher-appointed Reaganite Republican is matching him-self against the Marxist *enfant terrible* of the British trade union movement. The deep orange curtains, which have remained permanently drawn since a long-forgotten spate of IRA bombings, combine with wall-to-wall carpeting in the same remarkable colour and an array of huge wall mirrors to create an effect of suffocating claustrophobia. The layout, with tables ranged round the outside of the room to leave a gulf of central no-man's land, lent the proceedings, in the phrase of one participant, 'the air of two eighteenth-century generals, with their armies, facing each other before a battle'. 'Armies' was not too much of an exaggeration: MacGregor, never at his best in gatherings of more than six people, was flanked by nineteen people on his own side, with another nineteen from the NUM, eight from the managers' union and four for the pit deputies. After lunch, when the deputies and the managers departed and the Board were left closeted alone with the NUM, tension moved up several notches. The session started late. Scargill had commandeered the room to discuss the proposals with his own executive, and was reluctantly forced to break off when Board officials finally insisted that the formal talks must resume. By then Mac-Gregor, who had been kept waiting for several minutes outside the door, had gone back grumpily to his own office. When he returned, his attitude was characterised by one of his own directors as 'very casual and take-it-or-leave-it', while Scargill was 'of course, very emotional'. It was no recipe for a true meeting of minds. Three months later, on 28 June, at a tense meeting with the main steel union, ISTC, from which he was unsuccessfully seeking support, Scargill gave his own succinct summary of the 6 March exchanges. 'Mr MacGregor met the NUM,' he said, 'and made it obvious that he had nothing but contempt for the procedures of the NUM and all other trade unions. The NCB intimated their intention to take out four million tonnes capacity at once, and the NUM had no alternative but to oppose such a concept.'

No real attempt seems to have been made to soften that interpretation and it would have been difficult for anyone but MacGregor himself, in the circumstances, to offer even a small olive branch. There were serious divisions of opinion among the senior NCB managers, not all of whom were enthusiastic about the timing and nature of the 6 March announcement. With the strike already solid in South Yorkshire and certain to engulf the whole county by the following Monday, 'it hardly seemed like the best tactics to announce a substantial job cut right across the country', as one leading critic put it. But in this they were opposed to MacGregor, who would have liked to move even earlier. Even the hardliners had found themselves fighting to make sure that nothing precipitate was done until winter electricity demand was well past its peak. Several would have liked at least another fortnight of spring sunshine, just to improve the safety margin. But they were hardly likely to pursue that debate in public, and certainly not in the presence of the parties most intimately concerned.

There was little or no disagreement about the ultimate objective: cutting 20,000 jobs in twenty pits. But especially outside London there was a worry about the wisdom of specifying the whole programme in advance. Siddall, it was discreetly pointed out to MacGregor, had managed to achieve the same sort of result without any bothersome early warnings, closing, in McGahey's expressive phrase, a score of pits 'by stealth'. But although there was undoubtedly some dissent along these lines, it was pretty muted. 'There was a spirit of MacGregorism abroad, and everybody who didn't attack the bull with a red rag was regarded as a bit of a softie,' one director now recalls. For MacGregor and his deputy there was no hesitation that this was the right course. As Cowan later confirmed, they deliberately 'timed' the presentation to bring the overtime ban, one way or another, to a head. Few NCB men, in retrospect, doubt that was indeed the case.

To understand the vehemence of the rejection, however, and the cataclysmic events to which it gave rise, it is necessary to look a good deal deeper than the words which were actually exchanged: partly at the personalities involved, and their previously adopted positions, and partly at the things which were left unsaid or undefined at the 6 March encounter. Scargill, in particular, had talked so much about the existence of secret 'hit-lists' and was so committed to opposing commercially motivated closures that any publicly admitted intention of this kind had to be taken as a challenge he could not refuse. But of equal importance in swaying his colleagues on the NUM executive (and likewise, to a considerable extent, the leaders of Nacods and BACM, the deputies' and managers' unions, who were also present and almost equally unhappy) was the rather offhand way in which the Board presented its plans. There was, for instance, no mention of improved severance terms for those men willing to accept early departure – though in fact an extremely generous and attractive new package had already been agreed and was announced, with considerable fanfare, only two days later.

Similarly there was unwillingness at the meeting to offer assurances on the crucial subject of compulsory redundancy. Much of the miners' opposition stemmed from fear that the closure programme was reaching the point where the Board would be forced to renege on its long-standing promise to provide alternative jobs for all those wanting to stay in the industry. MacGregor himself came in on this, and went out of his way to tell Ken Sampey, the moderate chairman of Nacods, that there could be no such guarantees. Later in the dispute, though, the Board made it clear that there would in fact be jobs for all. If that had been said from the beginning, it would have been much more difficult for the miners' leaders to maintain even a partially united front. But that was not the way the game was being played. If Arthur Scargill wanted to go out on a limb, no premature lifeline would be thrown to dissuade him.

However strong Scargill's determination, there was no certainty that he could get his armies to march. True, Yorkshire was already grinding to a standstill, and the first brick had been thrown when a management team at Yorkshire Main colliery, near Doncaster, tried to force its way through a picket line to relieve safety men working on a gas leak underground. And Scotland, where six pits and 4,000 jobs had been allowed to go with no more than token protest over the past eighteen months, finally wound itself up on the Tuesday evening to agree a strike against 'the provocative and bullying' tactics of the NCB, as outlined earlier in the day. Cowan, at the London meeting, had explicitly singled out Scotland, along with South Wales, Kent and parts of the North-East, as the source of 'ninety per cent of the Board's losses', and warned it was 'inevitable' that the main cutbacks would occur in these areas.

Yet even in the most threatened coalfields, support at that stage was far from total. And elsewhere it registered mostly between the reluctant and the half-hearted. On Wednesday the Nottingham president, Ray Chadburn, though himself in favour of action, laid down one marker by saying that his

29,000 members would do nothing without a formal ballot. In Edinburgh, though, McGahey offered another. 'I want to make it clear,' he said, and repeated it throughout the day for the benefit of an assortment of media outlets, 'we are not dealing with niceties here. We shall not be constitutionalised out of a defence of our jobs. Area by area will decide, and in my opinion it will have a domino effect.' The next day, Thursday, 8 March, the twenty-four voting members of the NUM national executive, together with the non-voting secretary, Peter Heathfield, and the president, Arthur Scargill, who enjoys only a casting vote in case of a tie (which he has never in fact exercised), met to adjudicate between these two fundamentally divided views. The choice was indeed fateful – the word chosen by Roy Ottey, one of the three-man minority who came out in favour of a free vote. In its ramifications, social, legal, geographical and political, it affected and to a large extent determined the whole course and denouement of the year-long strike.

The day before they met, decisive steps had already been taken by the Finance and General Purposes committee, an inner group of the more senior executive members: it approved a proposal to give the national officials *carte blanche* to switch the union's funds into any 'joint stock bank and its subsidiaries' in the event of sequestration to enforce any future court order. The government's new employment laws were what they principally had in mind, like most other union finance people at that time, though these, as it turned out, were by no means the biggest legal threat they faced. To ensure that officials would not have to waste time in an emergency on tracking down authorised signatories, it was agreed that Scargill and McGahey, who would always be on hand, should replace Sammy Thomson, the Yorkshire vice-president, and Henry Richardson, the Notts secretary, as trustees. As extra insurance they put £1m. into a newly established fund for 'education and other benefits'. Such cash would not be available to finance a strike, of course; but nor would the sequestrators, it was hoped, be able to touch it. These arrangements had been fixed up well before MacGregor's 6 March announcement, mainly in anticipation that the overtime ban would escalate. By the time the finance committee convened, though, it was obvious that the executive were on the brink of much more momentous decisions.

The NUM rulebook – the 'constitution' to which McGahey had referred – dated back to the formation of the national union in 1944 (and still referred to the wartime miners' leader, Will Lawther, as 'president'). It contained two rules explicitly dealing with strikes. Rule 43, which had governed all previous major disputes, laid down that a 'national strike shall only be entered upon as the result of a ballot vote of the members' and required at that time approval by at least a 55 per cent majority, changed a month later to a simple 50 per cent, as it still remains. But there was also Rule 41, which was primarily designed to give the national executive control over industrial action in individual areas. Such action, it laid down, could only go ahead after approval had been sought and granted at national level; and it prohibited any strike activity which had not received such endorsement. Until last year Rule 41 had never, on any occasion, been used as the constitutional platform for a countrywide stoppage (though Scargill had briefly canvassed the idea during the Tymawr Lewis Merthyr discussions in 1983, before the rest of the executive had ruled it out of court). The union's present leaders, however, had recognised for some time that, with sufficient backing and careful preparation, a national withdrawal of labour might be engineered in this way without submitting the proposal to a national vote. That was the basis of McGahey's 'domino' approach.

A large, noisy crowd had already gathered to greet, and in some cases harass, the executive members as they arrived at the NUM's stark headquarters at Sheffield. Some were already reading the NCB's inviting new redundancy offer, issued that morning, which gave men aged up to forty-nine, even those with only a few years in the pits, greatly improved terms if they volunteered for early departure. With ten years' service the pay-off was now almost £11,000, almost three times the old figure, and after thirty years it was more than £33,000. As Owen Briscoe, the Yorkshire secretary, laconically remarked, such sums 'take some refusing'; but not many that day appeared to be tempted as they barracked and cat-called the recognised moderates of the union, and those identified with its less militant areas. One particular target was Henry Richardson, the Nottingham general secretary, who said bitterly and prophetically once he got into the hall: 'Calling us scabs will not help. If Notts are scabs before we start, Notts will become scabs.'

Inside, after disposing of the usual routine preliminaries, Scargill announced that letters had been received from both Yorkshire and Scotland asking that their strike calls be recognised under Rule 41, and urging general support. On the other hand Lancashire, where the board had just carried out a long-foreshadowed threat to close down Cronton, near Liverpool, with its 550 jobs, wanted the go-ahead for an immediate strike ballot. But the Lancashire secretary, Sid Vincent, promptly undercut any impact that might have made by saying he did not believe the men in his area could produce the necessary majority. 'Personally I believe it's now or never,' he said, apparently adding his voice to the Rule 41 group; and although speaker after speaker paid lip-service to the desirability of getting a national vote – and several deplored McGahey's remarks about 'being constitutionalised out of a strike' – there seemed little conviction behind the words. In the end Trevor Bell, leader of the colliery clerical workers' group, Cosa, put up a formal motion demanding a Rule 43 ballot, with a recommendation for strike action against the NCB's 'savage new rundown in mining'. But that was immediately overtaken by Emlyn Williams, the South Wales president, who moved endorsement of the Scots and Yorkshire requests.

After some desultory discussion of the risks that the two alternatives might involve, the president summed up. Scargill underlined the 'simple fact of life' that in the NCB's view no fewer than 115 of the industry's 179 pits, and a large proportion of its workshops and coking plants, were irrevocably uneconomic, and announced: 'It is now the crunch time. We are all agreed we have to fight. We have an overtime ban. It is only the tactics that are in question.' Those were quickly decided. The Emlyn Williams motion was put first, and approved by twenty-one votes, with only three against – Trevor Bell, Roy Ottey, who later resigned, and Ted McKay, from North Wales, who at the height of the strike was hounded out of his home and driven into hiding by men who deemed him insufficiently wedded to the cause. The Bell proposal was never put to the meeting, and Scargill, when the proceedings broke up, felt able to assure the assembled newsmen outside that the decision had been 'unanimous by virtue of a substantive motion', just the way it was later recorded in the minutes.

Bell, once Joe Gormley's industrial relations officer, and one of the candidates decisively defeated by Scargill in the 1981 presidential election to succeed him, confesses himself still mystified that the pro-ballot vote was so low. It is possible that, with Yorkshire still trying to limit the use of flying pickets, several moderates had convinced themselves that local strikes could be prevented from engulfing their own more sensible areas. But a more likely explanation lies in the general weakness and disarray that had lately beset the NUM's once all-powerful right wing. Thanks to a debilitating combination of circumstance and disinclination, this had almost ceased to meet as a coherent group.

Under Gormley, when the union's HQ was still in London (one of Scargill's first big decisions had been to move it to Sheffield), every monthly session had necessitated an overnight stay in the capital, thus providing a natural occasion for pre-planning and tactical decisions. The left-wing patronised the County Hotel in Upper Woburn Street; the right congregated in the Cora, just across the road, and after a meal would invariably drift over to the nearby Marquis of Cornwallis pub for further talk. Scargill's switch destroyed this convenient arrangement. Distances were now so short – from Cosa's base in Wakefield and from the other moderate strongholds in Bolton, Mansfield, Burton and Coalville – that overnight stopovers seemed extravagant and pointless. Moreover, there was now no natural harrier, like Gormley's former lieutenant, Les Storey, to bully them into an effective combination. While the left, forced to travel from Scotland, Kent and Wales, continued to meet and plot as before, the right began to disintegrate. If they had a plan, it was merely, as Bell ruefully described it months afterwards, to allow Scargill enough rope to hang himself. 'Arthur's got a tiger by the tail,' was the conventionally optimistic wisdom. 'Sooner or later it will hang him.'

It was hardly a formula for effective opposition. Ottey, who warned in the course of the 8 March discussion that 'if you take a decision today under Rule 41, then the strike will lead to civil war throughout the union and the country', always suspected that the whole business of the Scots and Yorkshire letters and the Emlyn Williams motion had been planned in advance. His suspicions were reinforced directly afterwards when he and other finance officers of the union were asked to endorse the arrangement designed to thwart the sequestrators. Such moves, he was convinced, could only indicate a premeditated intention, sooner or later, to breach at least the secondary picketing laws, and he for one wanted nothing to do with it.

His doubts were well founded. Picketing did indeed now move to the centre of the stage. Area after area justified the leadership's fears, as they insisted on local ballots. In every case where these were held – Cumberland, the Midlands, North Wales, Northumberland, Lancashire, South Derbyshire – they failed to produce anything like the requisite degree of support, so efforts multiplied to overturn these results by intimidatory force. At first there were serious efforts, especially in Yorkshire, to keep these activities under tight and responsible control. At an executive meeting in Barnsley on 9 March, Jack Taylor cautioned pickets to restrict themselves to six per pit, keep within the county boundaries, and remain in close contact with the area's central control room, which would be manned on a rota system, twenty-four hours a day, seven days a week. But even before he spoke, the Manvers Main miners, busy blockading Robert Taylor's pit, Manton, had been telling local reporters: 'We'll be in Notts next week.' As the strike teetered in the balance that weekend, with 103,000 more or less definitely out,

Leicester's 2,500 committed against, and 76,000 still un-decided, the cars, coaches and mini-buses started to fan out across the country in search of solidarity, imposed or otherwise. A MORI poll, carried out for the Weekend World television programme that Sunday, showed 62 per cent in favour of the strike, 33 per cent determined to work, and 5 per cent don't knows. With all the arrests, injuries, pitched battles and switches of sentiment that followed, those figures were never more than marginally improved.

Solidarity was patently not the word. At Bilston Glen, Scotland's biggest pit, 1,900 attended a stormy three-hour meeting, and several came to blows as local officials refused to call a vote, and a large part of the labour force expressed its intention to work on regardless. In South Wales, men at sixteen pits and several transport and washery plants initially voted to ignore the strike call, causing Emlyn Williams, who had set the whole dispute in motion, to reflect: 'I've been leading the South Wales miners for twenty-five years and never before encountered a rejection like this.' But the six Welsh collieries which did down tools provided enough pickets to bring out the entire coalfield by the end of the second week. Lancashire, Notts and Derbyshire were over-run by flying Yorkshiremen – mostly from the always militant Doncaster branches, like Hatfield Main and Armthorpe – and all three of the area secretaries, Sid Vincent, Henry Richardson and Gordon Butler, appealed to Jack Taylor to get his men off their members' backs until they had a chance to decide for themselves.

On Monday, 12 March, Taylor was still asking, vainly, for 'a disciplined approach' and some adherence to his earlier guidelines. Within twenty-four hours he had given up the struggle. The Yorkshire executive committee unanimously accepted the picketing of other areas 'forthwith', and man-dated the control centre to take over the organisation, as Taylor announced publicly that 'the gloves are off'. Richard-son in Nottingham, though he personally supported the strike throughout (and as a result found himself suspended from office by his working members), took a bleak and accurate view of what this was likely to do to the highly independent

57

and self-sufficient miners in his county. 'You cannot win a long strike battle if you haven't got the men with you. You cannot force them out,' he warned. And the following day the strike claimed its first major victim, as David Jones, one of the Yorkshire 'flying pickets', died, underlining the cost of ignoring the Richardson appeal.

Ollerton, where David Jones met his death, is one of the least threatened of the NCB's pits, profitable, producing over 1 million tonnes a year, currently enjoying a £25m. modernisation programme and credited with reserves that will last well into the twenty-first century. It was first sunk in the 1920s, and completed in the year of the General Strike. Many of the pickets who descended on it in the spring of 1984 had undoubtedly been briefed by their fathers and grandfathers that 'Ollerton was even built with scab labour'. But in the postwar years it lost much of its pure Nottingham character. The majority of the 1,150 pitmen there arrived during the 1960s, when pits in Durham and Scotland closed by the dozen (the council houses to the north of the village are known as 'the Geordie estate'). It was certainly not lack of experience that persuaded them to ignore Yorkshire's most determined efforts to keep them from work.

The first target for the invasion of pickets had been Harworth, the most northern pit in the Notts area (some of its workings actually extend under Yorkshire), which is famous in mining history as the site of the pitched battle, in 1937, which effectively marked the end of the hated breakaway 'Spencer' union. All but twenty of the Monday morning shift clocked on as usual, after shoving their way through an ominously growing crowd. By lunchtime, there were 200 militants outside the gate to stop any repetition. The twelve policemen on hand were completely outnumbered, even with encouragement from a line of angry wives who were trying to cheer their menfolk into work. The manager reluctantly agreed to close down, provided only that a skeleton safety staff was allowed. That evening, at the biggest branch meeting in years, the furious Harworth men agreed to defy 'the Yorkshire mob' and go in the following day. But when they saw the strength of the Tuesday reinforcements that had been pouring down the A1 – at least 450, it was estimated – even the toughest changed their minds. Harworth stayed closed for the rest of that week. With a first, morale-boosting victory under their belts, the Barnsley and Doncaster battalions moved on to Ollerton. By then, Wednesday, 14 March, both pickets and police were well organised. With six pits out of action in Nottinghamshire and North Derbyshire, strikers by the car, van and coachload swarmed south from Yorkshire to every colliery that was still working.

David Gareth Jones, a twenty-four-year-old miner at Ackton Hall, near Pontefract, had not been on the picket lines before. His car didn't start, so he had to take it to a garage for repairs, but three days into the strike he decided to join his elder brother Trefor in one of the two coaches which were leaving that day from his home village, South Kirkby. Their orders, received in a sealed brown envelope from the Barnsley strike control centre, were to slip through winding back roads to Gedling colliery, fifty miles away in South Notts. A CB radio set, carried on one of the coaches, would pick up warnings from other pickets, locating the police roadblocks now being set up close to the Yorkshire border as hundreds of extra police were drafted in, from as far away as Essex.

Jones was dark-haired, clean-cut, with good-looking sharp features and a natural arrogance which had already landed him in trouble at school and in the tough surroundings of a Yorkshire mining community. His father describes him as 'a lovable rogue' who was not frightened of a fight. Although unmarried, he had two children by different girlfriends. He came from solid mining stock, Welsh rather than Yorkshire. His father, Mark, had moved from a South Wales pit while still in his twenties. There was little politics or trade unionism talked in the house: just an unquestioned loyalty to the NUM. 'He wasn't politically minded,' says his father. 'He cared because that was the way he was. He used to say that they were intending to close down Ackton Hall. He said the Board and the government wanted to close lots more down as revenge for 1974.'

Twenty-five miles from their objective, the Jones brothers' coaches were heading along a road in Clumber Park, a wooded beauty spot in the Dukeries, when they came upon an unexpected police checkpoint. The drivers were persuaded to turn back, but David Jones, with two friends, Tony Short and Andy Slain, decided to get off and try to walk to Ollerton, five miles south, which heavy picketing had so far failed to close. They were soon picked up by other miners in a car that had found a way through the police cordons, and arrived outside the pit gates at 10.10 pm, just as the nightshift, flanked by about 200 policemen, was attempting to bypass a similar number of pickets. After their journey, the three Yorkshiremen were more interested in finding a drink, so they went into the crowded Plough Inn, opposite the lane leading to the colliery, where Jones had a pint of lager. While he was standing at the bar, a young Ollerton miner was brought in, floored by a brick thrown by one of the pickets. Jones, who as a teenager had attended weekly first-aid classes, got a kit from the barmaid and expertly cleaned up the nasty cut over the man's left eye, while someone else fixed up transport to get him to Mansfield hospital for stitches.

Outside, Jones and his friends found themselves in an increasingly violent situation. Many of the nightshift were clustered across the road, separated from the pickets by a wall of police. They joined the pickets. But they became separated for a twenty-minute period, during which there is some inconclusive evidence that Jones was crushed up against a car which was trying to get into the colliery. But he said nothing of this when he rejoined his group, who were now involved in a major mêlée. There was huge resentment among the locals at the aggression of the interlopers, who had imposed themselves on the village for the second night running. Wives had turned out again to cheer as the police escorted their husbands through the scrum at the pit gates. Bricks, rocks, milk and beer bottles, and lumps of wood torn down from nearby garden fences were hailing down on the workers and their bodyguards. Then word reached the picket line that their own cars, parked fifty yards away in Ollerton's main shopping street, were being attacked and damaged by local youths.

Jones, in a crowd with his friends, ran to chase them. They were met by a shower of bricks and stones. At approximately 11.25 pm Jones, who until then had complained of no injury and shown no signs of pain, was struck on the chest, just below the throat, by a half-brick apparently thrown by one of the retreating vandals. He collapsed, unconscious, on a grass patch opposite a shopping parade, and an ambulance which had been standing by for casualties took him to Mansfield Hospital. He died there at eleven minutes past midnight.

It took an hour for the news to get back to Ollerton. When it did, those with CB radios spread it right round the area, and pickets poured in from other pits. In an hour the crowd had swollen from 200 to 400, and an hour after that it was at least 600. The atmosphere grew more menacing as they stood in the cold darkness, watched by an ever increasing number of police. At the suggestion of the commanding officer, NUM officials were summoned to appeal for calm. Scargill and the Yorkshire president, Jack Taylor, were woken and agreed to drive immediately to Ollerton to take charge. Meanwhile the pit manager, Walter Standage, was asked by the local NUM representative to close the colliery – at least until after the area vote, which was due to start on the following day, suitably enough, in the pit surgery. He agreed. As the Notts secretary, Henry Richardson, said, it was 'surrender'. But it was the safest thing to do.

It had turned three in the morning when Scargill arrived and climbed on to a car roof to appeal for calm. When he called for two minutes' silence for Jones, the police were the first to take their caps and helmets off in a gesture of respect. Most of the pickets went home, but a hundred or so, enraged at their colleague's death, moved off to Thoresby, an even bigger and more profitable colliery two miles away, where ugly scuffles with the police produced a number of arrests, and injuries on both sides. In Ollerton, the working miners woke up to find a scene of carnage, with gardens ripped apart and cars scratched, stripped and vandalised. If they had considered voting in favour of the strike before, they were certainly against it now.

At Mansfield the post-mortem revealed a surprising result. Jones had not been killed by the brick. He had suffered a 'massive but short and sharp' compression to the chest, probably against an immovable object. This had torn the roots of nearby blood vessels and slow bleeding then took place, causing tension to build up until his heart stopped beating. A tear in the liver had caused a pint of blood to accumulate in the stomach. At the inquest, concluded three months later, the pathologist, Dr Stephen Jones, told the jury that the victim had probably been pinned against a wall, post or vehicle, probably during the crush at the pit gates.

The incident was very heavily investigated. Early rumours suggested that the police might have had some responsibility for the death. The Nottinghamshire chief constable, Charles McLachlan, promptly ordered a full independent inquiry, and Detective Superintendent Norman Thompson, from Northumbria, spent seven weeks taking and analysing a total of 227 statements before concluding that there was no way to discover what had happened to Jones during the missing twenty minutes before he rejoined his mates. There was little option but to return an open verdict.

That did not prevent the NUM from declaring Jones a martyr. In a consoling letter to his parents, Scargill wrote: 'His name and the cause for which he stood will be written in the history books of our land.' The funeral at South Kirkby, with 5,000 people in attendance, was like a trade union demonstration, with innumerable colliery branch banners held high as the procession wound its way from the Joneses' council house to the local cemetery. His mother and father, Mark and Doreen, were propelled into the forefront of the strike, writing memoirs, appearing at rallies, meeting leaders of the Trade Union Congress at their annual gathering in Brighton, and Labour's Neil Kinnock at his party conference in Blackpool. A year to the day after their son's death, the family took wreaths to Ollerton and laid them on the grass patch where he collapsed. Significantly they were quickly removed. The locals, still bitter at the intimidation they had suffered, considered them 'a provocation'. But David Gareth Jones's name will be made to live on. When the NUM's planned new head office is finally completed in Sheffield, a plaque to his memory – alongside others, commemorating another picket line victim, Joe Green, and also the work of the women's support groups – will take a prominent place just inside the front entrance.

The official dispute diary kept by South Yorkshire's chief constable, Peter Wright, opens: '9 March 1984. strike commenced. Incident room set up in police headquarters.' Three days later, on the Monday, he dispatched his first Police Support Units (PSUs) – each consisting of one inspector, two sergeants and twenty constables – into Nottingham to help contain the picketing. On Tuesday, 3,000 officers from all over the North of England were there too, reinforcing the massively outnumbered local constabulary, just 2,260 strong, in their fight to keep open the county's twenty-five pits. The National Reporting Centre, located in Room 1309, New Scotland Yard, was put into 'monitoring phase', ready to coordinate the biggest mutual-support police operation ever mounted in peacetime Britain.

But Mrs Thatcher was openly angered by the very partial success being achieved. As reports flowed in showing that of the eighty-three pits open at the beginning of the week, only twenty-nine were now working normally, she spoke witheringly to a group of new young Tory MPs about the 'fourth-rate' chief constables who were failing to hold the line. That afternoon, the Wednesday, 14 March, the NRC went on full operational alert, and the home secretary, Leon Brittan, prepared an uncompromising statement for delivery in the House of Commons the following day. 'The legal position is clear,' he affirmed. 'Any attempt to obstruct or intimidate those who wish to go to work is a breach of the criminal law. The mere presence of large numbers of pickets can be intimidating. The police have the duty to prevent obstruction and intimidation.' As he further made clear, they had all the powers necessary to do the job, and his full support in their use. Sir Laurence Byford, Her Majesty's Chief Inspector of Constabulary, and a key figure in the public order hierarchy, had been dispatched to Nottingham as a matter of urgency to make sure that they were put to good use.

The Reporting Centre soon became a subject of controversy. Because of the scale and effectiveness of its operations, and its lack of clear accountability, it was widely seen, especially on the left, as the unacknowleged beginnings of a kind of national force to handle riots and civil disturbance. This has always been strenuously denied, both in Whitehall and by the police themselves, jealously guarding their traditional local autonomy. But there is no doubt that the NRC, whatever its status, played a key role in blunting the picket weapon. It was probably the most significant new institution to come of age during the strike. As with the Civil Contingencies Unit, Scargill himself was largely responsible for its birth, which stemmed directly from the Saltley Gate débâcle of 1972. But it had been only intermittently used in the intervening years (never during the period of the 1974–9 Labour administration) and none of the tasks it was involved with – the 1980 prison officers' dispute, the 1981 Liverpool riots or the 1982 visit of Pope John Paul II – had been any real preparation for 1984. On its performance during the strike, however, its designers can certainly claim to have built a formidably flexible and efficient machine.

The man in charge of it at the start was David Hall, chief constable of Humberside, who had been elected to the job by his 200 colleagues in the Association of Chief Police Officers (they represent the forty-three English and Welsh forces, the Metropolitan and City of London police, and the Royal Ulster Constabulary, but not, for historic reasons, Scotland) at their annual meeting the previous September. Six months later his place was taken by McLachlan, whose Nottingham fiefdom had always been on the hottest part of the firing line.

On 13 March, when the Yorkshire pickets first stormed into Notts, Hall travelled to London to set the NRC in motion. Most of the time it consists of little more than a dusty thirteenth-floor cupboard full of telephones and office equipment. After this was moved out and assembled, Hall and his hastily recruited team started to gather all available information from local forces on how many men they could send to the coalfields and how many were needed. By the end of the first week, the NRC was fully active.

Hall had two groups assisting him. The decision-making team was supplied by ACPO. It consisted of Hall's Humberside staff officer, Tony Galloway, a South Wales superintendent, John Rowling, who was given overall charge of running the centre, and a Bristol inspector, Dave Leach. The second team, who manned the phones and communications network, consisted of six police, headed by a chief superintendent, all seconded from the Metropolitan Police. When Hall was not there a rota of chief constables and deputy chief constables from southern England took overall charge on behalf of ACPO.

The National Reporting Centre is housed in an oblong conference room. All along one side windows look out across south London. At one end of the room a large force-by-force map of England and Wales showed which forces were giving and receiving aid. Coloured symbols (kept in a biscuit tin) attached to the map showed the detailed picture. A brown circle showed a force was receiving help. A pink triangle indicated that a force had its own men available. Green and red arrows showed availability from other areas. Later in the summer a more detailed map of the Midlands coalfield was installed, showing every pit and power station.

Along the long wall opposite the windows were hung charts and tables showing current dispositions from and in each police force area. At a glance it was possible to see who had sent how much to whom, along with daily and cumulative totals of arrests, injuries and damage. A separate table logged the numbers of pickets and sites involved. The 'mood' in each area was classified 'peaceful', 'hostile' or 'violent'. The charts were updated twice daily, morning and afternoon, following changes of shift in the coalfields. At the far end of the room a further table listed forthcoming demands for police manpower throughout, so that non-strike needs were

65

taken into account. All this was logged in a desk-top computer as well as on the charts. The computer was acquired after the dispute had been some weeks old, because the cramped centre was running out of filing space. Messages to and from the centre went by phone on direct lines through the Scotland Yard main exchange and, at the start of the dispute, by teleprinter. As the strike wore on, however, the teleprinter was abandoned in favour of a terminal and keyboard which enabled the NRC to access the Metropolitan Police's own message-switch system. This in turn lightened the load on the NRC team, as the message system operators in the basement of Scotland Yard were then responsible for collating the daily reports to and from forces.

Each morning the NRC received a report from every force in the country. Later a report, combining the raw statistics and giving a detailed breakdown of pit incidents, was compiled by the Centre's staff for the ACPO president. Then a representative of the Home Office's F4 division, in charge of public order, came to receive a copy of the report and to be briefed.

The Centre was manned twenty-four hours a day. At night and at weekends, the cover was reduced. 'It's a Monday to Friday strike, so we can get off home on Friday afternoons,' one stalwart said, though that was hardly true early on when the policing operation was being constantly revised and no day was free.

All police officers have to know how to control crowds. Now that there is reluctance to call out the troops, and because the number of volunteer 'specials' has sharply declined and élite units like London's 'special patrol groups' are too few in number to be effective in a really widespread disturbance, police forces have had to turn to their own ranks. The chosen method, endorsed by the 1974 police Home Defence Report, has been to train a proportion of the younger, normally male, constables and drill them into police support units (PSUs).

These are the principal resource of the modern mutual-aid system. The total number of PSUs in England and Wales is 599, a total of 1,377 officers, which is rather more than 10 per cent of the total male strength (women are not members of PSUS and are not normally trained for riot control, an omission which caused a row at the 1984 Police Federation conference). Most PSUS are trained to use riot shields and to operate in conjunction with other groups, such as mounted police and dog handlers. But not all are, an omission which has caused some frustration during the 1984–5 operations. The organisation of PSUS has greatly improved, however, and become more standardised as a result of a Home Office review of 'arrangements for handling spontaneous disorder' in 1980.

As a result Hall was able to command by far the largest and most effective mutual-aid operation ever undertaken by the British police, completely transcending anything done by the NRC during its previous eleven-year existence. Within three hours of taking over, Hall had mobilised 1,000 officers for Nottinghamshire from five other forces. A week later the figure stood at a maximum of 6,990, with a further rise in the next seven days to 7,500. By then all but two of the country's forty-three police areas had become involved. Ten weeks into the dispute the rest had become either givers or receivers of PSU aid. A total of 220,000 officer assignments was made up to mid-May, and the NRC operation reached a fresh peak in mid-June, the week of Orgreave, when it was finally made clear, with a total of 8,100 police reinforcements on stand-by, that the days of the invincible flying picket were over.

By the weekend of 18 March, it was clear that the police, even if they had not yet established the upper hand, were more than holding their own. Three army camps had been commandeered in Nottinghamshire to billet the reinforcements, and although a glowing account of the conditions there inspired some bitterly complaining letters in *Police Review* (spartan beds; 2 am calls; no hot water; beer whose price went up overnight from 50p to 75p a can) the underlying stituation, as reported by Byford, was well under control. Riot shields, helmets with reinforced protective visors and 'cricket boxes' were now on general issue. Suspected pickets were being halted and rerouted as far away as Scotland (twenty-three turned back at the Border) and Kent, where the first of the much-criticised Dartford Tunnel roadblocks was used to deflect sixteen carloads of miners expressing a wish to 'visit' Leicestershire.

Things had looked much more threatening the previous Tuesday, when the Coal Board made its one attempt to use the government's new trade union laws. Disturbed, if not actually panicked, by the upsurge in violence, MacGregor authorised application to the High Court for an injunction to ban flying pickets. The next day, after 133 of the country's pits failed to open, this was duly granted by Mr Justice Nolan. The Yorkshiremen then started to withdraw, but this had little to do with respect for the law. A deal had been done with the Notts leaders that for forty-eight hours the area would picket its own pits, while the 29,000 members there were left free to conduct their ballot. It was merely a temporary truce, and in Barnsley the Yorkshire executive agreed unanimously to ignore the court and 'continue the normal established trade union practices to win solidarity for our members in their effort to save their pits and jobs'. If Nottinghamshire voted to continue working – as it did, by a 75 to 25 per cent margin – the pickets would be back to change their minds.

On Friday, therefore, MacGregor sought leave to pursue contempt proceedings against the Yorkshire NUM. No less a figure than Labour's deputy speaker, Harold Walker, went on Radio Sheffield to say it was 'the daftest thing he's done since he took office' (a statement for which he later half-apologised to the House, saying 'there are occasions on which it is impossible to keep silent'). But by Monday the NCB had been persuaded to see things in a different light. As 2,000 Yorkshire pitmen surrounded the baroque battlements of their Barnsley head office to defy sequestrators, the NCB decided to stay its hand. MacGregor's own explanation is that by then the police had firmly re-established control. There is no direct evidence that the government used its influence to persuade him to drop that very hot potato, but there is no doubt that Peter Walker, in particular, attached great importance to keeping the Employment acts as far as possible out of the firing line. Given the deep-rooted opposition of both the Labour party and the whole trade union movement to these laws, their careless use – though vociferously demanded throughout the strike by the more died-in-the-wool Tory supporters – was seen as the one factor that could solidify Scargill's otherwise very fragmented support. Walker feared their use would turn 'Scargill's strike' into a general unions vs. government confrontation.

Much effort was made behind the scenes to dissuade employers, private as well as public, to deny themselves this legal remedy, even when their businesses were being badly hurt by the dispute. Junior ministers like Alan Clark, at employment, spent earnest hours explaining how important it was to hold off. British Rail, whose valuable coal trade was particularly vulnerable, sent out copies of the acts to all their managers as the disruption started to bite, but they steered very clear of actually invoking them, even when action by the two big rail unions was running them into costs approaching £80 million. In the end, only two small West German hauliers and a group of North-East shipping firms made any attempt to flout the informal ban. It was other, and much longer-established applications of the law – often instigated by miners themselves – which in the end did more serious damage to the NUM cause.

Some of the legal powers claimed by the police – particularly those justifying the large-scale halting and rerouting of traffic – generated disquiet. For days at a time parts of Nottinghamshire became a virtual no-go area as would-be visitors ran a gauntlet of roadblocks and spot traffic checks. In the first twenty-seven weeks of the strike, according to the chief constable, Charles McLachlan, 164,508 'presumed pickets' were prevented from entering the county, many of them just ordinary people attempting to go about their business with no notion of 'causing a breach of the peace'. But whoever they were, they either turned back when ordered or faced immediate arrest. Attempts to clarify the position, or impose tighter definitions, met with short shrift and minimum sympathy. Two days after the Dartford Tunnel incident, 150 miles and three hours' driving from the Midland coalfields, Kent miners were briskly refused an injunction to raise their travel restrictions. In a written parliamentary answer, the attorney-general, Sir Michael Havers, said: 'There is no doubt that if a constable reasonably comes to a conclusion that persons are travelling for the purpose of taking part in a picket . . . he has the power at common law to call upon them not to continue their journey.' It was some months after that Mr Justice Skinner set some restrictions on those powers, requiring that the police should only act when the anticipated breach of the peace was 'in close proximity both in time and place'.

Meanwhile the battle for Nottingham's soul surged on. On Wednesday 21 March, the area executive issued orders to the men who had overwhelmingly rejected the strike motion that they were to respect picket lines at all the twenty-five pits. This was widely rejected, as a high proportion ignored the crowds, missiles and abuse and forced their way, with heavy police support, into work. Main roads on the Yorkshire and Derbyshire borders, and on all the minor routes and back lanes near a colliery, were heavily patrolled, often with a police helicopter overhead. Windscreens were smashed with crowbars on the Thursday, and the following Monday, 26 March, roadblocks and road-narrowing cones went up on every motorway sliproad leading into the region. Frustrated would-be pickets retaliated by blocking the M1 entirely, as one hundred cars crawled north from Balborough, taking several hours to cover fourteen miles. Another convoy closed twelve miles of the A1 between Blythe and Doncaster, where 200 protesters were encircling the NCB's local headquarters, Coal House. Eight police were hurt and twenty-one miners arrested – part of a swelling countrywide total which topped 300 the following day.

Magistrates embarked on another much-questioned practice: issuing standard printed bail forms to all charged with picketing offences, major or minor, which embodied a number of onerous conditions on residence, movement and avoiding any form of NCB property. Critics like Tony Benn claimed that these smacked of house arrest and the South African pass laws, but legal challenge on the whole brought no relief. The effect, as time went on, was a very significant thinning out of the potential pickets – especially when men who broke bail found themselves often serving longer prison sentences than could have been imposed for the original offence.

Chapter 3

The Ballot That Never Was

As March drew to a close, all the principal parties paused briefly to take stock. By that time the Yorkshire pickets, in particular, had amply demonstrated their ability to move with near-military precision, and to assemble in formidable force. But they had not been able to translate this capacity into any very clear-cut success. Everywhere that it mattered, the police had held them. Almost 45,000 miners were still working. Isolated pits had stayed open, or restarted, in Lancashire, Warwickshire, Leicestershire, South Derbyshire and the West Midlands, as well as the main body in Notts. Also it was becoming obvious that the NUM's central directing intelligence left a good deal to be desired. Workers at Old-bury nuclear power station were unimpressed when a cordon of picketing pitmen pleaded with them to take no more deliveries of coal. And although cooperative British Rail men succeeded in halving coke supplies to the main Scunthorpe blast furnace, it was common knowledge in the area that this was an installation British Steel would be only too happy to close.

Elsewhere, appeals for support from other unions were being widely ignored, even when reinforced, as they were on 29 March, with a ringing joint declaration from the transport and seamen's leaders. On 2 April, when 100 generating stations were systematically picketed, the power workers, by and large, just shouldered their way through, saying they saw little reason to show solidarity with people whose own ranks were so patently split. Coal supplies, with 25m. tonnes at the pithead, and rather more in the hands of the CEGB, were at least as high as they had been at the start of the overtime ban. Only a major collaborative effort now offered any real chance of falsifying Peter Walker's latest Commons prediction that there would be no power cuts 'at least for half a year'.

Increasing attention therefore refocused on the question of the missing ballot. Neil Kinnock let it be known that he was very worried at the way the NUM leadership was allowing internal arguments to drive its members apart, and many Labour MPs indicated, in private and in public, that they thought a democratic vote was the only way to give the miners even a fighting chance. Four face-workers at Hem Heath colliery near Stoke-on-Trent began a sit-in 3,000 feet underground to add their own support for this view; and within the NUM itself new hope flickered that Scargill and the left, faced with the realities of the situation, could be persuaded to change tack.

There was at least some basis for this. Heathfield, for instance, with his Derbyshire experience still freshly in mind, was on record, right up to the eve of the Cortonwood announcement, with the belief that 'our ability to sustain an attack on the National Coal Board and the government is dependent on winning the support of the miners in the Midland coalfields, in my coalfield, and in Staffordshire and Warwickshire'. Even the Yorkshire District Committee of the Communist Party, meeting early in March, had only very narrowly rejected a motion pressing the national ballot option. So now the moderates on the national executive decided, with much heart-searching, to make one more effort to undo the damage of 8 March. But although their intentions were sensible and sincere, their arrangements for what Heathfield later derisively dismissed as 'the secret public meeting' were amateurish to the point of farce.

Strike

Roy Ottey, Trevor Bell and Ted McKay, with backing this time from the mercurial Lancashire secretary, Sid Vincent, were again the moving spirits. With various slightly cloak-and-dagger arrangements (Ray Chadburn, for example, felt he could not leave London without 'blowing the gaff' and nominated the Nottinghamshire treasurer, Roy Lynk, later to emerge as one of the main leaders of the working miners, to vote in his place), they finally assembled a group of eight to meet at the Brant Inn, Groby, outside Leicester, on Tuesday, 27 March. The idea was to ensure a sufficient majority to swing the national executive when it held its next formal meeting to consider the state of the dispute, which had been set for 12 April. With pledges of backing from Northumberland, Durham, the Durham mechanics and the cokemen, they reckoned they could carry the day by thirteen votes to eleven.

If they had been able to spring their pro-ballot resolution as a last-minute surprise it might have worked. But they never got that chance. Thanks to inept organisation – the conspirators forgathered not in a private room, but in a corner of the saloon bar, and the whole place was stiff with police, reporters and TV camera teams – the whole enterprise blew up in a blaze of premature publicity. The agreed statement looked solid enough, urging Scargill and Heathfield to call an immediate executive meeting to organise a national ballot, but it gave the leftwingers plenty of time, if they wished, to set up a crippling counter-offensive. Meanwhile the moderates, as they tried to justify themselves to their various groups of often highly critical members, showed that they too were damagingly divided. Vincent, who had almost walked out when he first saw the TV lights, wanted it made clear that the aim was to solidify the strike and make it more effective, which was very largely the case; but by insisting on self-protective clauses encouraging working miners to cross picket lines and appealing for the withdrawal of flying pickets, too many of the others made it look as though they just wanted to call the whole thing off. In a storm of vituperation (in North Staffordshire the placards read 'Ottey is a Traitor') the whole effort was stillborn.

The Ballot That Never Was

But the ballot issue would not go away. To union officials across the country, anxious to help the miners but equally concerned not to get out of step with their own members, it was of central importance. For men like Dennis Widdowson, secretary for the National Union of Railwaymen at Shirebrook in North Derbyshire, its absence presented an almost insoluble conundrum. The general position of the transport unions had been stated by Jim Slater, of the National Union of Seamen, after a fraternal meeting with Scargill at the end of March. 'We can't afford to let the miners lose this strike,' he said. 'It would put us back to 1926. And it is doubtful if we would ever recover.' Like every other NUR and engine-drivers' branch, Shirebrook had received a head office circular endorsing that message and ordering a complete ban on coal movements. But Shirebrook was in a very special and delicate position. Sometimes known as the largest village in England, it sits right on the Nottinghamshire border and contains not only the biggest colliery in the district, but a rail depot for no fewer than forty trains a day running a non-stop 'merry-go-round' service to the big coal-fired generating stations in the Trent Valley – Ratcliffe-on-Soar, West Burton and Cottam. The Shirebrook pit was by then solidly on strike, despite a narrow local majority against such action. But most of the men in the North Notts collieries, just a few miles away, had equally firmly insisted on working, and the loaded wagons in the Shirebrook sidings testified to their productivity. As a result seventy-five of Widdowson's guards, calculating that the continued prosperity of Notts coal was the best guarantee for their own future jobs, had flatly refused to operate their union's recommended ban. On Sunday, 8 April, just four days before the meeting of the NUM executive, an impressive group of NUR leaders travelled to Shirebrook in an attempt to make them change their minds.

On his way to the local golf course that morning, Widdowson stopped to talk about his problem. 'My members have never disobeyed an executive instruction in the nineteen years I've been branch secretary here,' he said. 'But they feel this isn't their fight, and it could jeopardise our industry.' And he added wistfully: 'If the NUM held a national ballot,

75

got the 55 per cent majority, and then decided to strike, of course my members wouldn't move any coal.' He never got his wish, but in the end, with considerable bitterness, most of the guards were pressured back into line. But not all. British Rail continued to move some coal through Shirebrook for the entire duration of the strike. In turn the NUR was forced, as a significant concession, to change its rules and arrange to pay basic wages for the largely unwilling men who were sent home for refusing to work the coal trains; and again and again, in similar circumstances, the lack of a ballot was cited by other unions and groups of workers as a reason for withholding effective industrial support. As even NUM activists came to accept in the end, 'it was like a monkey on our backs'. In the post-strike inquests, even those conducted on the extreme left, it was singled out as one of the prime reasons for the miners' ultimate defeat.

A particularly virulent argument blew up on this topic after George Bolton, McGahey's deputy in Scotland and also president of the British Communist party, told a *Marxism Today* forum in the spring of 1985 that without mass picketing in Notts and the refusal to hold a ballot the strike might have been won. Peter Heathfield responded furiously, pointing out that Bolton himself had participated in the decisions he was now attacking; and careful inquiry establishes that scarcely any dissent about the Scargill Rule 41 strategy was ever expressed among broad-left activists at the time. Indeed, at the meeting they held before the crucial 12 April executive, the decision to exclude the moderates' pro-ballot resolutions and opt instead for a special delegate conference was explicitly endorsed. The main significance of the post-mortem row relates not to the period of the strike, in fact, but to future union attitudes towards the government's strongly pro-ballot labour legislation. With hindsight, it is widely seen that the most profitable policy may not be to avoid votes but to make sure of winning them.

It would probably have been physically dangerous, in any case, to express any such unpopular doubts in Sheffield during the week when it really mattered. The pickets' chosen anthem for the day of the executive meeting was the old

Welsh hymn tune, 'Cwm Rhondda', and 2,500 of them gathered in front of St James's House, roaring it out to the words 'Arthur Scargill, Arthur Scargill; we support you . . . ever more.' When a pretty girl passed they briefly altered the lyric and invited her, in the same solemn cadence, to take all her clothes off; but that was just a diversion from the main business, which was to make sure that whatever the arguments of logic and expediency, there would be no sell-out, and certainly no ballot. Yorkshire had agreed to provide finance and transport for 'peaceful lobbying', but only up to a limit of four representatives from each of the county's fifty-three remaining pits. The noisy, belligerent, mostly under-thirty crowd, eclipsing that modest figure by at least ten to one, offered no quarrel with the news headlines that labelled them 'Arthur's Red Guard'. Any member of the executive, like Ray Chadburn or Henry Richardson, suspected of half-heartedness over Rule 41, was shoved, kicked and vilified on his way into the hall, and twenty-four of the hecklers had already been arrested and hauled away by the 1,500 police in attendance before the assembled officials were ready to take their seats.

The extent of that highly visible and overpoweringly audible support constituted one of the key factors in making up Scargill's mind how to proceed. If industrial battles, as he remains convinced, are won and lost on the picket lines, then these were the front-line troops; and the overriding necessity was to keep them in good heart. He has never accepted the argument, embraced by his critics right across the political spectrum, that avoiding a ballot was wrong *in principle*. But there is also the major *tactical* question: should it have been called anyway, on the grounds that, as many believe, it would have been won with a clear majority, thus unifying the strike and sharply improving the odds on forcing the NCB and the government to back down?

When the dispute first began, Scargill was probably right in calculating, as he has frequently reaffirmed, that a national ballot would have been lost. But the passage of time and the ebb and flow of events and opinion were changing the balance. Five weeks earlier a MORI poll for Weekend World

77

had found 62 per cent of NUM members in favour of a strike, 35 per cent against and 5 per cent undecided. Assuming that the don't knows would have failed to vote, those figures translated into a 65:35 'yes' majority – but given the fallability of pollsters and the need for a clear 55 per cent endorsement it could still be read as too close for comfort. But now attitudes had significantly hardened. MORI's 13 April sampling, undertaken for *The Sunday Times* the day after the crucial executive, showed 68 per cent for, 26 per cent against and 6 per cent uncommitted. On the same basis as before, that would have produced an almost unassailable 72 per cent vote in favour. Even Nottingham, the most resolutely reluctant area, had by now apparently revised its view from outright opposition to a 42:43 dead-heat in the area council.

The assessment was still a good deal less than unanimous. Nottingham's real attitude, for example, would have been sharply questioned by Henry Richardson, himself a dedicated ballot supporter, who for all that felt impelled to tell his fellow-executive members that after recent events in his native village of Cresswell, where 1,000 pickets had rampaged through daubing on doors and smashing windows, 'we lost all the support we had in one hour'. Also Scargill's scepticism was widely shared within the government. On the basis of private polls, specially carried out by Harris and Gallup under the direction of Opinion Research Centre, Peter Walker was convinced that any ballot would come down against the strike – which is why he so consistently advocated holding one. The NCB, on the other hand, though using the same results, thinks that an April vote could easily have gone either way. What is not in dispute though is that the risks had been substantially diminished. With the required majority cut from 55 to 50 per cent, which was one of the proposals discussed and recommended at the executive meeting, most Labour party and trade union observers are now convinced that a pro-strike ballot would have been home and dry. Only the NUM president and the energy secretary are, for once, united in dissent.

Given the pressures, however, and the undoubted dividends that a successful ballot would have earned in terms of political legitimacy and the conversion of half-hearted into solid union support, it remains hard to understand Scargill's adamantine resistance. The best explanation, now embraced by much of the left in the course of various post-strike recriminations, is that the miners' leader had been just too effective in stirring up the emotions of his rank and file. The ballot issue, in the minds of the militants, had become a symbol of betrayal for those in favour, and virility among those who opposed. As Ken Capstick, the Labour-voting NUM delegate from Stillingfleet, in the Selby complex, later summed it up: 'The trouble was the national ballot had been made into an issue in itself. It was like giving in. You've got to remember that we had lads, masses of them, who were picketing every day, total commitment, never seen such commitment from people . . . They looked at it that Margaret Thatcher wanted a ballot, Ian MacGregor wanted a ballot, the media wanted a ballot, and they weren't going to have one.'

In the event, Scargill went along with that analysis. With his extraordinary charismatic sway over the mass of his members, particularly the younger men, he could no doubt have found words to justify even a 180-degree policy turn, but he chose not to make the effort – if only on the view that persuading them to accept a ballot which was then defeated would constitute just too big a gamble. He listened to speech after speech in favour of democratic voting, from all the Leicester conspirators and a variety of others, and then blandly used his powers as chairman to declare any pro-ballot motion out of order. He justified this decision on the technically debatable grounds that the same question had been proposed and rejected on 8 March, and could not be re-opened at another executive session. Although the moderates had their majority all sewn up, with many of their more radically inclined colleagues also mandated by area vote to support them, and the whole Scargill tactic had been signalled in newspaper leaks a full week earlier, no one, on the day, proved able to counter the president's gambit, and he swiftly passed to other business. The matter of the ballot, he blithely announced, would be resolved at a special delegate conference to be held in a week's time. And there, as everyone knew, the dedicated militants would be well in control.

The only faint hope now was that Scargill, with a recommendation to lower the ballot majority to 50 per cent safely under his belt, might have a last-minute change of heart. But few were prepared to put much money on that. Certainly not the government, which that weekend announced the composition of its special 'war Cabinet', formally charged with the task of spiking the miners' guns. Peter Walker and Mrs Thatcher were to be reinforced with a team including Norman Tebbit (industry), Tom King (employment), Sir Michael Havers (attorney-general), Nicholas Ridley (transport), Leon Brittan (home secretary), George Younger (Scottish Office), Michael Heseltine (defence) and Nigel Lawson (chancellor of the exchequer). Whitehall spokesmen made it crystal-clear that their ministers, with varied degrees of reluctance, were now resigned to a long, grim haul.

The sceptics were right, and the evidence was clearly visible on the windcheaters and donkey-jackets of the 7,000 rank-and-file strikers who were milling around the Sheffield Memorial Hall when the delegates duly assembled on 19 April. A freshly manufactured crop of lapel badges, echoing the headlines of the far-left press, carried the terse and contradictory, but also self-explanatory slogan: 'Simple majority; no ballot'. Among all the motley horde of dedicated newspaper sellers, only Fran Eden, of the Revolutionary Communist party, carried anything still advocating a democratic vote, and she was patently out of step with the mood of the crowd. Even Richardson and Chadburn had confessed the error of their ways and started calling on their ballot-seeking Nottingham members to change tack and join the strike regardless. The uncompromising response by the working miners was to push up coal production, for the first time since February, to over 500,000 tonnes a week. But the gesture brought the two beleaguered Notts leaders in from the cold; they were escorted through the centre of Sheffield, where a week earlier they had been in physical danger, by a distinguished bodyguard including Heathfield, McGahey, Scargill himself, and perhaps most usefully by the president's burly and inseparable driver, Jim Parker.

Inside the hall, as the moderates made their last, ineffectual efforts to roll back the anti-ballot tide, neither said a word. Two of their junior Nottingham associates, Roy Lynk and the area agent, David Prendergast, were left to support the principle of a free vote, and to oppose the 50 per cent rule change. The only really effective speech on the side of democratic choice was made by Lancashire's Bernard Donaghy, one of the three candidates defeated by Scargill in 1981. 'If you think at the back of your mind that a ballot vote will lose, and yet you are still urging your men to strike, then I think you are cheating on the membership,' he thundered. But his argument was swept away by the passionate eloquence of the other side. Heathfield, in his first big speech as secretary, charged that Ian MacGregor, in his quest for an efficient, low-cost, high-output coal industry, was also saying, unacceptably: 'Turn your backs on your comrades in Scotland, Durham, South Wales and Kent. Turn your backs on them and enable me to organise this industry to give you the highest wages in the world.'

To loud applause he faced the NUM's biggest tactical problem – the difficulty of getting effective support from other unions when so many miners were still at work. But he then dismissed this, with what had become the union's stock argument in favour of using Rule 41: 'I hope we are sincere and honest enough to recognise that a ballot should not be used and exercised as a veto to prevent people in other areas defending their jobs.' It proved an effective line. The moderate opposition tied itself in knots trying to demonstrate that, despite its belief in ballots, it was as eager as anyone to oppose pit closures. True to form, four distinct resolutions were proposed on the subject, each with wording more convoluted than the last, and all went down to clear-cut defeat. As Yorkshire's Jack Taylor told the various movers, in words that would later be quoted in a whole series of court hearings on the conduct and validity of the strike, the reason for their failure was that 'we don't really trust you'. When the tightly organised left, represented by the Kent leader, Jack Collins, put in its own, solitary proposal – making no mention of a ballot, and merely asking the conference, as the union's supreme decision-making body, to endorse a call for all working miners to down tools and join the dispute – it was passed, not overwhelmingly but convincingly, by sixty-nine votes to fifty-one.

Scargill summed up the session, before going out into the sunshine to address the seething crowds. Brushing aside any constitutional niceties raised by the proceedings, he affirmed: 'I am the custodian of the rulebook, and I want to say to my colleagues in the union that there is one rule, above all the rules in the book, and that is that when workers are involved in action you do not cross picket lines in any circumstances.' Outside the police paraded in self-consciously disciplined ranks, and were almost immediately called on to suppress a savage pub fight. For an hour they, press photographers, television crews and anyone who could be remotely identified as 'a lackey of the capitalist media' had to negotiate a hail of bricks, blows and strident verbal abuse. There were sixty-eight arrests and dozens of minor injuries. Billy Stobbs, a Durham member of the national executive, had two ribs crushed during a police charge while vainly urging his members to re-board their homegoing coach, and ended up in Sheffield Royal Infirmary. The conflict's first buoyant, all-over-by-Easter phase was now clearly past. Appropriately the characteristic picket-line chant changed around this time; henceforth it was no longer 'Cwm Rhondda', but the challenging defiance of the Sheffield Wednesday supporters' call: 'Here we go! Here we go! Here we go!'

Chapter 4

Battle for Orgreave

South Yorkshire, quite recently as throbbing an industrial landscape as the Ruhr or Tokyo Bay, is nowadays a grimy, silent wasteland. The M1 motorway cuts through a vista of dismantled steelworks, abandoned collieries and grassed-over slagheaps. In normal times the main sign of continuing economic life is a massive cluster of black, smoking chimneys, grey gasometers and huge coke-ovens which stands beside the main turn-off to Sheffield. This is the Orgreave coke-works, property of the British Steel Corporation, which takes coal from pits like Cortonwood, bakes it at high temperatures to drive out the volatile gases, and prepares it for feeding to the four big blast-furnaces still operating forty miles away at BSC's Scunthorpe plant. It was here, between 23 May and 18 June, that small armies of police fought pitmen in their hundreds, and frequently many thousands, in a sustained and ultimately successful demonstration that the mass picket, whatever its past successes, was no longer an irresistible force.

Electricity is far and away the biggest customer for coal – it burned 81.8m. tonnes in the last full pre-strike year – and closing the generating stations, or even inflicting major power cuts, would have been by far the most damaging tactic in the

83

miners' armoury. However, with record stocks in the hands of the CEGB and South of Scotland Electricity Board (23.4m. tonnes at the beginning of March 1984) and a warm early spring already eating away at demand, this was discarded as an unrealistic target. Despite anguished criticism from many rank-and-file strikers, particularly in South Wales, this view persisted to the end among the miners' leaders. Indeed, apart from an occasional foray to symbolic places like Didcot, most power stations remained largely picket-free throughout the dispute. Steel, on the other hand, though a much smaller user – its blast-furnaces took only 4.3m. tonnes in 1983–4, and that was a year of modest recovery – at least offered some chance of making an immediate and dramatic impact, particularly if the busy car and engineering sectors could be starved of their essential supplies. The decision was made, therefore, in the very earliest days of the strike, to concentrate maximum effort on cutting deliveries to the four biggest integrated steel complexes, Port Talbot and Llanwern in South Wales, Ravenscraig on the Clyde, and Scunthorpe in Lincolnshire.

It proved a decision much easier to endorse at national headquarters, though, than to implement effectively on the ground. The fortunes of coal and steel remain inextricably entwined, perhaps even more now that both have suffered a precipitate decline. In 1974, when Britain was at the peak of its last real boom, closing Scunthorpe's showpiece Anchor works was a near-knockout blow for the Heath government. But ten years later Anchor was just a shadow of its former dominant self, and shutting it was less likely to bring swift victory than to put even more miners and steelworkers on the dole. As a result loyalties and priorities, even at the highest level in the NUM, were in deep disarray. Men like Mick McGahey, a Communist party member who had fought for years and worked even with members of the Scottish Tory party to keep Ravenscraig open in defiance of industrial logic and crumbling markets, found it hard to give wholehearted backing to a blockade that might well close the rolling mills and billet forges for ever. With total non-cooperation from the steel unions, and sharp divisions throughout the rest of the Labour movement, coherent and effective action was close to impossible. Predictably, the attempt to impose such a flawed policy provoked endless confrontation and some of the bitterest clashes of the strike. When the final accounts were totted up, British Steel was able to report that output, far from falling, had exceeded all expectations for the year.

The campaign to get a stranglehold on steel began as early as 29 March, when, at Scargill's behest, the rail, road transport and seamen's unions called on their members to block all movement of coal. These groups made up the logistical end of the famous Triple Alliance, which since the 1920s had been supposed to bind the workers in coal, steel and transport together into an irresistible industrial force. But its notorious weakness and divisiveness under fire caused it long ago to be re-christened 'the cripple alliance', and Bill Sirs, general secretary of the Iron and Steel Trades Confederation, the main union in that industry, quickly demonstrated the aptness of the phrase. He instantly perceived the threat and within twenty-four hours had broken ranks, accusing the miners and their allies of threatening his members' jobs, announcing that he would never see them 'sacrificed on someone else's altar', and throwing in for good measure that the ISTC would unhesitatingly handle fuel supplies, 'scab' or otherwise, from any source that presented itself. A week later, his national executive unanimously backed his stand, and although the National Union of Railwaymen and the train drivers' union, Aslef, tried to step up the pressure, the predictable cracks quickly appeared. The assault on steel was barely a week old before the first of many compromise deals was agreed. On 6 April, McGahey gave the go-ahead for two trainloads of coal a day to go into Ravenscraig, after appeals from the steelworkers that this was the only way to save the furnaces from collapsing. On 10 April, Jack Taylor, the Yorkshire president, agreed that 15,700 tonnes of coal a week could be funnelled from Cortonwood, Silverwood and Barrow to provide a similar safety net for Scunthorpe. Emlyn Williams, in South Wales, underwrote parallel arrangements for Port Talbot and Llanwern.

Such fudged and inherently unstable arrangements were almost bound to break down. They regularly did, leaving the men involved on both sides confused and angry. The bitter irony of their situation was vividly illustrated at Polkemmet, the last pit left in West Lothian, west of Edinburgh, after a series of earlier closures. Its only reason for continued existence was to supply coking coal for Ravenscraig, the huge steel plant at Motherwell on the Clyde. But with the virtual collapse of the heavy steel users it had been built to service – the shipyards, like John Brown and Upper Clyde, the car and lorry plants like Linwood and Bathgate, and dozens of others – Ravenscraig's future was now in deep doubt. As every one of the 1,300 Polkemmet miners knew, any successful attempt to picket out 'The Craig' was 90 per cent guaranteed to cost them their own jobs. When the national strike was first mooted in early March, the pithead voting there was four to one against any action. As John Burns, the NUM branch delegate, said at the time: 'A lot felt there was too much at stake.' But they were overruled. Inside a fortnight there were picket lines outside every gate leading into Ravenscraig, and an eerie, often violent and ultimately destructive bout of shadow-boxing began, as the miners and their allies tried to inflict some dramatic wound without actually crippling or killing the victim, and the steelmen, however sympathetic some were to the larger cause, battled grimly and effectively to nullify their efforts.

The first phase ended with McGahey's two-train concession, when the steel union leaders, like Clive Lewis of ISTC, and Tommy Brennan, convenor of the Ravenscraig shop stewards, argued successfully for enough coal to keep the coke-ovens and furnaces in the plant safe from the really serious damage they would sustain if the fires ever went out. It was never intended, though, that there should be enough fuel for actual production. No stipulation had been laid down as to the acceptable length of 'a train' and it was with mounting suspicion that the pickets noticed the number of trucks were gradually growing, day by day. On 27 April, when the extra load reached eight and another locomotive had to be coupled up to pull it, the NUM and the railwaymen abruptly announced that from then on they would only allow one train delivery per day.

That was the signal for fresh trouble. The BSC announced 'emergency measures' to move coal by road, with offers of up to £50 a day for drivers ready to make the trip. Brennan indicated without any attempt to hedge the issue that 'our people will handle any coal that comes into this plant'. Fifty trucks roared down the Edinburgh-Glasgow motorway, mainly driven by 'cowboy' operators from the Borders and northern England. Local members of the Transport and General Workers Union, whose leader, Hugh Wiper, had pledged support for the NUM, now started pressing for a share in this lucrative business. The Ravenscraig blockade had failed, they argued through their representative, Willie Brand, and any resulting benefit to the haulage trade should accrue to properly unionised labour. On 3 May, Ravenscraig had its first and only experience of mass picketing, as police horses turned out to force a path for the trucks. The following day the single surviving train was withdrawn, and the road-runs doubled. The NUM effort was switched to Hunterston, the Clydeside dock complex where the coal was being unloaded (and where there had already been the first threat of a dock strike). On 7 May, 1,000 pickets clashed with police there, with sixty-five arrests. But fifty-eight more trucks still got through, winding their way through a maze of secondary roads and finding a little-used back entrance to get into the plant. McGahey, who had been calling in public for a total shutdown at both Hunterston and 'The Craig', sat down in private with the transport unions to hammer out a new two-train formula, announced on 11 May, which allowed for deliveries of 18,000 tonnes a week – three times the minimum needed to keep the furnaces alight.

That pattern repeated itself throughout the summer. Whether concessions held, as they did for almost three months in South Wales, or intermittently broke down, made little difference. But after the first burst of action none of the three plants concerned ever looked to be at serious risk. The response was less than wholehearted. As one Polkemmet man put it: 'Picketing Ravenscraig went right against the grain. We did it, but I can't say we believed in it.' And geography militated against success. The Craig, Llanwern and Port Talbot were all close to deep-water ports, with excellent and under-utilised facilities for loading both coal and the more bulky iron-ore. But Scunthorpe presented a very different and much more propitious set of factors, being landlocked and in normal times wholly dependent on home-produced fuel supplies. Its ore comes in via Immingham on the Humber – a fact which later gave the government a nasty moment or two when it led to a potentially crippling but in the event short-lived national dock strike – but its coal-handling capabilities are entirely geared to cope with the NCB's modest export trade. So the denial of coal and coke supplies to Scunthorpe was, on paper, a much more practical proposition than Cardiff Bay or the Clyde. It was there, and more particularly round the Orgreave coke-ovens thirty miles away, that the real battle for steel was fought and won.

From 23 May, when the first brick smashed through a lorry windscreen, to the final cataclysmic encounter almost four weeks later on 18 June, the violence rose in a series of tidal waves. Thanks to television, with its long-focus cameras positioned behind the police lines on top of a concrete-roofed bus shelter conveniently close to the works gates, the nation had an armchair view of the violence: uprooted telegraph poles, rolling down the hill towards the police cordon; a workmen's hut dragged into the road and going up in petrol-fed flames; a lone policeman with his truncheon repeatedly laying into a recumbent miner; the wall of riot shields parting like the Red Sea as groups of police, in black one-piece suits and NATO helmets, dashed into the crowded pickets while a senior officer, with loud-hailer, encouraged them to 'take prisoners'.

But the most enduring memory of Orgreave, to those who were present or who saw any of the hundreds of dramatic pictures, is of the police horses and their riders: squadrons of visored figures, reins in one hand and wooden batons in the other, cantering across a vast cornfield, scattering pickets by the thousand. It is a picture without modern precedent in

Britain: all serious confrontations between police and mobs had normally taken place in city streets where buildings on either side created solid boundaries and confined the action to fairly small areas. Orgreave's semi-rural location provided a far wider front.

The works stand about 250 yards down High Field Lane, leading out into the country from Handsworth, one of Sheffield's outermost suburbs. On the right, going down the hill, is the fenced cornfield; on the left, a pavement, a steep embankment and another field. Just before the plant entrance, the police regularly took up position: a solid wall often ten men deep, facing up the hill, and a second line, three deep, stretching across the level field. The sheer numbers of miners present on the crucial days – running up to 10,000 and more – meant that whatever their strategic intentions they spread off the road and into the field, about the size of two first division football grounds. The fence was torn up and used as ammunition, as waves of horsemen deployed in pincer movements to break up and disperse the pickets. Men with blood streaming from their head wounds stood defiantly hurling stones. A police rider fell from a horse stunned by a half-brick. Constables with small, round, Perspex shields, like latter-day gladiators, engaged in hand-to-hand combat with miners. Helmeted ambulancemen loaded casualties into an armoured Land Rover, bought for the purpose from the army. Smoke from a burning barricade further up the hill hung in the air. Often only the absence of sabres and bullets differentiated it from full-scale war.

Despite the fierce challenge and response, there had been no headlong rush to confrontation. Scunthorpe, like Scotland and South Wales, had originally been granted a coal concession designed to keep the plant at least ticking over. In April, the local representatives of the Triple Alliance had agreed that 15,700 tonnes a week should be carried by rail from various pithead stockpiles in Yorkshire – including specifically Cortonwood. Asked by the ISTC whether they also needed coke, which would have come from Orgreave, the British Steel management replied that this would not be necessary – it was coal they needed, to keep their own on-site coke-ovens safe. Orgreave, with 22,000 tonnes of coal and coke in its stockyard, would just go on gradually converting one into the other until things sorted themselves out. But despite the initial good will, the arrangements soon proved unsatisfactory. According to BSC it was getting far less than its full quota – only 7,600 tonnes in the first two weeks, and less than two-thirds of the promised total over the first month and a half. Even more important, the quality was very poor: after months lying around at the pithead much of the coal was waterlogged, and in quite the wrong mixture to make good metallurgical coke. As a result Scunthorpe's iron and steel production plummeted – first to 25 per cent of normal, and then, by the end of April, to 17 per cent. Worse still, the low-grade material started causing serious technical problems. With temperatures being erratically raised and lowered to conserve fuel supplies, and air vents clogged, volatile gases started to build up and the 1,000-tonne 'burden' of cinder, coke, lime and ferrous pellets from which the molten pig-iron is produced, began to shift out of control.

About 5 am on Monday, 21 May, there was an explosion in the oldest, smallest furnace, affectionately known as the Queen Mary. Firemen and furnacemen fought for two hours to douse the flames, and another eight to stop the liquid iron bursting out through the brickwork. 'It was a very hairy experience,' according to Ray Hill, the local delegate for the National Union of Blastfurnacemen. It was also the spark that ignited Orgreave.

Both Hill and Roy Bishop, the ISTC's divisional officer, had foreseen the danger and warned the NUM that sub-standard deliveries would lead to trouble. Scunthorpe's plant, already drastically reduced, now faced terminal damage, they insisted, and neither the government nor BSC was likely to accept that situation for long. If substantially more fuel was not made available, they confidently expected the Steel Corporation to seek an alternative source. Hill had several 'clandestine' meetings with the miners, trying to explain the problem. 'But the Yorkshire executive had difficulty in convincing their national office,' he recalls. 'They were very naive.' Bishop, who had a number of fruitless telephone

90

conversations at the same time with Jack Taylor, got an even more candid rejection. The Yorkshire NUM president 'couldn't see Arthur giving BSC any more coal'.

As it now transpires, BSC was not waiting around for Scargill's permission. Already it had purchased all the coal it was likely to need, and specifically to supply Scunthorpe it had ordered a huge consignment from Poland, scheduled to start arriving at Flixborough, the Corporation's wharf on the River Trent, at the end of May. Altogether 1.55m. tonnes of this coal were to reach the Lincolnshire plant by the end of the strike. Even without Orgreave, that would have attracted the miners' anger. But now the Queen Mary explosion shifted the timetable forward, and dramatically changed the venue.

On the morning the Queen Mary blew up, Bishop was due at an industrial training meeting at a restaurant in the West Midlands. On arrival he found a telephone message, scribbled on the back of a menu, asking him to ring BSC's personnel director at Scunthorpe, Mike Live. 'Major slip on Mary furnace,' it said. 'Now unstable.' When he got through it was to receive a request that 5,000 tonnes of top-grade coke should be released from Orgreave and delivered immediately to the steelworks. As Bishop well knew, the best way to cure a faulty furnace is to blast it through with as much hot air as can be made available, and that was certainly not possible with the inferior material which had been arriving at Scunthorpe from the Yorkshire pits. But almost since the start of the strike, Orgreave had been locked up tight, with a miners' picket installed permanently on a nearby railway bridge, ensuring that no NUR or Aslef man would take a train in or out. While they sat there the forty-mile journey to the steel plant might just as well be 40,000.

Bishop did his utmost to resolve matters. From the restaurant foyer he telephoned Jack Taylor in Barnsley and explained the need for the coke. Taylor said 'No' and then asked to have the request in writing. The steel official then rang his secretary and dictated a letter, for hand-delivery to the NUM, explaining the urgency of the hot-air blast, the need for it to go on for several weeks to save the furnace, and proposing it for prompt discussion at the NUM's dispensation committee, which he knew was due to meet the following day. 'I would hope that your committee would look upon this request with favour,' he wrote, 'bearing in mind that the present situation is creating a position where not only are the employees in some physical danger within the blast furnace area, but that the blast furnaces are now in serious danger of irreparable harm.' The NUM refused to accept the urgency. The Yorkshire secretary, Owen Briscoe, told him that only an area executive or area council meeting could alter the dispensation terms, and the nearest was on 30 May, a full week away.

Perhaps an approach to national headquarters might be more productive? So Bishop then spent a frustrating day trying to reach someone senior at the miners' Sheffield headquarters. At teatime he finally reached the general secretary, Peter Heathfield, only to be told that nothing could be done without speaking to Scargill, 'and I don't even know where Arthur is'. That was the final straw, as Bishop at that moment happened to be watching the miners' president, on his desktop TV, giving a news interview somewhere in London. But it was still not possible to reach him. Bishop, with no further options, was left feeling that the miners thought he was overreacting: they just could not be persuaded that a 'responsible management' like BSC would have postponed any really vital request so dangerously close to the eleventh hour.

If that was the case it was a bad misjudgement, because BSC, far from dithering, was moving fast. In the forty-eight hours following the Queen Mary blast, the Corporation's supplies and transport offices in Scunthorpe telephoned every South Humberside haulage firm with which they had ever had regular dealings and made a simple but tough request. They wanted as many twenty- and twenty-five-ton bulk carrying trucks as could be made available, and they wanted them the following day – with a non-union driver at the wheel. By Tuesday night, they had fifteen lined up. The drivers were no problem, as few transport firms operate a closed shop and the rates on offer – £80 a day, as against a normal £95 weekly average – were mouth-watering. Several firms were worried about reprisals, having read reports of strike-busting lorries and buses being set on fire in Nottinghamshire, but BSC, fully prepared, just offered them huge stickers with the Corporation logo to slap over the company names painted on their cabs.

On Tuesday evening, 22 May, Danny Ward met the senior officials from all the Scunthorpe steel unions. Orgreave and its 20,000-tonne stockpile was at no point explicitly mentioned. It was merely made clear that BSC would not wait for Scargill or the Yorkshire NUM to give their blessing: the prime priority was enough fuel, of the right quality, to keep the works going. But Ward was at pains to remind his audience that the only effective cure for a temperamental furnace was to blow through as much hot air as possible, with the minimum of delay. The men left his office convinced, correctly, that the Corporation was already committed to repossessing its coke.

That night, the NUM's Barnsley office was tipped off by a friendly steelman that there might be activity at Orgreave the following morning, 23 May. At first light there were twenty-five pickets at the gates, four times the usual number. But they were powerless to interfere. The fifteen hastily collected lorries, with a police Range Rover at the nose and tail of the convoy, swept into the works. There was no chance of talking to the drivers or trying to persuade them to abandon the job. When the first truck emerged, loaded to capacity, its windscreen was smashed with a well-aimed rock. It was the first of tens of thousands of increasingly malignant missiles to be thrown on that stretch of road, and from then on, all lorries on the Orgreave run were routinely fitted with sturdy steel window grilles. Many drivers organised additional protection for themselves, wearing motorcycle helmets and fixing foam padding to every exposed area in the cab.

There was little coverage that first day. The media were too occupied with the first face-to-face MacGregor–Scargill meeting of the strike, which broke up in bitter recrimination that same morning (see p.124). But the pitmen quickly realised that an important gauntlet had been thrown down.

On the second day, 24 May, there were 400 pickets strung across the road, and twenty-one lorries, fuelled up to do a double run. The police responded by matching the NUM forces one-for-one, and as the lunchtime convoy snaked in, two miners were hurt in a scuffle, one falling unconscious. Stones and lumps of wood rained down on the assembled policemen, and both the Yorkshire NUM president, Jack Taylor, and his vice-president, Sammy Thomson, were frustrated in their efforts to talk to the drivers inside the works. The atmosphere grew progressively more tense.

Still hopeful for fraternal support, Taylor and Thomson went straight from their picket-line rebuff to a Triple Alliance meeting, called at the ISTC offices in Rotherham. There they appealed to the steel unions to 'black' the coke when it arrived at Scunthorpe and refuse to feed it into the furnaces. It was a forlorn hope: since 1980, when their own strike-for-jobs had so ignominiously failed, employment at Scunthorpe had slumped from 20,000 jobs to 8,000, and the surviving steelmen had no stomach for putting any more of their numbers at risk. Earlier in the day they had agreed to handle any fuel needed to keep the furnaces intact, and the discussion quickly degenerated into an acrimonious shambles. There could be no more 'dispensation' deliveries, said Taylor, to men who were so clearly acting in collusion with BSC, and he added bitterly as he left: 'It is difficult in some cases to tell the difference between union and management.'

Back in Barnsley, Taylor started to plan a picket which he thought would quickly bring the convoy to a standstill. The police earlier that day had not put on a very impressive performance, and plenty of miners had got close to the gates. What they lacked was sufficient numbers to make their presence effective. Orders were sent out from the Yorkshire strike control centre to scale down the daily effort to breach the police roadblocks protecting the working pits of Nottinghamshire and Derbyshire, and concentrate instead on Orgreave and Scunthorpe. The five telephones were no longer used, in the belief that they were all subject to police tapping, and the switch in picket targets was signalled in a series of brown envelopes delivered to the branches by a dawn patrol of volunteer messengers. At first light, an estimated 1,500 miners, in cars, vans and mini-buses, poured across the Trent and took up position outside the main gates to the steelworks. A huge police presence, already in place, led them to believe that they were not a moment too soon, and they braced themselves for the first lorries bursting through the early morning mists. Several hours later, however, they realised that they had been comprehensively bamboozled. The police were a decoy. The trucks used another entrance two miles up the road.

At Orgreave, forty miles away, things were little better. South Yorkshire police, anticipating trouble, had asked the National Reporting Centre for full-scale help, and it arrived in a continuous stream throughout the morning: transit vans and coachloads of twenty-three-man Police Support Units from West Yorkshire, Lancashire and Greater Manchester, on a scale that eventually swamped the miners' presence. Six mounted officers impassively guarded the gate; the 1,200 pickets who turned up were neatly and expeditiously divided, like wedding guests, into two groups, one each side of the entrance approach, at a distance far too great to approach any of the wagons. The rules, which, if strictly applied, would have precluded any NUM pickets – Orgreave being owned, not by the National Coal Board but by British Steel – were graciously bent on this occasion to allow six men, as 'a goodwill gesture', to talk to the lorry drivers. It was a fruitless exercise. The truckers indicated that they were unimpressed by the miners' case, and intended to keep the convoys running 'to save Scunthorpe steelworks'. When the 300 transport union members in the plant, furious at the use of non-union labour to load the trucks, tried to mount their own picket line, it was swiftly and efficiently broken up by the police.

That weekend, the first of the spring bank holidays, Arthur Scargill himself decided it was time to take a hand. With 300 tonnes of coke a day on the move, the miners' president decreed that it was pointless sending men to cover the numerous entrances to Scunthorpe and that henceforth all picketing power should be concentrated at Orgreave, where he would assume full personal charge. Citing the 1972 Saltley precedent, he implied that closing the coke-plant, on this later occasion, was scarcely more than a formality. Indeed, in article after article, and in endless radio, television and newspaper interviews, he had made clear his guiding conviction that no force in the land could prevent a determined well organised mass picket from shutting any designated factory gate.

He arrived at Orgreave, on Sunday, 27 May, in a steady downpour. His chauffeur-bodyguard dropped him off among the semi-detached villas of Handsworth, on the other side of the hill, and in his unvarying uniform of charcoal trousers, black anorak and navy baseball cap, he strolled down in the rain to survey the scene of what was to be his most decisive defeat. After a few jokes about who should have the benefit of the bus-shelter, he successfully argued with the police commander that he should be allowed to talk to the drivers, but soon came back saying it had been a waste of time as they were 'all non-union'. An untidy scuffle, as police tried to push miners off the road and on to the pavement, left him lying in the field and complaining to an inspector about bruised ribs. It was all over in a couple of moments, and as he got ready to leave, one of the senior policemen told him there would be no point coming the next day, as all convoys would stop for the holiday. 'Do you think we've just fallen off a Christmas tree?' said one of the pickets, and Scargill, equally sceptical, added grimly: 'We'll be here.'

It was not his shrewdest judgement. There were no coke movements the following day and a mere sixty police were on hand to watch 1,200 pitmen and their president take three hours to realise that their mission was pointless. To rub it in further, news broke later that afternoon that British Steel had pulled off a far bigger coup: the first of the Polish coal ships had unloaded its 6,000-tonne cargo at Flixborough on the Trent, and the 500 police laid on to make sure it reached Scunthorpe safely had not seen a single picket on the narrow, winding backroads it had traversed. This was potentially a far bigger threat to the success of the miners' strike than

Orgreave, where stocks, at the rate they were diminishing, would run out completely in less than a month.

Some of the steel union leaders firmly believe that Orgreave was mainly a diversion, a place to tie up the main army of pickets while the real action was elsewhere. But it was not a view that Scargill could easily embrace. The Trent wharves were immensely well protected against industrial disruption – four bridges, including the mighty Humber bridge, had to be traversed to reach them, all easily controllable by the police and any would-be pickets faced a detour of over 100 miles through the South Lincolnshire lanes even to get near them. Scargill weighed the possibilities and decided that symbolic victory at Orgreave was a great deal easier to achieve, if only because most of his keenest activists lived virtually on the doorstep. By the time news came through of the Flixborough coup, the word had already gone out for a mass picket at the coking plant. At the end of his long, frustrating bank holiday he told reporters: 'I suspect it will be different tomorrow.'

Tony Clement is a dapper, sharp-faced policeman with a David Niven clipped moustache and a stylish line in TV interviews. As South Yorkshire's assistant chief constable (operations) he was in command at Orgreave. He was the kind of law officer who did not exist when Scargill closed Saltley. In 1972, the Birmingham police had nothing more violent than the occasional Aston Villa–Birmingham City football derby to stretch them and they could not easily get help even from a neighbouring force (the National Reporting Centre was still a couple of years away). They certainly had no experience with visored helmets and shields. But in 1984, men like Clement were the product of a decade of planning, training and hard street experience. The NRC stood ready to provide all the manpower asked for. Following the inner city riots of 1981, and the recommendations of Lord Justice Scarman's report, the police had not only the equipment but also the systematic training to deal with a large hostile crowd. Clement, aged fifty-five, with thirty-two years' service, had

been in the front line at the steelmen's 1980 mass pickets –
'a picnic compared with the miners' – and he had recently
put himself through a full riot-control course, since Scarman
had specifically said these should include all ranks up to
assistant chief constable. 'When the miners came over the
hill,' he says, 'they did not find untrained police holding
dustbin lids as happened at Brixton and Toxteth. They were
confronted with a well-trained, well-equipped and confident
force.'

He needed all his experience and training that Tuesday
morning. Under Scargill's guidance, the miners had made
careful preparations of their own. There were maps, detailed
instructions on where to stand and how to coordinate for a
big push. 'It was great,' as one picket commented later.
'Best guidance we ever had.' But the police, with superior
discipline, ample resources and a good deal of tactical improvisation, just about managed to hold their own. Far from the
city streets, it was necessary to tackle situations Scarman had
never envisaged with methods he had never mentioned or
probably imagined.

The day began badly for Clement. Down the hill from the
works gates, on the route that would be taken by the lorries
when they swept into view, ten minutes' drive away, as they
left the M1 sliproad, about 600 miners were already formed
up when the police arrived from their army camp billets in
Nottinghamshire. The first convoy was not due for almost
two hours, but at 7 am the pickets suddenly charged up the
slope in an apparent attempt to storm the plant. Immediately
four dog-handlers, the only police nearby, formed a line
across the road and unleashed their Alsatians. Several colliers
were bitten as an inspector wrestled on the ground with one
of their colleagues and reinforcements arrived to push the
crowd back into a carpark well away from the gates.

Having some hint of the scale of Scargill's plans, Clement
had assembled the biggest force he had ever commanded –
ninety-six PSUS, totalling over 2,200 officers from twelve
different forces, with twice as many more in reserve, parked
in lay-bys along the Derbyshire, Nottingham and Humberside borders. Thirty-two mounted policemen waited in rows

of eight, and when the entire fleet of vehicles was assembled, one seasoned sergeant whistled and remarked: 'My God. It looks like the Police Transit of the Year competition.' The miners' main strength was gathered in High Field Lane, looking eastward down the hill towards the massed police. When the lorries were sighted, roughly two miles away, the pickets, directed by Scargill, with his Saltley-style loud-hailer, and several other 'organisers' who regularly showed up on the videotapes the police were filming from the roof of the works canteen, would marshal them down the road for a massive heave. If successful the result would be a total blocking of the sole entrance to the plant.

The decisive incident which transformed police strategy and created many of the most indelible images of the dispute, took place that morning well before the trucks arrived. When the miners made a brief preliminary surge down the lane, the police wall more or less held. But a group of six, told to make arrests, became detached and were quickly surrounded by over forty pickets. 'There's half a dozen of our lads getting a good hiding here,' one constable called back to Clement, and he had a sudden inspiration. He ordered the wall to break momentarily so that a line of eight mounted officers could move in to rescue the stranded six. The miners, who had never seen anything like it, fled instantly up the hill. 'To see the effect those horses had on them, the way they backed off and ran scattered,' says Clement, 'it immediately suggested that if you were about to be overwhelmed, the horses could be invaluable. At no time before had I envisaged using them that way.'

The effect was electric, especially on those who had not witnessed the original incident. Seeing it as 'an unprovoked demonstration of force against the pickets' they poured back down High Field Lane, with chunks of the cornfield fence stakes as improvised weapons – and ball-bearings, suggesting that the attack was a good deal less than 100 per cent spontaneous. Clement held off the riot squads as long as possible – 'Once you bring the shields and helmets out you've got to keep them there until ninety per cent of the crowd decide to go home.' But once the lorries came into view, and a young constable was knocked senseless with a brick on the back of his neck, he radioed the reserves in the Transits to break out the first of the 5ft by 2ft transparent shields, and come forward to take the strain.

It was not enough. As the mood worsened, a red smoke flare went off, a firecracker exploded and the pickets' cheering and the police chant of 'Thrust! Thrust!' was increasingly punctuated by the warnings of 'Brick coming!' from senior officers watching the hail of missiles. Protective hands and forearms went up like a ritual dance, and when the thirty-five-vehicle convoy finally arrived, with its endless chain of police escorts, there was still one more brief moment when it looked as though Scargill's strategy might actually work. The ten-deep wall of blue uniforms broke at one point under the sheer weight of the picket-line scrum, and a few miners spilled through. They were too bemused and incredulous, though, to consolidate their advantage and they were all quickly arrested. The breach was soon repaired with re-inforcements, ambulancemen patched up face wounds and badly cut heads on both sides, and a steady stream of victims were dispatched to hospital in Rotherham.

The horses went into action again, stopping the pickets from reaching Orgreave's perimeter fence, and then, as so often happened on such occasions, the disturbance died down as fast as it had originally flared. Many miners, shocked at what they had seen, just went home, and when the lorries, now loaded to the limit with coke, reappeared ninety minutes later, there was just a giant chorus of 'scab' and no further resistance. The afternoon run, after some heavy lunchtime drinking, produced a renewed storm of bottles and half-bricks, but this was largely unfocused aggression. It took only two minutes for the horses to clear the lane and put the pickets to flight. As the riders trotted back in pairs, the police applauded them, with the soon-to-become-familiar drumming of truncheons on riot shields. Up the hill, a tight-lipped Scargill told reporters it was the kind of tactic he would expect from the authorities in Bolivia and Chile.

Similar criticism, though in more muted terms, was levelled by local Labour MPs and the Labour-controlled South Yorkshire police committee. The chief constable responsible for Orgreave, Peter Wright, was accused of policing without the consent of the community – a charge with some substance in an area where the NCB, with 41,000 miners on its payroll, was by far the largest employer. But Wright was unmoved: 'The only way I could have satisfied the local politicians was by not policing the dispute.' His policy, he later expanded, was that anyone who wanted to work or carry out legitimate activities would get assistance. 'Whatever resources were needed would be provided. It was I who decided that Orgreave should stay open. I was well aware that if the pickets pulled it off at Orgreave they would move on and try it elsewhere.' When the police committee tried to curtail his activity by curbing his expenditure – and particularly by questioning the cost of maintaining the police horses – he went to the Home Office and the High Court for rulings that effectively gave him *carte blanche* to police the dispute in whatever way he saw fit. But throughout, he maintains, he received no direct orders from either the home secretary or the National Reporting Centre. 'The image of someone centrally pulling strings was wrong – we acted purely locally,' he insists. 'But it really is difficult to get that across.'

The following day Scargill, who had left the battlefield calling for an even larger mass turnout from 'the wider labour and trade union movement' in order to ensure a repetition of the Saltley triumph, returned to find that his support, though ferociously armed, with nails and bolts twisted together with wire for piercing horses' hooves, and saddle-high cables stretched across the lane to unseat their riders, had regrouped at only half its previous strength. At about 7.15 am he was leading a group of about ninety pickets down the pavement toward the works when he was approached by that day's ground commander, Chief Superintendent John Nesbitt, who asked him to stand on a grassed area opposite the works. When Scargill said: 'Lads, we're staying on the footpath. He can't tell us where to go' and refused to stop, he was promptly arrested. Six months later, after pleading not guilty and claiming that a deliberate policy decision had been made to apprehend him that day, he was fined £250

101

with £750 costs. Renewed peace talks with the NCB, which had been set for that day and were looking moderately promising, had to be postponed for twenty-four hours while bail was arranged. They broke off in an atmosphere of mutual recrimination.

For the next two weeks, the miners' leader seemed to lose interest in the coke question. The occasional flurry of picketing action achieved nothing and the trucks moved in a steady, 300 tonnes a day procession. Police, with little to do, played cricket with a tennis ball, using truncheons for bats and a pile of helmets for a wicket. The horses grazed peacefully in a nearby field. But as midsummer approached, Scargill decided the time was ripe for one more major effort. The coke pile was rapidly running out, BSC was getting more coal with every tide that washed up the Trent, and although it was clearly much more difficult in 1984 than in 1972 to forge the 'Red Guards' into an effective fighting force, a couple of developments had noticeably stoked up the miners' general aggression. Another death had taken place: Joe Green, an underground worker at Kellingley colliery, North Yorkshire, was hit and killed by a trailer while trying to dissuade lorries from supplying fuel for the Ferrybridge 'A' power station. And there were a series of nasty encounters at Maltby, just six miles away from Orgreave, where a large group of young pit-workers had besieged the police station on Saturday, 9 June, and the heavy response, which left the village more or less cordoned off for several days, had generated a great deal of resentment. The following Sunday, 17 June, speaking at a big rally in Wakefield, Scargill made his most impassioned plea so far. All that was needed to close Orgreave, he said, was determination and numbers, and Monday, 18 June was the day when it would be finally achieved.

Behind the scenes, plans had been carefully prepared. This was to be a truly national picket, with strikers from every one of Britain's coalfields bussed in to take part. Among the first fifteen men to face riot charges arising out of events that day, there were miners from Gwent, Seaham in County Durham, Fife and Ayrshire, and militants from Mansfield and Newark as well as a hard core of Yorkshiremen; and fleets of coaches had been laid on to bring demonstrators from all over Scotland, the North-East, Kent and South Wales. Jack Taylor, after his own early rebuff, had expressed much scepticism about the effectiveness of the Orgreave effort and was widely accused of weakening the offensive by directing his members instead into the working areas of Nottingham and Derbyshire. But he had agreed to change tack for this one last assault and use his 'brown envelope' system to mobilise every available participant under his command. In the event more than 10,000 men were in position that morning ready to swarm down High Field Lane and block the entrance to the beleaguered coke-works.

The first assault, however, took quite a different form. A phalanx of pickets, some accounts putting the number at over 1,000, climbed the back fence and penetrated the works itself for the first and only time. Some attacked the pump house, others set about unloading and immobilising the coal wagons which were waiting to move that day. The main body, fighting toe to toe with the relatively small group of police who had been told to confront them, gradually pushed them back within 200 yards of the main picket line.

Clement, again in charge of operations, had assembled a formidable army of his own on the site: 181 police support units, totalling some 4,163 men, together with twenty-four dog handlers and forty-two mounted policemen. But at this point his forces were awkwardly divided. Reinforcements, trying to get through to swell the cordon protecting the plant entrance, met a hail of bricks and other missiles. Had there been a concerted heave at this point it is just possible that the police line, caught in a pincer movement, might have been breached, and it is now part of the mythology of far-left groups like the Socialist Workers party that this was the moment where a failure of will cost the miners their best chance of a decisive breakthrough. But the NUM organisers, who were supposedly directing operations with their megaphones and loud-hailers, never managed to coordinate their orders to 'charge', and the moment of opportunity was lost. Fifteen minutes later, as the men inside the works were being gradually thinned out and forced backwards, there was a huge heave in an attempt to smash the police barrier. By now, though, they met what was virtually a solid wall of Perspex shields, and the assault, mounted by men who by this time had in many cases removed their shirts to avoid the heat of the early morning sun, just bounced backwards into the crowd.

That was the end of any real chance of a miners' victory and the start of several hours of sustained but ultimately irrelevant violence as the pickets tried to relieve their frustration. The police, under Clement's direction, made a determined effort to clear them right away from the battlefield. At the height of the resulting confusion, television cameras caught a vivid and horrifying sight: a policeman, standing over a cowering picket, repeatedly lashing out at his head with his truncheon. The officer, from Northumbria police, was later traced, and the director of public prosecutions, after long deliberation, decided not to press charges. But as Yorkshire's chief constable, Peter Wright, now admits: 'That incident very nearly lost us Orgreave, in the eyes of the public. It gives credibility to all the other statements of police misbehaviour which were rife.' Some of the most virulent of these came from Scargill, who had spent the whole day either in the thick, or on the inner fringes, of the action. At the height of the final push, the NUM president himself was injured. But there is disagreement, and contradictory testimony over the circumstances. He claims he was standing on a grass verge when he felt himself struck violently on the back of the neck by the edge of a riot shield. This is corroborated by two pickets standing with him at the time but is flatly contradicted by Clement, who has always insisted that he was the policeman closest to Scargill when he went down. His version is that the miners' leader tipped backwards over some fencing, hit his head and suffered mild concussion. He called for an ambulance, and Scargill, with another injured picket, was taken off to hospital. He was one of eighty-nine victims recorded that day, thirty-seven of them police. There were ninety-three arrests, including many for the serious offence of riot.

Sporadic trouble went on for several more hours, with cars

burned and Molotov cocktails ineffectually thrown. But the gestures were so patently futile that the police did not even bother to respond. After a night in hospital Scargill refused to admit the extent of his setback. 'Does it heck mean we've lost,' he said. 'We shall go on picketing at Orgreave and anywhere else, until we've won.' But it was empty bravado – underlined by the fact that the 18 June convoys, almost unnoticed in the heat of the fighting, had cleared out the very last of the Orgreave stockpile. There were no more lorries for several weeks, until enough coal had been brought in from the Flixborough deliveries to start coke-making again, and then there was barely even a token attempt at a picket. As far as steel was concerned, the miners had suffered a comprehensive defeat.

The full magnitude of this was already becoming apparent elsewhere. Another attempt at a complete ban on coal movements, agreed between Scargill and the rail unions on 7 June, had temporarily interrupted the 'dispensation' deliveries to Port Talbot and Llanwern. But on 12 June, Emlyn Williams, saying 'I run South Wales; no one else,' had restored matters with a guarantee of two dozen trainloads a week. On 14 June, the NUM national executive agreed to end all dispensations, with Jack Taylor affirming that from then on there could be 'no secret meetings, no sell-outs and no secret deals'. Scotland and Wales finally acceded, but with ill-concealed reluctance, and although there was 100 per cent support from Aslef and the NUR, who now refused to carry iron-ore as well as coal, the ban had minimal effect. British Steel, now confident of its ability to bypass the blockade, merely stepped up the lorry runs, and the local NUM branches, after the reverses at Orgreave, just let them get on with it.

On 29 June, at a special meeting convened at Congress House, the TUC's London headquarters, Scargill played his last forlorn card. Marshalling all his arguments for union solidarity and the universal interest of everyone concerned with industry in the protection of jobs, he appealed to the members of the Iron and Steel Trades Confederation to respect picket lines and refuse to handle any material that crossed them. 'Every trade union principle was violated,' he pleaded, if such an understanding was not observed. Bill Sirs, the ISTC leader, listened with cool politeness, and responded with a carefully worked out, seventeen-part answer. It made all the right noises about recognising the justice of the miners' cause, wanting to help, needing to consult with all the other steel unions (who, he reminded his audience, represented half the men in that industry) and being much happier if only the NUM had agreed to work with the TUC rather than going it alone. At the end of the day, though, he could go no further than to confirm that 'the ISTC could not enter into a commitment or assurance beyond what could be given without further consultation'. That, as far as the steel phase of the Scargill strategy was concerned, was effectively that. The blood-stained heads, broken limbs, blighted lives and long prison sentences arising out of Orgreave had all been in vain.

Chapter 5

UDI for Nottinghamshire

Nottinghamshire, as Ian MacGregor conceded as early as 11 May 1984, was the key to the strike. The coal from its twenty-five working pits ensured that the nation's lights, even at mid-winter, would not even flicker. Its giant Trent Valley power stations – Cottam, West Burton, Ratcliffe-on-Soar – never missed a shift. The independence of its miners denied the NUM any claim to unity of purpose, and ultimately brought the union close to falling apart. In the meantime, their determination to defend their right to work, both individually and collectively, started the process of tying up Scargill and his national executive in a straitjacket of legal actions and financial penalties. The failure to win over Notts flowed essentially from the refusal to countenance a national ballot, and this proved a fundamental error from which it was impossible to recover.

On 19 April, the day the ballot option was formally voted down by the Sheffield delegate conference, that failure was still not a foregone conclusion. The 31,000 Nottingham miners, after a month of violence, intimidation, heavy anti-strike votes from the rank and file, pro-strike speeches ranging from passionate to ambivalent from their elected leaders, and almost total confusion over the rules on crossing picket lines, were angry and jittery. A large majority of ordinary branch members were going in for every shift, facing down the brick-throwers, the scab-shouters and the paint-daubers, and there were never more than 6,000 in the county who even temporarily answered the strike call. But these included, almost without exception, the union officials, the branch secretaries, the compensation agents and the delegates on whom they were accustomed to rely, not only for political guidance, but to deal with all the everyday problems of colliery life – pensions, discretionary coal, injury benefit, bonus disputes and all the rest.

Suddenly the whole comfortable safety net was removed, in circumstances that in many villages and estates often approached civil war. Rumours proliferated, riots and police raids became routine, Welsh and Yorkshire pickets, who had evaded the roadblocks, hid up in strikers' houses like resistance-fighters or prisoners on the run. Some of them, in Blidworth, were said to have joined a fifty-strong 'hit-squad' which went out at night smashing working miners' windows and vandalising their cars. Many men, already committed to respecting the overtime ban (because it had been constitutionally agreed), now lost more work as they refused to go in on the nightshift so that they could stay and protect their homes. Chris Butcher at Bevercotes, who later won national prominence as a working miners' spokesman, under the soubriquet 'Silver Birch', recalls that one of his friends – 6ft 4 in and 17 stone – took the insults and the missiles for five weeks, and then gave in: 'His branch officials were on strike and his area leader was telling him to stop scabbing. He didn't know who to trust. He didn't know who to turn to. I thought there must be hundreds like him. I always said, if 50 per cent came out, I'd join them.'

That was one risk; that men would just get fed up and vote with their feet. The other was that Scargill, despite everything, might suddenly decide it was an appropriate time to call a snap ballot, get his 50 per cent endorsement, and then Notts, however they themselves had polled, would swing behind the national decision. The government, with its own private opinion-polling resources, was convinced that this would never happen. Plenty of managers in the Coal Board were much less certain. Even Colin Clarke, the Pye Hill ex-face-worker who soon emerged as one of the most aggressive defenders of the right to work, said later: 'I wasn't frightened of a strike. What annoyed me was having one imposed on us against our wishes. If they had held the ballot after they changed the rules to a simple majority and got a simple majority, I would have accepted that vote. Colin Clarke would have organised pickets and a soup kitchen at the welfare.'

But that was not to be his role. On 25 April, at Mansfield, a tense meeting of branch officials and committee members was called to sort out the increasingly chaotic state of affairs in the county. Two thousand more Notts men had joined the strike that week, and the NUM secretary at Bolsover, constantly under siege by pickets swarming across the nearby Notts-Yorkshire border, was telephoning every hour with pleas to declare the dispute official, at least for the 1,000 beleaguered men at his pit. Scargill and Heathfield attended themselves that night, making powerful speeches arguing that the Nottinghamshire miners now had no choice but to come out. The atmosphere was stormy, but the heckling seemed weak, and many there thought they detected all the signs of a cave-in. Only two questioning voices were raised. Roy Lynk, the NUM finance officer for the area and rather fortuitously one of Roy Ottey's 'moderate conspirators' at the abortive Leicestershire cabal, now loudly asked under what rule the strike could be declared official. Colin Clarke wanted to know how any national strike could be called without invoking Rule 43. Both were ignored or brushed off with a reference to the special conference decision, and Clarke, normally a shy, rather hesitant speaker, was gripped with rage. He went straight up to Scargill and said: 'If you try to impose this strike on the membership, I'll take you to court.'

He was not taken very seriously. Although, at fifty-four, he was a veteran NUM officer – past president of his own branch and a formidable authority on the rulebook – he had been voted off the area executive in the general swing to the left, and was regarded as a spent force. When he repeated his intention to Henry Richardson, the area secretary, he was just told: 'You try, and be a martyr then.' It was a challenge Clarke was not prepared to let pass. He went back to his 700-strong branch, near D. H. Lawrence's home village of Eastwood, and told them that, with all the area officials set on strike action, the alternative avenue led through the courts. A whip-round raised £200 and on 30 April, with the Nottinghamshire area and NUM national rulebooks in his hand, he called on the family solicitors, Ellis Fermor, who had done the conveyancing on his house twenty years before. There he met a young partner, David Negus, who quickly decided there was no justifiable way, under the rules, in which the Nottinghamshire strike-call could be described as 'official'. But he recommended getting a proper supporting opinion from leading counsel, and warned that, if it went before a judge, the legal fees could hardly be less than £10,000. As Clarke remembers: 'I wondered what the hell to do. I couldn't see how I could find so much money.' But the events of the next day quickly persuaded him to raise his sights.

May Day had been picked by the 24,000 men still digging coal to communicate their anger and frustration to the officials who, they felt, no longer properly represented them. It has always been the contention of the left that this was deliberately fostered by the Coal Board: men like Jimmy Hood, the pro-strike secretary at Ollerton, claim that the NCB contributed the equivalent of £1.5m. in the shape of transport and the declaration of an extra day's holiday. But there is little hard evidence. What is not disputed is that Neil Greatrex and Colin Bottomore, at Bentinck colliery, two of the few branch officials still working, had become tired of the threats – removal from office, expulsion, physical retribution – and decided to fight. Ringing round all the pits in the county, they persuaded 11,000 men to give up one of their eight annual rest days and travel to Mansfield, where the area executive, headed by Richardson and Chadburn, was due to meet. But when they started to arrive, around 7 am, the Berry Hill Lane offices with their surrounding lawns and carparks were already occupied by 4,000 striking miners, who had taken possession at two in the morning. Three men were particularly active in the chaos of the May Day rally. Each deplored the way in which the strike had been forced on the miners, and had the beginnings of a plan to restore the rights of members who wanted to work and to vote. All, in their different ways, had a significant – and collectively, perhaps, decisive – influence on the course of the dispute. But beyond that, they had little in common, either in temperament, in position in the NUM, or in their ideas as to what should be done. Often they were bitterly critical of each other's approach.

Chris Butcher was the outsider. Aged thirty-three, he worked as a blacksmith at Bevercotes, the most modern pit in North Notts, but had only been in the mining industry for five years – before that he was a market trader. He freely admits he was one of those who never attended branch meetings and apathetically allowed leftwingers and militants to take control. But he had been sickened by the violence, particularly David Jones's death at Ollerton, and by the attitude of the union's area leaders. 'We had a meeting at the Welfare, and Henry Richardson came and called us scabs. I thought, what's it coming to when we're not striking and this man who's supposed to represent us is calling us scabs. I was offended.'

At the end of March, Butcher decided to organise something. He started making telephone calls to people he knew in other collieries and listing names. Forty or so met at a pub in Stanton Hill, and were frightened enough to tell the police what they were doing and ask for protection. Most were from North Notts, as there was virtually no contact with the South Notts pits, even a few miles away. 'Areas were islands, we weren't united.' But then, at Mansfield on 1 May, there were thousands of working miners, all milling, leaderless, in a large field. Butcher had brought little slips of paper with his name and telephone number, and started circulating, introducing himself as a rank-and-file member who didn't like what was being done. He found himself often talking to forty or fifty at a time, and when he got home that night, the phone started ringing. Eighty men attended the second Stanton Hill meeting, and the Nottinghamshire Working Miners' Committee was born.

Clarke, the long-time union man, shared his disquiet. The leadership, he argued, 'have got to accept that the union is not a vehicle on which to go on a political rampage, a vehicle for their own political aspirations, to become the paymaster for their political objectives'. Even before the Notts ballot, on 16 March, he had seen the way things were going. A car drove into his own pit, Pye Hill, saw the pickets, and started to reverse. 'They stopped this young fella, he was prepared to go back home, but before he'd moved half a yard they were kicking at it. It alienated him against what they were trying to do, so he parked his car and went to work. That for me was the start of things that said, no way.'

At the rally, Clarke found himself with the working miners, herded behind a link-fence and a line of police, while strikers, many of them from outside Nottinghamshire, occupied the offices and monopolised the public address system which had been installed for the occasion. Clarke found himself angrily haranguing a small crowd. 'We're Notts miners paying contributions to run these offices, yet we can't get in to speak to our officials.' With him in the lead, they vaulted the fence, ran a gauntlet of abusive pickets, forced their way into the building and reached the first-floor balcony where Ray Chadburn, purple in the face with the effort of making himself heard above the shouts of 'resign, resign' from the working pitmen, was again calling them 'scabs' and telling them to 'get off their knees' (a remark which, later in the year, helped to get him expelled from his area president's job). Clarke tried to reach the microphone, to tell him that he had been elected to serve his members, but was forced back and nearly fell over the guard rail.

After that, he found a ready audience for his views that the only way for the members to regain control lay through the courts. Many miners from other pits said they would help raise the money to fight the cases that he and Negus had sketched out the previous day. An old friend whom he met in the crowd, John Liptrott, NUM secretary at Sherwood, promised that his branch would go fifty-fifty in getting the actions off the ground. It was enough to light the legal touch-paper. Within a month, in the first of a long series of critical decisions, Clarke and Liptrott had won a declaration from the lord chancellor's deputy, Sir Robert Megarry, that the strike had been illegally called, under the NUM's own rules.

To a greater or lesser extent, both Butcher and Clarke were committed to a go-it-alone strategy, outside the union structures to which, as they saw it, access had been denied. But the third key figure at Mansfield that day, Roy Lynk, had no such option. In his position as area treasurer and third in the Notts NUM hierarchy, he could work only within the established framework of national and local rules. In the first three months of the strike this meant that his freedom to act, and even to speak, was tightly and very uncomfortably circumscribed. After making his initial position clear, and crossing swords publicly with Scargill in April, he found himself excluded from many union affairs. He still reported for work at Berry Hill Lane offices, but these had been turned by the area executive into a strike headquarters. 'It was a traumatic experience,' he recalls now. 'There was a hostile atmosphere. I knew that everyone else had an opposite view and that many were involved in violent picketing. They were always in groups. It really honed the nerves.'

Frustration was fuelled also by a long-standing area council decision that only the president, Ray Chadburn, and the secretary, Henry Richardson, could make public statements. So Lynk's interventions at this stage were limited, and made only under almost intolerable strain. One came at the May Day really, when Lynk, though ringed by strikers, seized the microphone and told the working part of the milling audience: 'They can't fetch you out without a national ballot, and whatever decision you make I will support,' before falling back under a shower of spittle and a hail of clods of earth. The dividend came eight weeks later, when the Notts working miners, mobilising their majority, voted overwhelmingly to expel the militants from their branch and area posts and replace them with men who believed in the right to democratic choice. Lynk, and his like-minded colleague David Prendergast, the area compensation agent, were the leading beneficiaries of that switch, and as a result look like winning national prominence, either within a more moderate NUM or heading a powerful, independent, breakaway union, based on Nottinghamshire, if the national body, as is very possible, breaks apart. But none of that would have been possible had Butcher and Clarke, in their different ways, not paved the way.

Butcher's contribution was to create an atmosphere where working miners could believe it possible to organise and resist the enormous pressures, moral, social and intimidatory, to support the majority line. He was not, at least initially, interested in promoting a back-to-work movement. His address book, a blue-covered NCB notepad, was lettered on the cover 'The link-up of friendship', and the threefold objectives of his committee were to set up an information network among the twenty-five Notts pits 'to stop rumours spreading' throughout the coalfield; to assist miners who were still working, especially those being threatened or attacked; and to 'reaffirm democracy within the NUM . . . not to break or replace it'. Numbers swelled, the meetings were changed to the Green Dragon at Oxton, where the landlord was an ex-miner and there was a large room upstairs, and funds started to build up, with a growing account at the Trustee Savings Bank.

This proved useful to Clarke and Liptrott as they struggled to get their legal campaign off the ground. The day after the Mansfield rally, Clarke and his solicitor David Negus travelled to London, where they were introduced to Michael Burton QC, a relatively young, extremely able barrister who, at Oxford, had been active on the moderate wing of the Labour Club. He quickly emerged now as a master strategist, weaving from the NUM's rules, minutes and decisions a web of injunction, precedent and contempt-of-court judgements that by the end of the strike had virtually tied the leadership hand and foot. But cash, as Negus had warned, was needed to get the process started. When Clarke and Liptrott came to one of Butcher's meetings, they disclaimed any interest in his general objectives, but outlined their need for legal funds. At that time they had collected £500, but needed much more now they knew they had a case. The Notts Working Miners' representatives said they would all appeal to their own pits – Butcher took five rest-days off to collect £216 at Bevercotes – and the required total of £10,000 (actually £10,908) was put together in a week. When the application got to court and Clarke was asked to identify his financial guarantors he was able to list 900 names who had signed and donated.

On 26 May, the vice-chancellor announced his finding that there was no basis for calling the Notts strike 'official'. But three days earlier there had been an even more important decision. On 10 May, the miners' national executive had ordered the postponement of 'branch elections in those areas where industrial action is currently being taken'. That would have meant that the pro-strike officials in Nottinghamshire would have remained unassailably in office for the duration of the dispute, despite a clear area rule that there must be an election every year before 30 June. On 23 May, Sir Robert Megarry decreed that the NUM ruling was void, and that ballots should go ahead.

The effects of the two judgements was dramatic. The week after the spring bank holiday, 2,000 Notts miners abandoned the strike and returned to their pits. The curtain went up for a fiercely contested and unprecedentedly ill-tempered election campaign. With an overwhelming majority of members now solidly committed to working, and an even more solid majority of incumbent officials supporting the dispute, there was bound to be an upheaval. When the results came through, only three seats on the 31-member area council remained in the hands of strikers, where they had previously had twelve or thirteen. But that was the least unexpected change. At branch committee level there was almost a clean sweep, with only four of the 310 places still held by Scargill supporters. Many of the newcomers were men who had never before stood for union office. Experienced people like Colin Clarke warned against over-enthusiasm, pointing out that too many nominations for a particular job carried a danger of splitting the vote; but equally it was recognised that many of those putting themselves forward against, say, a striking secretary, as at Ollerton or Cresswell, were taking a real risk. 'They'd got Yorkshire miners and Kent miners lodging in the villages. They had windows smashed. But they were still man enough to stand up.' Feelings ran equally deep on the other side. Jimmy Hood, the long-serving Ollerton secretary who was one of the many who lost their positions, said afterwards: 'It would have been an insult to win. I had little in common with men who were breaking the strike.'

In July, the area executive elections repeated and reinforced the switch. Overnight, the leftwing complexion was erased, with only one active striker left in place. Chadburn and Richardson, though still technically the senior representatives, were now heavily outnumbered, and Lynk and Prendergast, despite their nominal status as No. 3 and No. 4, moved to the centre of the stage. Almost the first move of the new-broom committee was to lift the 'gagging' rule (in fact it was swept away so thoroughly that any union member, worker or striker, was henceforth given formal freedom to discuss with outsiders union affairs in the coalfield), and at last it became possible to formulate an open, forthright defence of the Nottinghamshire stand. Lynk denies any desire to seize the lead – 'Six weeks into the strike Ray and Henry decided to change sides,' he says. 'That left a hole and somebody had to fill it.' But inevitably events have propelled him into greater prominence. Even before the end of the strike, he decided to stand against McGahey as the union's national vice-president.

As the summer wore on, divisions between the main working miners' groups became deeper and more abrasive. All three had played key roles at the start in giving Nottinghamshire the will and the weapons to go it alone. Butcher offered a rallying voice for many confused and beleaguered men, at a time when every pit in the county was an isolated, rumour-ridden outpost surrounded by threatening pickets and ringed by police. Clarke and Liptrott, through the law, found ways to blunt the NUM's power to discipline and coerce. Between them they provided the time and opportunity needed to vote men genuinely representing the local majority into positions of effective union authority. But once the need for mutual support was past, the underlying differences of temperament and approach meant that increasingly they went their separate ways.

Although most Nottingham miners remained at work, there was always a significant minority who took a different view. Hood's pit, Ollerton, with its 1,050 NUM members, was divided fifty-fifty in the first weeks of the dispute, and after 19 April, when it was declared official, the number on strike went up to 700. It was Megarry's court decision rejecting this, on 26 May, which dramatically turned the tide. By the end there were only 150 still out. But looked at the other way, it was amazing that even that number stood firm. There were no union funds to help. As Hood says: 'We had to raise every penny to help our families. We became experts in fund raising.' The women's support groups were just as important here as in the strikebound areas. Brenda Greenwood, the only woman to go to prison during the strike, came from Ollerton – in the end she was found not guilty on breach of the peace charges, but only after spending seven days on remand.

Hood's own car was vandalised and his garage set on fire, and anonymous phone-callers claimed, falsely, to have kidnapped his five-year-old daughter. He maintains that there was a great deal of unreported violence against men like himself who supported the national line, but fully accepts that the decision to sidestep a national ballot was 'a fatal error'. He does not believe, however, that the decision to carry on working indicated deep-seated support for the Board or the government. It merely provided men an easy option to hang on to their substantial privileges, including bonuses which amounted in many cases to 100 per cent of basic pay. 'We've been deliberately spoiled,' he argues, 'to a point where Nottingham men felt so trapped by their lifestyle and their financial commitments that they could not afford to support the strike.'

Liptrott and Clarke, both active branch officials with long

experience within the NUM, soon cut loose from Butcher's Nottingham Working Miner's Committee, which they thought too much of a one-man band. Clarke was particularly angry at Butcher's refusal to admit his identity when he was attracting enormous national publicity as the mysterious 'Silver Birch' – especially after he himself had been accused of hiding behind the pseudonym. After some hesitation, they set up their own alternative organisation, the National Working Miners' Committee, whose main purpose was to coordinate the use of the law by non-strikers.

By 6 July, when Clarke got together a group of some twenty pitmen and interested solicitors to pool their experience, there had already been a spattering of successful court cases throughout the main coalfield districts. But they were very haphazard: as Clarke told David Negus, who was now working almost full-time on miners' business: 'We seem to be going off in a hotch-potch way.' Jim Lord, for instance, the branch secretary at Agecroft, one of the two pits in Lancashire which produced coal throughout the dispute, had in May won an important injunction against his area executive, blocking their declared intention to suspend him and all his working members for a period of five years if they crossed a picket line. But he had had no idea where to turn for advice until 'a lad in the canteen' produced the name of a solicitor who happened to live in the same street. Till then, he had thought, the only way out would have been for the whole branch committee to join the strike 'while they sorted themselves out'. In Derbyshire, however, rather more support was at hand. When two individual miners, Roland Taylor and David Roberts, decided to seek a Nottingham-style declaration that the strike in their area was unofficial, they were brought together by the Coal Board and put in touch with the Mansfield law firm of Shacklocks, where the partner who took the case, John Lewis, happened to have been to school with Negus. The beginnings of a network were forming – strengthening Clarke's view that 'if you've got to do this sort of thing, you might as well try to do it at one fell swoop' – and by the end of the year this had become a formidable force.

After a first wave of mainly defensive action, during which the strike was judicially deemed unofficial in the Midlands, North Derbyshire, Lancashire and North Wales, as well as Nottinghamshire (though not in Scotland, where several such applications failed), the committee and its advisers moved to the attack. As more and more professionals mastered the NUM's intricately overlapping national and local rulebooks and the fruitful discrepancies they contained, it proved possible to get an array of important judgements: limiting the number of pickets (in Wales), banning aggressive picketing at named pits (Yorkshire), preventing union officials from spending funds on prosecuting an unofficial dispute, and in one case (Derbyshire) making them personally responsible for an overspend of £1.7m., though this was not enforced.

In fact the Inns of Court grew so enthusiastic that many working miners, initially sympathetic, became seriously worried over their role. Increasingly Clarke and his colleagues faced accusations, and not only from the extreme left, that they had allowed themselves to become Coal Board tools. Such suspicions did not lack fuel. Early meetings of the committee had been attended by David Hart, a colourful and conspiratorial figure who was demonstrably close to Ian MacGregor and, by his own account, to Mrs Thatcher. The NCB chairman never bothered to deny newspaper stories that he had personally masterminded the legal strategy. Large advertisements placed on behalf of the committee in *The Times, Daily Mail* and *Daily Express* were designed by Tim Bell of Saatchi and Saatchi, the Tory party's publicity advisers, who also wrote one of its promotional brochures. In September, one of the founder-members, Bob Copping, the Barnsley winders' secretary, resigned, claiming that the committee 'was turning into an anti-union organisation with a Conservative orientation'. Also there was endless sniping, both from outside critics and between the rival groups, over the sources of their funds, which were held, without much supporting evidence, to have been provided to an unacceptable extent from big business sources.

Clarke, whose twelve-year-old daughter Tracy was the subject of a death threat at the start of his campaign, has

119

always vigorously rebutted such claims, though he freely admits that he set out to find allies with experience of fighting the left wing. But the constant accusations weakened the committee's political influence. Although in late autumn it finally came out with a public endorsement of the Board's back-to-work drive, this was already in full swing and the backing had little discernible effect. In the end the impact of the National Working Miners' Committee – though not that of Clarke himself – was limited, almost entirely, to its un-doubted successes in court.

Even these, though, did not include the most important cases of all, the series of actions brought by two Manton men, Robert Taylor and Kenneth Foulstone, whose ramifications finally engulfed the NUM leadership in a quicksand of writs, receiverships and sequestration orders. These were launched separately, with the backing of Chris Butcher, and pressed independently to their highly damaging conclusion.

Butcher remains somewhat bitter at the way he was de-serted, after his efforts to give the working miners unity and heart, but he was certainly not prepared to give up. Early in May he had sought legal advice of his own on how best to proceed. After an initial rebuff – the first office he ap-proached was in Ollerton, next door to the spot where David Jones had died, and all strike issues there were still regarded as dangerously sensitive – he struck lucky. Hodgkinson and Tallent, in Newark, are a large partnership by provincial standards, and although they had little previous experience with industrial relations or mining they quickly saw the significance of Butcher's ideas. The senior partner, David Payne, a former mayor of Newark and a prominent Midlands Conservative, thought it inappropriate at this stage to get directly involved. Instead he handed over the new client to Andrew Fearn, who had previously specialised in the rather arid business of trusts, but now set about turning himself into an all-round expert on the multiplicity of contentious issues that the strike had spawned.

Fearn's first, not very exciting task was to take in hand the 'Chris Butcher Fund for Democracy' which had been set up to accumulate small contributions and help men and families who had suffered from intimidation. But that elementary function was soon outgrown. Butcher, under his 'Silver Birch' alias, was rapidly developing from a parochial to a national figure. When news broke out in May of the troubles at Agecroft, he had a fifty-minute telephone conversation with Jim Lord, immediately followed by a meeting with eight of the working Lancashire collieries and his first public speech, which drew cheers from a 450-strong audience assembled in Agecroft's pithead canteen. At Lea Hall, in Staffordshire, where he went next, there were 600 gathered to hear him. Then it was South Wales, in a better car which he had borrowed for the trip, and a £100 handout to some miners there who wanted to work. That was when he acquired his *nom de guerre*: there had been jokes about his silver-streaked hair, and when a South Wales reporter called to ask his name, he just said: 'Call me Silver Birch.' When the *Mail on Sunday* did a big feature on his travels, the phrase appeared in the headline and immediately acquired the status of a household expression (predictably perverted by the strikers to 'Dutch Elm'). When he got to Scotland in July, the nine defiant men at work in Bilston Glen had all heard of him. Within weeks of his meeting there, another fifty had joined them and there was £13,000 in the fighting fund, and all the way through he provided a source of encouragement for the many ordinary miners who merely wanted to get back to a paypacket and a peaceful life. But his approach was always too gentle and personal to bring any really decisive break. The nearest he came to that was when he put up the cash to propel Taylor and Foulstone towards the High Court.

He had met the two Manton miners early in July, when they had only begun to explore the chances of testing the legality of the strike-without-a-ballot which had forced them both to sit idly at home since being forced back by the pickets in the second week of March. They had spent the intervening weeks assiduously collecting all the union minutes, reports and resolutions that they could lay hands on, and in particular they had obtained copies of both the national and the Yorkshire rulebook – documents which, though nominally available to any member who wants them, are in fact like gold dust and have been seen by only a minute fraction of the union's rank and file. Now Butcher recommended that they get in touch with Fearn, and the appointment was made for Thursday morning in late July.

The Newark lawyers, at that point, had no idea what to expect. As Fearn cheerfully admits, it had never crossed their minds that the very calling of the strike might be open to serious legal challenge. It was one thing to win exemption for Notts, which had explicitly voted against taking part; but quite another to question the whole procedural edifice on which Scargill and his executive had decided to rely. Like most people outside the coal industry, and many within, they knew almost nothing of the complex formalities required, under the NUM's constitution, to validate the operation of Rule 43 or Rule 41. But when Taylor and Foulstone turned up with their pile of papers, and started to explain the significance of things like the 1981 Yorkshire ballot, the lack of consultation since, and the failure to provide adequate opportunity for branch debate, it quickly became clear that there was real meat here.

Naturally, there were still many difficulties. Even with the extensive documentation provided, there remained very important gaps – notably the minutes of various area conference meetings, and the proceedings of the national and Yorkshire executives. Taylor and Foulstone, however, were fully prepared. They had a 'mole', they explained, strategically placed within the Yorkshire area's Barnsley headquarters, and he could lay his hands on virtually anything that might be required. Armed with a detailed shopping list, they went off to test their source's capabilities, and when the first handover came, some days later, in a Barnsley lay-by, he proved to be even better than his word – not just minutes, in many cases, but actual verbatim reports.

The main outstanding problem now was money to get the action off the ground, and here Chris Butcher was able to play the fairy godmother part. His funds, though generously supported by all sorts of well-wishers, had been heavily depleted by his extensive tours round the country. The weekly get-togethers at the Green Dragon, where he would cheerfully buy pints for a hundred working miners and petrol for any reluctant strikers who cared to turn up (and where Fearn and Payne, who were now taking a very close interest, found many of their most valuable supporting witnesses), represented another significant drain. It was therefore a generous and unselfish gesture when he made over the entire available residue to give the Manton pair a fair wind. It was far from enough to cover the whole costs of the case, but it got them to London and paid for a decent hotel, while Payne, who had appointed himself chief publicist as well as legal adviser, set out to persuade Fleet Street that a big story was about to unfold. With the *Daily Express* he struck gold, and the paper offered to append a box number, seeking cash contributions, to the article that appeared. It produced £10,000 within the week and a final total of £34,000 for what Fearn and Payne christened 'The Miners' Ballot Fund'.

At the end of September the case, based on an affidavit stuffed with quotations from NUM internal papers, which had taken sixty-two concentrated hours to prepare, finally came before Mr Justice Nicholls. In the absence of any representative from the NUM, which had declined to appear, he found that both the Yorkshire and national strikes were 'unofficial' and 'unlawful'. When Scargill appeared that same night on ITV's Channel 4 news to declare that the decision 'as far as we are concerned will not be accepted', the contempt of court machinery, which finally deprived the NUM of all access to its funds and control over its affairs, was primed and ready to go.

From Nottinghamshire itself, though, the solid core of the working miners' movement and the one area whose continuing coal production was of more than propaganda significance for most of the strike, the spate of legal actions drew a very mixed response. Roy Lynk, who after the July elections emerged as the main spokesman for the working majority's views, gives Clarke and Liptrott, in particular, full credit for their early initiative. Several of the decisions they caused to be made gave crucial help at a time when there was a real

123

risk that Notts's resistance would crumble. 'But after that,' in Lynk's dismissive assessment, they seemed to want to go to court at the drop of a cap, as if they enjoyed the glory. 'They became an embarrassment to us . . . They went all over the country and gave folks the impression that the Notts miners were trying to subvert the strike, and we weren't. All we wanted was to work, keep our noses out of everyone else's business and wait for a national ballot.'

This was and remains an extremely sore point. Nottinghamshire, with its rich, profitable pits, its high productivity bonuses, its relatively assured future, and its tradition of hard-headedly putting its own interests first, has, for most of this century, been the object of bitter suspicion and deep-seated envy to the rest of the coal industry. Ever since the great six-month miners' lockout, which followed the short-lived General Strike of 1926, when the Notts men, under the leadership of George Spencer MP, negotiated their own return to work and subsequently formed a notorious breakaway union, they have always had to live with their reputation as potential betrayers. In 1984 'Spencerism' had not lost its potency as a term of abuse. In NUM demonology, Nottingham is always expected to sell the pass: hence the premature and violent picketing that characterised the first days of the dispute, and solidified the county's determination not to be pushed around.

There are plenty of reasons – historical, geological, social and economic – to explain why Nottingham is different, but none of them are really needed to understand the events of 1984. The fundamental split that emerged within the NUM was between those who emphasised loyalty and solidarity, without too much concern for the niceties of the fine print, and those who, however sympathetic to the cause, gave their highest priority to the rights of democratic choice. As Lynk has said, a preponderance of Notts miners, including men like the area president, Ray Chadburn, and the secretary, Henry Richardson, to whom on many issues he is diametrically opposed, feel it is of overriding importance to test the feelings of the membership. 'We're traditionally committed to the ballot. It was good enough for Henry and Ray and good enough for all the militants.' But problems started when the ballot came out the wrong way. 'They left us and deserted us. They can't select the results they like. They've got to stand by them all. That's democracy.'

It did not take long for that democracy to come under threat. Almost as soon as the July elections had upended Nottingham's pro-strike executive, the NUM's extraordinary annual conference passed its new, complex, four-page-long Rule 51, which sets up disciplinary committees (immediately dubbed 'Star Chambers') to deal with members who commit 'any act (including omissions) which may be detrimental to the interests of the union . . .' Assurances from the president that the change was in no way designed or contemplated 'with the issues of an Industrial Dispute in mind' were seriously undermined by delegates, like Jack Collins from Kent, who spent most of their speeches talking about 'scabs' and the disciplining of 'anyone who breaks ranks to our collective disadvantage'. The Nottinghamshire men, having tried, with only limited and temporary success, to get the courts to block the threat, moved in December to put themselves beyond the reach of Sheffield's future inquisitors. The Notts area council voted to delete that portion of its rulebook which gave the national union the final say in any matter of dispute between them, and thus took a long step down the road that could still lead to total separation and the setting up of an independent, as opposed to merely autonomous, Notts-based miners' union.

That would run counter to everything the current Notts leadership wants, or thinks necessary. Although it was Clarke, in his capacity as union official, who proposed the December amendments, Clarke's Working Miners' Committee, which was widely seen as a breakaway union in the making, was expressly disowned as 'an embarrassment' by the local NUM. As Lynk said, after the final return to work in March 1985: 'I don't think a split is inevitable, but I'm under a lot of pressure to do it. I don't want to do it. I want to stay in the national union. I would like to curb some of Arthur's excesses and I would like to see the union work as a union.' But he may not be given the option, in which case he, for one, is perfectly happy to relax and take the consequences. 'If a split happens, then I feel the future of the Notts miners would be strengthened. We compete economically with anyone,' he affirmed, and then added, in an apt summary of the county's basic attitudes: 'We feel a moral responsibility to the folks in Yorkshire. I don't want to be in a position where I'm all right, Jack. But I don't want to be in a position where we are ordered what to do. It's like feeding the people of Ethiopia – everyone wants to do it, but you don't take the last crumb off your own table. You give your surplus, but you don't inflict hardship on yourself.'

Chapter 6

Finding Another Word for Peace

On 9 July, at the Norton Park Hotel in Edinburgh, the NUM and NCB negotiations came as close to a peace agreement as they ever achieved. Nine days later the talks foundered – over the single word 'beneficial'. Many leading trade unionists think Scargill, through intransigence and miscalculation, threw away his best chance of victory at this point. But an equally important factor was undoubtedly the government's determination not to endorse what Walker and Thatcher regarded as an over-generous deal. And from then on the energy secretary established firm control over the strategy of the dispute. There would be no more off-the-cuff concessions when Ian MacGregor thought he detected the chance of a compromise.

The search for conciliation began as early as 17 April. MacGregor met the representatives of BACM and Nacods at Hobart House for a regular session of the consultative Joint Policy Advisory Committee (which the NUM, though normally present, did not attend) and surprised everyone by his flexible approach. Norman Tebbit, the secretary for industry, had just made the startling suggestion that coal might be a candidate for denationalisation once the strike was over. Peter McNestry, the Nacods general secretary, opened the meeting with an angry complaint about this, and the NCB chairman was quick to reassure the unions that the remarks had been quoted out of context and given an exaggerated importance. But the real surprise came when he was asked whether the closure plans, as announced in March, were in any way negotiable. Out of the blue, and to the visible astonishment of his own senior officials, he said, according to the minutes, that 'the phasing of the adjustments needed to meet these problems could be a subject for negotiations'. McNestry, recognising this as a possible face-saving formula, quietly set about trying to bring the warring parties together for more extended discussion.

This proved a delicate and frustrating exercise. When MacGregor's idea leaked out a week later, Scargill's first public reaction was to reject it out of hand, and although Peter Heathfield gave it a slightly warmer reception it never explicitly figured on any agenda. But McNestry, with some delicate diplomacy, engineered a triangular exchange of letters between himself, Heathfield and Ned Smith, the NCB's personnel director, and laid the foundations for a face-to-face encounter – the first since 6 March – which was fixed for 22 May. This too was fraught with problems. A phrase of the NUM letter to Ned Smith was quoted in a news broadcast, and when Heathfield and Scargill heard it on their respective car radios (they were both travelling on various motorways at the time) and totally failed to recognise it, they each drove immediately to the nearest telephone and angrily rang Sheffield to find out what was happening. Each assumed that the other was responsible for the wording, only to discover that the drafting had actually been done, without reference to either of them, by the union's chief executive officer, Roger Windsor. But in any case MacGregor decided that the miners had set unacceptable preconditions – basically they were insisting on a total withdrawal of the closure programme before any serious talking could start – and at the last moment cancelled the whole arrangement.

Nevertheless the two sides did meet the very next day, 23 May. The occasion was a regular biennial meeting of the NCB and the whole union executive (one of many such consultative engagements in the coal industry calendar which were always available for a bit of quiet diplomacy, but almost all of which the NUM skipped during the conflict). Neil Kinnock and Stan Orme, of the Labour party, had spent much of the previous evening persuading Scargill to attend this one, and after sorting out the problem of the venue—it was fixed for Hobart House, and the miners said they could not possibly cross the Kent picket line, which was at that time permanently established outside the Board's headquarters – the key figures finally got together.

It was not a success. With the atmosphere already soured, and Scargill determined that there would be no negotiations – they were merely to listen and then demand that the closure plans be dropped – no progress was achieved. After sixty-five minutes, MacGregor growled: 'So – no comment' and closed the proceedings. Scargill emerged furiously and told waiting reporters: 'It is very apparent that we are fighting government direction.'

This was to become a constant refrain. Throughout the dispute Scargill, and on many occasions also the Labour leadership, Kinnock and his colleagues, maintained that it was only the intervention of Walker and the Prime Minister which prevented the Coal Board from concluding a mutually acceptable deal. Publicly, the Downing Street line was to deny this. Indeed, for the first ten weeks of the strike, there was only one major ministerial speech on the subject outside the House, and that came only on 16 May, when Walker, at the coal trade annual lunch, made an appeal for miners to accept what he described as 'the best offer ever'. Behind the scenes, though, there was a plethora of strike-related activity throughout Whitehall. Walker, right at the start, had set up his daily coal committee, which pulled in senior officials from all the key departments, notably transport, employment, industry and the Home Office. It met without fail not later than 10 am each morning – which was why the energy secretary missed the Brighton bombing later in the year – to hear detailed reports from the Coal Board and generally monitor the latest developments. This committee played a central role in shaping and controlling the wider aspects of the dispute.

But there were also very important decisions made at a higher level. Very early on it was agreed in Cabinet – with Mrs Thatcher siding with Walker against the differing inclinations of Nicholas Ridley, Nigel Lawson and initially Norman Tebbit – that there should be no recourse by the government to its own new labour laws, and that efforts should be made to discourage any excessive zeal in applying them by anyone else. As Lord Denning accurately argued when the subject was later debated by the House of Lords: 'It must have been a matter of high policy . . . not to go to the courts of law but instead to call out hundreds and thousands of police.'

Similarly, there was great wariness over potentially inflammable statements. When Tebbit made his 'denationalisation' remarks, the whole government information machine moved in to minimise the damage; and when one of the Treasury ministers, John Moore, told two journalists over lunch in early May that coal might become a candidate for privatisation, both the editors concerned, at the *Daily Mail* and the *Daily Telegraph*, were heavily leaned on to kill the story (it leaked out only when another newspaper correspondent oveheard the angry complaints of one of the reporters concerned). Finally, as was revealed in the *Daily Mirror* on 6 July, Mrs Thatcher herself, and several other ministers, had taken active parts in encouraging a British Rail pay settlement in April for reasons directly related to the strike. As John Selwyn Gummer, the chairman of the Tory party, had written then to Nicholas Ridley, the transport secretary: 'It seems to me to be central at this juncture to avoid the risk of militants being strengthened in their attempt to block the movement of coal by rail and to make wider common cause with the miners.'

But did this involvement extend, as the miners' leadership maintained, to the setting, and if necessary vetoing, of terms on which the strike might be resolved? The answer, at the beginning, is no. MacGregor operated with a very considerable degree of autonomy. He did not himself report directly to Peter Walker on any regular basis. Instead the NCB's marketing director, Malcolm Edwards, and its secretary, David Brandrick, neither of whom were Board members, were deputed to deliver the daily progress reports.

Exasperation started to mount at the beginning of June. On 31 May, Scargill, released on bail after his Orgreave arrest, had a 'secret' meeting with the NCB's Jimmy Cowan in an attempt to set up, for the first time, a round of genuine peace negotiations, which the two men agreed should start on 8 June. The miners' leader went straight from his two-hour session with Cowan to a rally in Islington Town Hall where he talked exuberantly to the crowd about the imminence of a 'quick victory' and to supporters afterwards about substantial concessions he was now confidently expecting on the scale and timing of the Board's closure plans. These remarks were reported only obliquely and without attribution, but up in his Bolsover constituency Scargill's closest parliamentary confidant, Dennis Skinner, was characteristically less circumspect. That same evening he announced that he had 'inside information that the miners were on the verge of a great victory'. The government was visibly rattled by such talk, and a damage limitation exercise was set in train. In a *News of the World* article on 3 June, Peter Walker wrote that, whatever happened, four million tonnes of high-cost capacity had to be eliminated from the coal industry within the year; and in private conversation during the weekend he firmly predicted that the 8 June talks would break down.

The high-level alarm was not diminished when the discussions opened, in an atmosphere of surprising affability. MacGregor referred to his 'friends' in the NUM and called them, familiarly, Arthur, Mick and Peter. More significantly, the two sides reached some degree of accommodation, albeit very limited, on the issue that lay at the very core of the dispute, with the mineworkers agreeing to explore at least the possibility that there might be grounds for closing a pit beyond those of safety and complete exhaustion. Scargill acknowledged Cowan's point that it would be stupid to spend eighteen months opening up coal reserves that would only provide six months' work, and although he stopped well

131

short of accepting this as a 'third category' of justification, there did seem to be some faint signs of movement.

By the time the two teams met again, in Rotherham on 13 June, the whole mood had changed. MacGregor, talking to *The Economist* earlier that week, had predicted that the strike was still 'only half way through'. Even more provocatively, in an interview with *The Times*, he had reaffirmed his intention to establish the Board's right to manage, to eliminate uneconomic mines, to develop a high-wage industry with fewer jobs, and to produce a new Plan for Coal. This infuriated the NUM negotiators (who were wholly unappeased by MacGregor's other newly announced aim, to sell 125–150m. tonnes of coal a year by the end of the century) and the talks collapsed in mutual recrimination and acrimony.

There were several reasons why *The Times*'s article produced such a strong reaction. They were clearly spelt out at the time by Peter Heathfield. The general feeling at the Edinburgh session, he said, was that foundations had been laid for a 'pretty rapid conclusion' to the dispute, that there were no 'insurmountable problems' to finding an acceptable definition of a pit that was no longer worth keeping open, that there would be no further 'ultimatums' blocking the road to agreement, and that the Board was ready, as a result, to withdraw its 6 March demand that 4m. tonnes of capacity must go. Although the NCB chairman's attitude, in the miners' view, had been 'very belligerent' and could almost be described as 'arrogant', there had appeared to be the beginnings of a meeting of minds. But any such hopes had been dashed when the interview came out. In Heathfield's eyes, Mac-Gregor had 'decided to rewrite the Plan for Coal and go back to the language of ultimatums'. And that was not the only place where the 'language' set hackles rising. According to its new boss, the NCB had to 'recover the management of the industry' – implying that the Board had not been running things since 1947 – 'and it seemed to us that by the use of that language he was turning the clock back to the free-market situation that prevailed in the past. Obviously we, as leaders, would not be prepared to accept and tolerate that situation.'

In addition the NUM leadership were upset by the way MacGregor had spelt out his ideas on the industry's future – not only for what they contained, but particularly for the total lack of prior discussion. 'We had been denied access to any conversations on that topic,' Heathfield bitterly complained. The spirit developed in Edinburgh, he thought, 'would surely have enabled Mr MacGregor to talk aloud . . . rather than publishing five days later an interpretation of the Plan for Coal that certainly was not acceptable to us'.

What was particularly unacceptable, of course, was the insistence that in the short term 20,000 jobs had to be shed from the industry, despite MacGregor's stated confidence that in the future there would again be expansion and new recruitment. That, to the NUM negotiators, 'seemed a nonsensical approach' in a business where proficient, experienced workers needed years to train. It was surely 'daft' to dispose of 20,000 skilled men when in a relatively short period they were likely to be needed again. But as so often happened, such practical matters barely figured on the formal agenda. Most encounters failed to get beyond the increasingly metaphysical question of what constituted an 'uneconomic pit', and to that, as became ever more apparent, there was no mutually agreeable answer.

The Rotherham breakdown in itself did not worry the government: it was what Walker had expected, and it effectively scotched the Scargill – Skinner victory claims. But ministers were less than happy with the way it had been handled in presentational terms. As soon as it became clear there would be no basis for agreement, MacGregor just folded his papers, rushed out of the meeting leaving uneaten sandwiches on the table, and swept back to London. Walker was left in the dark for two crucial hours with no direct report of what had happened, while Scargill, with blanket coverage on radio and television, was giving his own characteristically coloured version of events. This was not an isolated snub, either, by the independently minded Coal Board chairman. It stemmed from MacGregor's well-documented distrust of politicians.

One of his favourite jokes is the one about the three lies of modern society: 'Our cheque is in the post; I'm working late at the office; and I'm from the government and I'm here to help you', and he did not hesitate to apply it to his current political masters. Worse still, he had taken to spending much time in detailed discussion with Stan Orme, the shadow energy secretary, while distancing himself from the government's own key ministers (which was doubly irritating, as it had been in direct response to a challenge from Walker that Orme first decided to try his hand at mediation).

This arm's-length relationship, and the erratic unpredictability it often entailed, was becoming increasingly unacceptable, and Walker was now determined to assert greater influence over the management of the dispute, and particularly to effect some improvement in the Board's often lamentable presentation of its own case. But to manage this without either damaging MacGregor's authority or abandoning the government's ostensibly neutral stance proved a tricky challenge, and it was not until October that the delicate transition was fully achieved.

One manifestation of MacGregor's lack of finesse in the public relations department had been his letter, dated 21 June, addressed to the home of every miner on the NUM books. He had been under pressure for some time to communicate directly with his workforce, and when he finally complied, a full week after the Rotherham débâcle, the results were less than overwhelming. Fewer than 1,000 men responded, even by post, to his invitation to 'join your associates who have already returned to work so that we can start repairing the damage and building up a good future'. Meanwhile, most of the leftwing press had a field day with his 'Dear Colleague' opening, publishing spoof replies to the effect that few miners recognised colleaguehood with a man committed to butchering the industry.

Another blunder was the Board's £1m. 'propaganda offensive' – seven full-page advertisements under the heading 'How the miners on strike have been misled' which started to appear in national newspapers on 4 July. Not only was this heavily criticised for its content – ICI, who were said in the first of the series to be having 'second thoughts' about a big coal conversion programme on Teesside, complained that they had not been consulted and that in any case the copy was wrong – but it also coincided with renewed attempts to start up new peace talks. Miners were bemused to read, two days after the Board initiated its latest approach to Scargill, Heathfield and McGahey, a call to reject their own executive. The strike, said the second advertisement, had been 'called by the miners' leaders. It now needs to be called off by the miners themselves'.

The clear implication was that negotiations were not seen as the way to end hostilities. But negotiations did indeed start that very day, and, after nine hours at the Rubens Hotel, near NCB headquarters, were cautiously described as 'constructive'. Again attention had focused on the elusive 'third category', and the debate continued – for another five hours at the Rubens on 6 July, and then transferred to the Norton Park Hotel, Edinburgh, for an extended session on 9 July. There, at last, the two sides produced written drafts of agreements on which they would be prepared to end the dispute.

Both versions contained four clauses (though the numbering was unhelpfully inconsistent) and they embodied a remarkably high degree of unanimity. They agreed, with minor variation in wording, that 'in the light of the changed circumstances' – mainly the loss of output and markets during the first four months of the dispute – the Board would revise and re-examine its 6 March proposals. They concurred that five pits explicitly named by the NUM – Polmaise in Scotland, Herrington in County Durham, Cortonwood and Bullcliffe Wood in Yorkshire, and Snowdown in Kent, would be either 'kept open' (NUM) or made 'the subject of further consideration' (NCB). And they accepted that they would 'jointly discuss the Plan for Coal and any proposed revision'. The only substantial point of argument – though this turned out to be critical – concerned 'the parameters for exhaustion of reserves'.

The key issue was embodied in, and subsequently became notorious as, Clause 3c of the Coal Board's version (it was

135

2c for the NUM, but the distinction got lost when the debate restarted at the Advisory Conciliatory and Arbitration Service later in the year). The NUM draft provided that where 'a colliery has no further mineable reserves that are workable or which can be developed, there will be agreement between the Board and the union that such a colliery shall be deemed exhausted'. The NCB formulation added just one word to this crucially important statement. It insisted on expanding the central phrase to read 'reserves that are workable or which can be beneficially developed'.

'Beneficially' was far from being the first word considered in this vital context. It was the latest and far from final product of a wide-ranging semantic debate which prompted McGahey, at one stage, to call for Roget's Thesaurus; and when the NUM, later in the autumn, produced a dossier of the various formulations that had been proposed it formed one of a series lettered comprehensively from (a) to (z). Like all the others it proved insufficient to bridge the still yawning gap. The meeting broke up inconclusively, with an agreement to convene again in London on 18 July. In the meantime MacGregor wrote his second, much simpler letter to the country's 180,000 miners. The NUM, he told its membership, were saying that 'pits should be kept open even when they are of no benefit to the industry, while the NCB could not sanction a policy that might harm the industry'. It was, he summed up, 'a small but significant point'.

It was also, as things turned out, a clinching point. When the two sides got together once more at the Rubens Hotel, the talks swirled for hours round the inclusion or exclusion of beneficiality, and in the end they foundered. At 11.15 pm the union suggested a midnight adjournment and a continuation in the morning. MacGregor said he had an important alternative engagement and could not attend, so the search for verbal accommodation went on, fruitlessly, into the small hours. Finally it was the Board that decided that enough was enough. There were no further meetings until September, and by then the whole picture had changed.

Was Scargill right to balk at that single, obstructive word? MacGregor, for one, argued that although its inclusion was necessary to preserve any economic sense in the coal industry, it still left ample room for fruitful compromise. He strongly hinted that 'beneficial' could apply not just to the profit-and-loss account but to the totality of miners, their communities and the industry in which they worked. But that was not a universal view. As *The Times* argued, in one of its more forceful leaders: 'It is not an innocent word. It symbolises the division between two philosophies – one that seeks to run pits, regardless of costs, as a kind of occupational therapy for miners; the other which wants to apply the usual commercial criteria to pits, as all other industrial enterprises do, particularly in the harshly competitive field of energy.'

Many experienced trade union leaders, then and later, thought the miners were crazy not to pick up the July package. But while it was easily the best offer made to Scargill in the course of the dispute, it is important to recognise that it would still have represented a retreat. Nothing till now – even the reverses at Orgreaves – had diverted him from his quest for total triumph, and indeed between Edinburgh and London outside events seemed to have moved sharply in his favour, and against the government. There appeared to be little immediate case for compromise.

The most important development was the one the Cabinet had most feared – the opening of a 'second front' in the ominous shape of a national dock strike, called on 9 July, just as the 'beneficial' debate was in full swing. This had an immediate impact on business confidence and the financial markets, and when Scargill was presiding over the NUM's foreshortened national conference in Sheffield on 11 July, he was able to punctuate the proceedings with a series of bulletins on the falling state of the £. At one point he offered to adjourn the meeting for coffee, before the parity dropped any further, and he made it clear, at every opportunity, that he thought final success was now in reach. One delegate, David Crowther from Warsop in North Derbyshire, summed up the euphoric mood when he burst into song, transforming the pickets' familiar 'Here we go' slogan, into an operatically aggressive 'Here we are! Here we are! Here we are!'

Chapter 7

Danger in the Docks

The two worst moments for the government came in July and October. One was the autumn threat by the deputies' union, Nacods, to strike and close all the working collieries (see Chapter 9). The other, the dangerous opening of a 'second front' which would end the NUM's isolation and bring solid aid from another major union, was sparked just after 10 am on Friday, 6 July, when an excavator driver at the Immingham bulk terminal on South Humberside dipped his shovel for the fiftieth time that morning into a heap of iron-ore pellets. That precipitated a national dock strike. Eight days later the Prime Minister was talking, for the first and only time, about states of emergency and the possible need to bring in the troops.

The clock started ticking on Tuesday, 3 July when six pitmen took up position on the railway bridge at Eastfield Road, South Killingholme, which spans the line leading into Immingham docks just a mile away. Before sitting down to play cards and enjoy the sunshine, they draped a banner over the girders saying that this was an official NUM picket line. Soon one of the thirteen trains that normally ferry iron-ore each day from Immingham to British Steel's Scunthorpe works, just recovering from the Orgreave coke siege,

138

was brought to a halt below the bridge by its Aslef crew. That, it was thought by all concerned, would be that. According to the calculations of local union leaders it would need 1,200 truck journeys a day to carry anything like the same tonnage: iron-ore is an extremely bulky commodity. However, just in case, on Thursday, 5 July, Transport Union officials issued a formal warning: any attempt to move the material by road without the dockers' approval could provoke a national stoppage. Responding to an NUM request to black any lorries not complying with this ruling, John Ibbett, the T&G's district officer in Grimsby, said categorically: 'There is no way we are going to allow anyone other than registered dock workers to do the work.'

This was the time that Scargill and MacGregor were holding their early, relatively friendly meetings. The Immingham dockers had postponed close consideration of the NUM request in the hope of an agreed settlement. Like many groups affected by the miners' struggle they were in something of a cleft stick, dependent for their own livelihood on the continuing health of both Scunthorpe steel and the NCB's coal export trade (in normal times worth 90,000 tonnes a week to the port) but at the same time anxious not to undermine either the coal-workers or the train-drivers. They finally called their branch meeting for Friday morning at 10. On a split vote (figures have never been published, and there was some talk of threats to withdraw union cards from any open dissenters) it was agreed to go ahead with the ban.

Under the intricacies of the dock labour scheme, the statutory arrangement that governs working practices in Britain's 'registered' ports, ore-loading can, if necessary, be done by 'non-scheme' labour. This includes the drivers of the big front-loader shovels which are kept in reserve at Immingham for precisely those occasions when it is not possible, for some reason, to dispatch ore by train. The deal, however, allows this only if the outsider is 'observed' or 'shadowed' by at least one registered docker. This is normally a pretty informal, loosely controlled arrangement – the T&G men concerned claim they get no extra pay for the 'shadowing' job and merely keep an occasional eye on the interlopers in the intervals of other duties. The union's view, though, is that, as a matter of principle, work in the absence of such supervision must not proceed.

On the crucial morning, the dumper driver had started his morning shift with not one but two 'shadows', so when they both went off to their 10 am union meeting and he just carried on, he had broken the rules. In fact British Steel, as the transgressing employer, later apologised and paid the appropriate fine. For the purpose of extending the dispute to other ports this was presented as a threat to the jealously guarded integrity of the dock labour scheme. But the real crux of the matter was that he was loading ore on to trucks, and on a massive scale. The first lorries moved out later that afternoon, and between 3 pm on Friday and 6 am on Monday, working flat-out round the clock, an endless convoy shifted 27,000 tonnes through the Lincolnshire country roads. When they knocked off, the huge Immingham stockpile, which on Friday morning stood at 60,000 tonnes, had been reduced by almost half.

The response was swift. The T&G executive met on Monday morning and called out all 35,000 docks and waterway members on indefinite strike from midnight. Only 13,700 of these, though, were actually in the port labour scheme which had been guaranteeing work and generous fall-back pay since 1947 to all men who remained on the register. Retirement and hefty redundancy payments had cut the numbers by almost three-quarters since 1972, when the last countrywide stoppage had brought export shipments to a near-halt. The impact in 1984 would depend crucially on the degree of support the union could mobilise, particularly among the non-registered groups: lightermen, tugboat crews, canal workers, and above all those who now worked the new, booming container ports like Felixstowe and Dover and were not covered by the scheme. That in turn would be largely determined by the majority's assessment of just what they were being asked to fight for: backing the miners; defending their industry's traditional labour arrangements, despite their dwindling importance; or, as many militants advocated, taking deliberate advantage of the coal crisis to re-extend

140

these arrangements so that they again embraced the great bulk of Britain's seaborne trade. Failure to clarify the objectives turned out to be a crippling weakness for those seeking to prolong the dispute. But for the two weeks while the dockers held fire, they presented a serious threat.

Before the first week was out, all fifty-three of the registered ports were at a standstill. A steadily growing proportion of the 150-odd unregistered ones – mostly small, but including the two crucially important container handlers, Folkestone and Dover – were gradually grinding to a halt. Two sets of peace talks had ended in stalemate, and a belated confession by British Steel at Immingham that they had broken the rules was treated as an irrelevant aside. Felixstowe's 1,100 men voted on Friday to join in, as did Dover, where the halting of freight traffic also meant large-scale disruption of the summer holiday exodus to Europe. Commentators deplored the state of Britain, where life could be paralysed the moment a union decreed that an unskilled job had been improperly filled. Mrs Thatcher in her Finchley constituency gave due warning that 'the government will do everything necessary to keep the country working'. The nation, she added, was being held to ransom by 'a tiny minority' – 200,000 at the most – who were determined to impose their will on the other 55 million.

The curt dismissal of BSC's act of contrition deepened the government's fears. Nicholas Ridley, the transport secretary, assured the Commons that there were 'no plans to change or abolish' the dock labour scheme: now that the Immingham position had been corrected there was 'no reason whatever for the strike'. John Connally, the TGWU's national dock organiser, equally vehemently denied that the dispute had anything to do with the miners – though Arthur Scargill had spent the weekend welcoming the dockers' support. At the Civil Contingencies Unit, the secretary, Brigadier Tony Budd, took the precaution of dusting off his regularly updated file on dock disruptions and checked the arrangements for bringing in troops to move essential supplies. The armed forces, in the last resort, are geared to release a maximum of 20,000 soldiers and seamen for such work – 7,000 more nowadays than the number of registered dockers. Although no more than 5,000 have ever been used in recent times (the last occasion was April 1950) they are always available to act as labourers and drivers, and at a pinch to ferry supplies to such remote spots as the Orkneys and the Hebrides.

The plans remained in their pigeon holes, but by Tuesday 17 July the strike was pretty solid, and customers – from farmers needing imported foodstuffs to Yorkshire woollen mills awaiting Australian fleeces – were hastily improvising emergency supplies. Only the tiniest of ports, like Wivenhoe in East Anglia and Teignmouth in Devon, were even nominally working. Industry was reluctantly accepting that the only real alternative open would soon be expensive air freight. A thousand lorries, which had missed the deadline for closing Dover, were stranded outside Calais awaiting passage. On the Kent side of the English Channel, 153 articulated vehicles, mostly from the Continent, took up a five-mile stretch of the M20 which had been coned off for emergency parking. The only break was at Swansea, where a few tugboat men went back to work and docked an oil tanker which had been waiting to discharge. Elsewhere, the national employers' organisation, the CBI, sombrely warned that roughly 75 per cent of industry would soon be at risk – far more than had in any way been affected by the miners.

Throughout the week an anxious debate raged as to the dockers' true motives. The NUM took aid and comfort, the pound slipped well below $1.30 for the first time and the stock market plunged. John Connally reiterated that the TGWU's only formal objective was to win a pledge that there would be no further breaches in the rules for using non-registered labour in the port. Nobody, even in his own union, was quite sure how far it was safe to believe him. Then, suddenly, the whole thing was over – blown away as unexpectedly and as inconclusively as it had begun.

The deciding factor was the anger of the stranded lorry drivers. Stuck with their vehicles on both sides of the Channel, they made it increasingly plain that they would not tolerate for long a situation which left them short of food, cash and anywhere to sleep but their own uncomfortable cabs. By Thursday tempers were fraying fast, and the six Transport Union officials responsible for Dover were under virtual siege in the cramped hut beside the lavatories in the corporation carpark which served as their strike head-quarters. Some 180 truckers, mostly French, West German and Italian, were stuck in the East Dock a mile away down Marine Parade, and they picked a large, expansive English colleague, Dave Rowley, to express their rising fury. He tackled the job with enthusiasm, and made it clear it was not only the Continentals who were fed up. 'I'm disgusted with these people who haven't the guts to stand up to the unions,' he fumed. 'All we've had is promises and no action.' But action was not far away.

Conciliation talks had been going on in London, and there was hope these would produce some indication of when the drivers could get back to Calais. The latest promise from the harbour authorities was that there might be some news at 6 pm, but somehow that got translated during the afternoon into 'We're going at six.' As the time neared, all the parked lorries started honking their horns, and around 5.30 pm Donald Soppitt, the port's director of operations, went to the strike-hut to warn the shop stewards that things were getting out of control. Almost as he spoke, three trucks with their horns blaring smashed through a metal barrier to join the cars and caravans waiting to board the holiday ferries. While police raced to stop them, more drivers formed a picket line of their own across the ramp leading to Number 2 berth. Régis Bouyssi, leading the French contingent, said angrily: 'We have run out of food and money. Why should the tourists go and not us?'

Soppitt managed to persuade them to end the blockade, but only after he had given them permission to drive into the loading area. When he pleaded for more time to give the London peace talks a chance, Bouyssi announced firmly that: 'We are leaving at 10 o'clock tonight whatever happens, whether the strike has stopped or not.' Dave Rowley under-lined the threat: 'There's been no violence so far, but after 10 pm I don't know what will happen. If the drivers can't leave they will burn the place down. It won't just be blockades, they'll go on the rampage.' As the evening wore on, Soppitt and the shop stewards persuaded themselves that these were anything but idle boasts. Telephone calls from across the Channel talked of fighting in Boulogne and an incident at Ostend where a ferry captain had been run down by a truck trying to board. Then a TGWU official arrived from the Eastern Docks with news of an anonymous tip that at 10 pm the drivers intended to leave their cabs, hunt down the men who normally operated the mooring ramps and 'beat the living daylights out of them'. It was decided that there were only two choices: to call off the freight ban or to pull all TGWU members off the docks and leave it to the police. At 8.30 pm, after phoning the London headquarters of Acas and hearing there was no progress with the peace talks, Alan Green, the union's district organiser, walked across to the harbour board offices and announced that the ban was to be lifted immediately. As far as Dover was concerned, the strike was over. When Soppitt told the drivers the news, he got a rib-crunching bear hug from Rowley and the verdict: 'We've cracked it. We've bloody well cracked it.'

Nationally, it lasted another two days, but there was little more heart in the struggle. Sixteen more hours of talks at Acas produced a five-point agreement, signed on the Saturday afternoon, which gave assurances that in future there would be 'no intentional breaches' of the dock labour scheme, and a seventy-eight to five vote by union delegates in favour of ending the dispute. John Connally, the strike leader, insisted that it had been 'necessary'. Nicholas Ridley, the transport secretary, denied it. And Mrs Thatcher, immediately she was told of the Dover collapse, said with some satisfaction: 'Arthur Scargill must now be wondering where he can turn.'

Right: The strike's first martyr.
Yorkshire miner David Jones who
died at Ollerton on 14 April 1984.

Below: Arthur Scargill emerges into
adoring crowd after the conference on
19 April rejects a ballot.

Above: The Alamo. The miners' own name for their picketing redoubt at Cortonwood, the pit where it all began. It was area director George Hayes 'bombshell' announcement of closure that triggered the Yorkshire strike.

Overleaf: Police charge in the battle of Orgreave, the South Yorkshire coke works which Scargill failed to close by mass picketing. The massive police operation ensured the coal lorries to Scunthorpe kept running.

Lorry driver and TGWU docker square up during the ports strike which opened up a second front in the government's confrontation with the miners. Lorry drivers proved the weakest link of all in the TGWU's uphill struggle to provide industrial support for the miners.

NUM delegation joins the vote of overwhelming support for the union at the TUC in Brighton's conference centre in September. The statement approved by Congress was put together in a tense meeting in Len Murray's hotel suite in the early hours of the previous Friday.

From left: Peter Heathfield, Mick McGahey, Arthur Scargill. Behind McGahey, Gordon Butler (Derbyshire Secretary), behind Scargill, Windsor Emlyn Williams (South Wales).

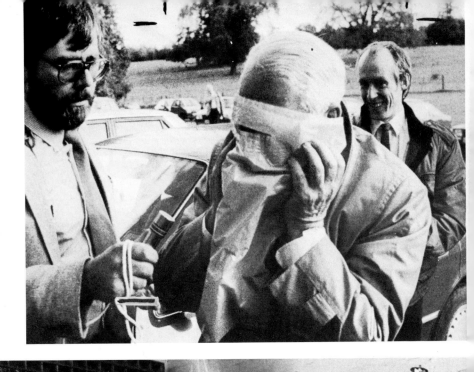

Above left: Ian MacGregor arrives at Edinburgh peace talks in September shielding his head from cameramen with a plastic bag. It was partly to cut out PR gaffes like this that Michael Eaton was brought down to London by the NCB the following month.

Above right: Roger Windsor and the Libyan connection. Windsor, the union's chief executive officer, on the way home from Libya before the storm breaks over *The Sunday Times'* revelation of his Scargill-authorised journey to Tripoli. Link man Mumtaz Abbasi has back turned.

Left: Dick Bryan (left) and Ken Cross, pit deputies at Ollerton colliery on the brink of what would have been their union's first ever national strike. The strike, averted at the end of October, threatened to do what the NUM had failed to do – and shut the Notts coalfield.

Police escort for miners returning to work at Whittle colliery: by mid-November t
advances and often heavily protected transport.

CB had mounted a carefully planned back to work campaign using publicity, pay

The taxi in which Cardiff cab driver David Wilkie (right) was killed bringing a working miner to Merthyr Vale colliery on 30 November 1984. A concrete block dropped from the bridge above went straight through the windscreen. At a rally the same night Arthur Scargill said the union was 'deeply shocked by the tragedy' and disassociated itself from 'acts of violence which occur away from the picket line.'

Left: Devoted picket in audience in Derby in November as Scargill goes on the stump in coalfields where support had started to crumble. In the previous week, according to NCB figures, 3952 more miners had returned, bringing the total not on strike to 65,000 out of 180,000.

Herbert Brewer (left) Derbyshire solicitor, prominent local Conservative, and the first Receiver appointed by the high court to control NUM funds handed over within a week to insolvency expert Michael Arnold (right).

Below: Peter Walker, post-strike, on 8 March 1985. The energy Secretary told backbench Tory MPs not to 'gloat' at the outcome of the dispute.

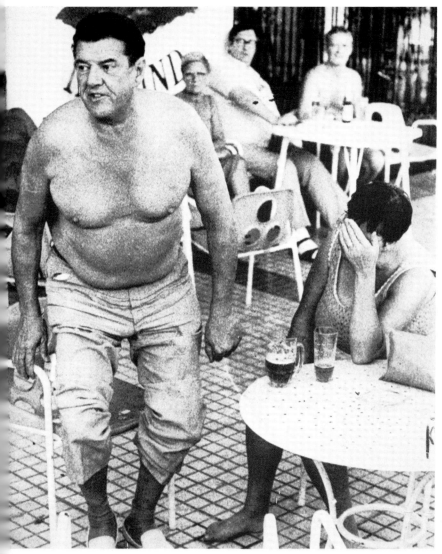

...l Vincent, Lancashire area secretary, with companion Joan Hodkinson, discovered on ... winter holiday in Tenerife ten months into the strike. 'I wish I'd never come,' he tells ...*e Sunday Times*. He flew home early and secured a unanimous confidence vote from ... area executive despite having not told them about the trip.

The men go back at Merthyr Vale colliery, in the shadow of the Aberfan tip. As at Mardy, the Merthyr Vale men marched back behind their banner proudly showing 'we are still united' as Bill King, the branch secretary put it. Much of the impetus for a return to work without an agreement came from South Wales.

Chapter 8

Am I My Brother's Keeper?

Superficially, the 1984 Trade Union Congress, which opened in Brighton on 3 September, was a triumph for the striking miners and their cause. Their president received a standing ovation. Their motion, calling for 'total support' was overwhelmingly endorsed. The general council, representing some ten million organised workers, decreed a full-scale blockade of both coal and alternative fuel. The general secretary, Len Murray, previously a less than wholehearted ally, had assured the 1,121 delegates that the entire union movement now stood 'shoulder to shoulder' with the NUM. Outside in the carnival sunshine, 4,000 pitmen demonstrated, with good humour and often moving dignity, while the extra police drafted in for the occasion stood around with nothing to do – except watch the brisk grounding of an unauthorised plane which had been trailing a 'Get Stuffed Scargill' pennant overhead.

But behind the scenes, and to some extent even in public, the strains were readily apparent. Eric Hammond, the electricians' leader, was angrily booed when he dismissed the general council's pledge as 'dishonest and deficient'. Mobilising the industrial strength of the power workers might seem to present a dazzling prospect, he warned. 'But are the

145

miners deaf? Can they not hear the backstage whispering?'
John Lyons, for the equally important power engineers, was
no less forthright. Without the backing of his and Hammond's
members the call to 'black' coal and its substitutes was
meaningless. 'We will not do it. Our members will not do it.
I predict that other workers in the industry will not do it.'

A determined optimist might try to brush such sentiments
aside. The Hammond and Lyons unions, though strategically
important, formed only a tiny minority against the ninety
or more (the exact vote was not recorded) who indicated
uncompromising support. But realists, whatever they said
for the record, already knew that the Brighton performance
was largely a hollow sham. The 'backstage whispering' was
no fantasy. The NUM leaders, with their determination to run
the strike their own way, their earlier aloofness from the
TUC, their lack of alliances in depth, and above all their failure
to heal the internal divisions exemplified by the defection of
Notts, had contributed to strengthening their enemies and
dividing and isolating their friends. As one white-collar
moderate tersely summed up the mood before the debate:
'They should give the gold badge of Congress to whoever
can arrange things so that the miners win and yet Scargill is
defeated.'

The tension, and often outright antipathy, that existed
between the miners' leaders and the rest of Britain's trade
union establishment manifested itself in a thousand subtle
ways. For instance, there was a tiny but telling incident
in May when Len Murray, the long-serving TUC general
secretary, arrived at Aberconway for the annual conference
of the Welsh TUC. On his way in he was accosted by a small
group of pitmen from Point of Ayr, in North Wales, who
asked him: 'Come on then, Len, are you going to support
the miners?' Although the dispute was already two months
old, it was the first time that the movement's chief functionary
had met any of the participants face to face. All he could
summon up was the flicker of a smile and a nod in their
direction. He walked on without speaking, and in his speech
that day the coal strike was not dignified with so much as a
single word.

The first twelve days of the strike, in fact, had already passed before the TUC was formally told of its existence. Normal practice when any official dispute is called is for the union concerned to notify Congress House and ask that all the other 109 members be circulated with a request for assistance. The insouciant communication from Peter Heathfield, however, made it clear that the NUM was not at that time seeking either intervention or assistance, and that if anything changed it would pass Murray the word. As one senior general council member growled: 'Basically the letter said: don't ring us, we'll ring you.' Indeed, it was clear from the outset that Scargill preferred to deal directly with likely allies, not through the labour movement's institutional structures. This coolness had developed inexorably since 1980, when the NUM president, then forty-two, had been elected as the council's youngest member. At an impromptu press conference on that occasion, he insisted that membership would not change his politics, which were 'deeply militant and socialist by nature', and that he would not allow himself to become infected with the TUC's notorious predilection for compromise. 'Compromise,' he said prophetically, 'is not a word in my dictionary.'

Once he started attending meetings, his impatience grew apace. He hated the 'Buggins's turn' tradition that consigned newcomers like himself to the less important committees, and he patently regarded much of the business as a waste of time. Often he skipped even the regular eve-of-council caucus meetings held by his natural colleagues on the left wing. When there was a change in the council's composition which left the NUM with only one representative instead of two, he unhesitatingly gave it up to his deputy, Mick McGahey. Even while he retained his seat, he was the only member who, after two years, had still failed to provide Murray with his home telephone number. Murray reciprocated, and freely revealed his suspicions that Scargill, through his cultivation of 'friendly unions' – mainly those representing the transport workers – in preference to the main body of organised labour, was deliberately aiming to set up a left-wing-dominated 'alternative TUC'.

147

The divisions that might have given substance to that charge were real enough, and went far beyond mere personalities. Murray's view, crystallised in the phrase 'new realism', that the TUC should only support those disputes which it regarded as winnable, was anathema to radical militants, who saw its failure to provide backing in such confrontations as the train-drivers' rejection of 'flexible rostering' and the National Graphical Association's struggle with the newspaper owner, Eddie Shah, as tantamount to a sell-out. The NUM, under its leftwing leadership and with its own bitter memories going back to the 'betrayal' of 1926, naturally gravitated to this group; and Scargill in turn drew two crucial and closely related conclusions – that he should in no circumstances risk the TUC taking charge of the 1984–5 struggle; and that he had enough allies for his purpose without need to use the machinery of Congress House. The first, however, proved unsustainable and the second plain wrong.

The mistake was compounded, from the miners' point of view, by a failure to weave together the members of the 'inter-union coordinating committee' – Murray's alternative TUC – to provide a fully integrated network of support. With all the main transport unions including the huge 1.6m.-member Transport and General Workers represented, it should have been possible, in principle, to get a comprehensive stranglehold on Britain's economic life, similar to that which precipitated the three-day-week working of 1974. But in fact the response was very patchy. It was the National Union of Seamen and the rail unions which made easily the biggest sacrifices. British Rail lost £250m. in the course of the strike, £70m. of it directly attributable to the blacking of coal trains. Aslef and the NUR contributed generously from their head office funds – £100,000 in the first three months – and had several hundred men a day suspended (in many cases with their wages made up to full basic pay) for refusing to man the footplates and signal boxes. Even in the heart of the areas where miners continued to work – Shirebrook, serving the Trent Valley, and Coalville, in Leicestershire – the railwaymen maintained a broad (though never quite total) ban on coal movements till the end. But all their efforts were undercut, to the point of futility, by the ease with which it proved possible to find alternative ways of delivering the loads.

The key factor was road haulage. Just as the British seamen, loyally rejecting coal cargoes, found the work switched to foreign flags over which they had no control, so the railwaymen, grimly sticking to their bargains with the miners, merely saw a large slice of their industry's staple trade transferred from the sidings to the motorways. Though independent owner-drivers were responsible for many of the lorry journeys which resulted – 25,000 a week at the peak – at least a substantial minority were TGWU members working in open defiance of their union guidelines. By the end of the strike the TGWU executive had donated over £3m. in money to help the NUM cause, but matters were very different when it came to practical support. Particularly in Nottinghamshire and the Midlands, where it would have been most useful to tie down coal stocks, drivers – and also TGWU workers in the power stations – took the view that, with 34,000 miners working, there was little reason for them either to defy management or pass up lucrative jobs.

The desire to cooperate was not always enhanced, either, by the often graceless attitudes of the NUM strike leaders. A polite request from Aslef to run just one experimental coal-train trip, from Bickershaw in Lancashire to the Fiddlers Ferry power station, was brusquely turned down. A gentle suggestion from George Henderson, the TGWU official responsible for open-cast coal workers, that support from his members might win them a little more sympathy in future from the deep-mining end of the industry (Scargill, at the 1983 Labour party conference, had successfully proposed a motion that open-cast, by far the most profitable part of the NCB's operations, should be wound down and eliminated) produced a furious demand from Sheffield that he be formally reprimanded. Henderson had to stand uncomfortably while Moss Evans, his general secretary, dictated a fulsome 'Dear Arthur' letter reaffirming that 'beyond any shadow of doubt the official policy of the TGWU is that we give the miners unequivocal support . . . both physical and financial'. But it was a promise easier to write than to fulfil. The open-cast miners, whose agreed contributions had been to stockpile their output for the duration, duly fell back in line – without any promise that there would be an NUM change of heart. But their efforts were without any element of overzealous enthusiasm. As one of them, Ian Partridge in Northumberland, wrote to Henderson: 'How can the NUM president expect to put out his hand for our friendship when he is preparing to stab us in the back?'

If approaches to friendly unions were heavy-handed, those to the less committed sometimes verged on the inept. Intelligence tended to be rudimentary and out of date – when a belated search began for 'sympathetic activists' in the field of power supply, one of the few names on file was Wyn Bevan, who had long since abandoned his formerly fiery Trotskyite views to become a loyal moderate member of the EEPTU executive – and there was little diplomatic sensibility on display. This was most strikingly exemplified by a letter which appeared out of the blue on the desks of all the main power union general secretaries in the eleventh week of the dispute. Written by Peter Heathfield, it made the routine request that all workers in the 'fuel and power' sector should refuse to cross the NUM picket lines, and then introduced, without preamble, a wholly new and revolutionary concept: that from henceforth every generating plant in Britain should be 'deemed to be picketed' and treated as though it was ringed by accredited strikers, even if there were none within twenty miles. When he recovered his breath, John Lyons, who is secretary to both the 28,000-strong Electrical Power Engineers Association and the Electricity Supply Industry National Council, which represents all the various employee organisations, wrote a clipped and dismissive reply. 'What you propose,' he said, 'would be so far-reaching as seriously to affect the whole country, and therefore the whole trade union movement.' He passed it to Len Murray 'for information' and nothing more was heard of that remarkable idea.

By the end of July, in any case, it was clear that appeals to individual unions, whether welcome or otherwise, could only have a limited effect. A belated effort to switch picketing from steel to power stations had ignominiously fizzled out (Kim Howells, the NUM's Welsh area publicity officer, when asked to organise it, pleaded he was too busy with other more immediate affairs). Also, the money for day-to-day strike activity was rapidly running short. The switch of £8m. worth of assets abroad immediately after the decision to call the dispute had left only £2m. in the union's general fund, and although donations by midsummer had already topped £5m., this was mostly earmarked for easing hardship in the pit communities. Now local NUM headquarters received warnings from Sheffield that the so-called 'campaign fund' – the cash set aside to help less well-off areas with general strike-related expenses – was exhausted. Heathfield and Scargill let it be known to an inner circle of supporters that they now needed at least £115,000 a week just to keep head office going. Friendly unions like Aslef, which had already put up £60,000, the National Union of Public Employees (£50,000) and the TGWU (£30,000) committed themselves collectively to meet the bill until September. But beyond that the financial landscape was shrouded in fog; another urgent reminder that the TUC could not much longer be totally bypassed.

It was against this background that Scargill began to consider the impending TUC congress – a mere five weeks away – and what might be secured from it in terms of support. This was not necessarily a U-turn. There was a large difference between entrusting the dispute to an unpredictable and uneasy TUC general council and its secretariat, and appealing, in the highly charged atmosphere of Congress, to the rank-and-file delegates themselves. Indeed there are senior TUC figures who still believe that had been Scargill's strategy from the start: to secure from the TUC's sovereign body exactly the kind of unequivocal backing he could never have secured from the general council on its own.

On 1 August, in the brown marble offices in Euston Road, London, which house the headquarters of the NUR, Scargill met the four union men who constituted his closest non-mining allies, and started to plan the change of tack. The miners had already submitted a motion calling in general terms for all-out support, but the question now for discussion with Aslef's Ray Buckton, the TUC's current chairman, Jimmy Knapp of the railwaymen, Jim Slater of the seamen, and Ron Todd, who is now general secretary for the transport workers, was how best to translate this into hard practical effect. Developing a strategy originated by Roger Windsor, the NUM's self-effacing chief executive (at least until his October trip to Libya), it was decided to tack on to the main resolution a series of far-reaching amendments. The first, to be proposed by Aslef, would demand a 10p a week levy from each member of the TUC's ninety-eight affiliated unions; the second, from the NUR, would extend the pledge to respect NUM pickets so that it embraced all unions; and the third, from the NUS, looking forward to an escalation in which attempts might be made to move coal from strikebound pitheads, aimed to bar the use of any material delivered by 'non-union labour or members of the armed forces'.

The first two amendments, in particular, embodied daunting demands. In cash terms the levy would represent close to £1m. a week. The picket ruling, if passed, could be used to prevent almost any worker from getting to his job. Scargill later told Len Murray that it was intended merely to deflect fuel from the power stations, but alarm bells started to ring. Many union leaders took fright at the prospect that they might pass and become official TUC policy, after which the miners' president would be invited to discuss their implementation. As one white-collar representative warned: 'He'll be like a bailiff with a court order to enforce.'

Since March, Murray had abided strictly by Heathfield's hands-off rules. Once a month, just before the regular meeting of the TUC's inner cabinet, the finance and general purposes committee, the two men spoke on the telephone. Murray would ask politely whether the miners' attitude on fraternal assistance had in any way changed, and the NUM secretary would reply, with equal courtesy, that it had not. Not everyone at Congress House was happy about this arrangement. David Basnett, for instance, with 500 of his

Am I My Brother's Keeper?

General and Municipal Worker members actually employed in the coal industry, had several times suggested inviting the NUM in to discuss the dispute. But this had always been rejected on the grounds that it would be embarrassing if they refused. One of the advocates of a more positive policy was Norman Willis, Murray's deputy, who was due to succeed him as general secretary immediately after the 1984 Congress. As relations between them were almost as cool as those between Murray and Scargill he had not pressed the point. But now, in early August, Murray was off ill after collapsing at the annual rally to commemorate the Tolpuddle Martyrs, and Willis seized the opportunity. He travelled with Buckton to Sheffield and informed himself at first hand about the state of the miners' finances. It was the first face-to-face contact between Scargill, Heathfield and a senior member of the TUC bureaucracy since the strike began.

After that, things started to move. Murray, recovered from his illness, quickly saw the dangers implicit in the NUM's Congress plans. On 19 August he wrote to Heathfield, saying that the inner cabinet had decided it would be 'helpful' to meet and discuss how the TUC might help. Specifically the suggested agenda would cover 'financial assistance, including interest-free long-term loans from the whole trade union movement . . . practical means by which effect could be given to the NUM motion; and ways in which the dispute could be brought to a conclusion satisfactory to the NUM'. Behind the ponderous officialese was a clear aim: to reach an agreement pre-empting the amendments, which as Murray realised must either split Congress down the middle or saddle it with a series of demands it almost certainly could not fulfil.

Getting the NUM round a table, though, was much easier said than done. Heathfield told Murray he could do nothing without consulting his executive, which was not due to meet until 29 August. A frustrated Murray pointed out that was the very day the TUC inner circle would be deciding their attitude to the miners' strike: could Heathfield not possibly move faster? Yes, he could; but the result only increased Murray's exasperation. On Tuesday, 28 August Heathfield reported, after telephoning eighteen out of the NUM's

153

twenty-four executive members, that there was no desire to meet the general council, and no plans to arrive in Brighton before Sunday: just in time to put their appeal directly to the floor of Congress, as Scargill had always planned, on the Monday morning.

By now the miners' leader had had second thoughts about one of the controversial amendments and had decided to drop the call for a £1m. a week levy. But the equally divisive claim for universal recognition of picket lines remained intact. After the miners had ignored yet another urgent invitation to talk, this moved to the top of the pre-Congress agenda. John Lyons, whose power engineers would be among those most directly affected, demanded a full general council debate on the miners' ideas of 'total support' before things went too far, and was only persuaded by Murray to hold off in order to make time for one more last-ditch appeal. By now though McGahey, in his role as member of the TUC general council, had become almost as worried as the rest about Scargill's intransigence, and he went off with Willis to call Sheffield, where the NUM executive had just ended. With Scargill and Heathfield both listening, on separate extensions, he told them bluntly: 'Comrades, you've got to come tonight.'

That morning, as it happened, Scargill had had an internal rebellion of his own to deal with. Jack Jones, the NUM area leader in Leicestershire, had committed what many of his colleagues on the miners' executive regarded as an unforgivable crime. The NCB chairman, Ian MacGregor, had been seen that week by millions on TV driving the first stake to start work on the brand-new £300m. Asfordby super-pit in the Vale of Belvoir. Jones had been the man holding the stake. In the most emotional of many denunciations, Idwal Morgan, of the Barnsley cokemen, accused him of 'driving a stake through the heart of the miners'. Although Scargill was able to point out that there was no power, under the rules, to sack him on the spot, he was unable to prevent a demand for his resignation going through by twelve votes to ten. Whether or not this affected his decision, he now accepted McGahey's advice and agreed, though with significant provisos, that he would go early to Brighton after all. The main stipulation was that the NUM team should talk, not to the whole inner cabinet, but only to Murray and his top officials, plus Buckton, as TUC chairman, and Basnett, representing the economic committee. With that accepted, Scargill and Heathfield set off to make the 220-mile Sheffield – Brighton drive.

When the meeting began at 8 pm, in the red-carpeted Louis xv suite at Brighton's Metropole Hotel, Murray spoke plainly. That morning, he said, the general council had shown it wanted to help; but it was fed up with the miners' apparent determination to bypass its efforts and appeal over its head to trade unionists at large. Many members were strongly critical of the way the strike was being run, particularly the violence of much picketing, and they needed to know much more clearly what the NUM was really after before giving full backing to their appeal for 'total support'.

Following diplomatic assurances from McGahey that there was no intention to snub the TUC, Scargill developed his familiar theme. After twenty-six weeks the strike was still 88 per cent solid; even in the working coalfields, production losses were heavy; the NUM was acting in strict accord with the 1974 Plan for Coal, which had not anywhere envisaged closures on 'purely economic grounds'; and although the NCB had sabotaged the July peace negotiations by introducing the word 'beneficial' the NUM was always ready to talk. On violence, as the confidential minutes show, Scargill said he could not condemn members who were suffering 'great hardship, frustration and in some cases provocation'. The hardship in the mining areas was now 'tremendous' and there was a crying need for financial aid. The basic thrust of the NUM motion and its amendments was to put pressure on the power supply unions to give their wholehearted support.

At that point Basnett stepped in to introduce the first sour note. As head of one of the two biggest unions in the electricity-generating industry, he could not accept the Aslef amendment on respect for picket lines. The prime objective for the miners should be to get a fully united trade union movement behind them; any proposal of that kind would

155

achieve just the opposite. After that it took four hours of intensive and occasionally bad-tempered argument to produce an agreed form of words that could go forward to the general council the following morning. This affirmed 'total support' for the NUM's objectives of saving pits, jobs and mining communities, launched a 'concerted campaign' to raise money for alleviating hardship and maintaining the union's finances, and neatly sidestepped the much-criticised ban on workers crossing picket lines. Instead it sought to make the dispute 'more effective by (a) not moving coal or coke, or oil substitute for coal or coke, or using such materials taken across NUM official picket lines; (b) not using oil which is substituted for coal'. However, there was a sting in the tail. These proposals would only be implemented after 'detailed discussions with the general council and agreement with unions which would be directly concerned'. This stipulation, which seriously diluted the miners' control over the strike, proved the major sticking point that night. At one point Scargill and Heathfield withdrew for private discussions. When they returned they tried hard to have it deleted. In the end though, they accepted defeat and the draft went forward in its significantly more circumscribed form.

The new wording virtually ensured Congress's enthusiastic acceptance, but the general council, when they met in the morning, were far from unanimously happy. They gave their endorsement only after a speech from Gerry Russell, representing the powerful engineering workers, who told his colleagues soberly: 'We can't promise the moon. There'll be problems delivering. But we'll do our best.' Three of the other moderate unions – and the three who would be most directly affected by the decision – all voted against. John Lyons and Eric Hammond, backed up by Bill Sirs of the steelworkers, rejected what they saw as a piece of blatant hypocrisy, cobbled up merely to preserve some pretence of unity. Condemning the resolution, even in its laboriously revised version, Hammond exploded after the meeting: 'Either it means the complete cessation of civilised life, or it doesn't mean what it says and it's a con-trick on the miners.'

The debate was far from academic. It went to the heart of

the TUC's agonising self-appraisal which had already been going on for a year, ever since Len Murray issued his warning that Britain's unions, with their declining influence and shrinking membership rolls, must start cultivating a 'new realism' and stop promising more than they were able to perform. Willis, for one, now sees the 1984 Congress as a case in point. The fulsomely offered support did indeed prove impossible to deliver, and he now believes that the price of unity – and of not being franker with the miners about the parlousness of their cause – may have been too high. At the time, though, the greater priority was seen as 'getting through Congress' without a major split. Murray, Buckton and Basnett, from their different standpoints, were all relieved that the outcome of the miners' debate was now a foregone conclusion.

On Monday afternoon, a packed audience at the conference centre saw Scargill achieve a notable oratorical triumph; but as he himself clearly recognised, a speech at least equally potent was the one made by Gavin Laird, the moderate and highly articulate general secretary to the engineers. Laird did not mince his words in criticising the fact that 'the NUM saw fit for many months to ignore the general council and the government of the trade union movement'; and he warned that there was 'no excuse for violence on the picket line', which he said was a 'disservice to the wonderful struggle and sacrifices of the men, women and children of the mining communities'. He acknowledged that the engineering workers in the power stations and the mining equipment business had so far refused industrial support, because the miners had not first gone to the TUC. But in a ringing peroration he signalled what was intended to be a dramatic change of heart. 'Let the government know, and the unions, moderate or what you will, that the position is changed from today; and that the AUEW and its 943,000 members are at one with the NUM and will resolve this dispute on the basis of victory.'

That was what the hall wanted to hear. There was a very different reception for John Lyons. Shouts of 'scab' and 'Tory swine' punctuated his text, as he warned the delegates

157

that 'the electricity supply industry is not, and never has been, available to solve industrial disputes external to it, not even for the miners.'

Yet curiously it was Lyons, the purveyor of unwanted truths, who now helped to get new talks started between the miners and the NCB. Robert Maxwell, the multi-millionaire printing magnate who had recently bought, and appointed himself editor-in-chief of, the *Daily Mirror*, had been in Brighton that weekend closeted with Scargill and Heathfield, and letting it be known that he was in the thick of secret peace moves: these, in the end, came to nothing. On Monday evening, after the delegates dispersed, Lyons was appalled to see Ian MacGregor, in a television interview, saying in his usual blunt fashion that whatever the TUC had decided, there was no point in any further negotiations unless the closure of uneconomic pits was at the top of the agenda. While recognising this as the central issue, the power engineers' leader thought that, by setting it as a precondition, the NCB chairman was going out of his way to ensure that no talks could even get started.

From his hotel room Lyons telephoned Roger Farrance, who runs labour relations for the Electricity Council and is one of Britain's most experienced and successful negotiators. After getting his anger with MacGregor off his chest, he laid out for Farrance a few basic facts about the electricity supply industry. He had meant what he said when he told Congress he would not see it used as a battlefield in the miners' strike. From the start, power workers had unprotestingly handled fresh-mined coal in the Trent Valley, and elsewhere cooperated fully in the use of oil and nuclear power to ease pressure on the coal-fired stations. But if the NCB or the government were seen to be stalling on talks, he could not guarantee that tolerance would continue. Farrance listened carefully and promised he would pass that message up the line. The next day, the Coal Board offered to resume negotiations.

In the event, these took place in a blaze of unwanted publicity, and produced as rich a mixture of farce and tragedy as was seen in the long course of the dispute, but there was at least one brief moment when the whole thing came within

158

touching distance of being resolved. Discussions began in Edinburgh, where MacGregor arrived with his face inexplicably covered in a plastic bag. Pursued at breakneck speed by a posse of newsmen, they proceeded in an erratic southerly direction via Monk Fryston in the Selby coalfield (where Scargill and MacGregor, for once united, appeared side by side before the TV cameras to protest at 'harassment' by the media) to a long nocturnal session at the bleakly imposing head offices of British Ropes in Doncaster. That was where many participants thought they had got a deal. But whatever agreement there was evaporated in the train somewhere between Yorkshire and London. Back at the ill-starred Rubens Hotel, where the last round has collapsed in July, the same thing happened again. In an atmosphere of even more bitter recrimination, the parties went their separate ways.

Nominally the breakdown occurred over just five crucial words. It is probably worth repeating the critical paragraph – yet another attempt to define a third category of closures, other than those on grounds of exhaustion or safety. The Board's version was that:

'in the case of a colliery where a report of an examination by the respective NCB and NUM qualified mining engineers establishes that there are no further reserves that can be developed to provide the Board, in line with their responsibilities, with a base for continuing operations there will be agreement between the Board and the unions that such a colliery will be deemed exhausted.'

For the words 'in line with their responsibilities' the NUM wanted to substitute, because of their more expansionist connotation, 'in line with the Plan for Coal'.

But there was a further complication. The first paragraph of the by now notorious clause 3c, which had already been much bandied between the two sides, now read that 'since the advent of the Plan for Coal there have been colliery closures that do not fall within the definitions of exhaustion or safety and in accordance with the principle of the plan it is acknowledged this procedure will apply'. At one stage at least in the round of post-TUC talks, the NUM had apparently accepted this formulation, though it insisted afterwards that it had always done so only on the understanding that it was simply a way of saying that the colliery review procedure would continue to operate. True or not, on the Friday the union draftsmen amended the paragraph to drop any explicit recognition of a third category, pleading the 'ambiguity' of the former wording.

MacGregor publicly accused the NUM of reneging. Privately, some NCB officials claim they were within spitting distance of a settlement in the early morning of Thursday, 13 September, but that Scargill and Heathfield changed their minds during the Doncaster–Euston journey, after analysing the wording with Mick Clapham, head of the NUM's industrial relations department. When they produced their suggested revisions at the Rubens, Scargill complained that MacGregor would not even look at it.

Whatever the cause of the breakdown, it was clear there would be no more talks for some time. Ned Smith, then running the NCB's industrial relations, now identifies September as the period when the government first took a direct hand in seeking a solution. Other Board men have a different interpretation: as the week-long Brighton Congress wore on, they suggest, Whitehall found the ringing expressions of solidarity with the miners increasingly less impressive. In consequence, there was rapidly diminishing eagerness for any settlement that could be seen as a fudge or a compromise. As one holder of this view put it: 'They knew the fox was on the run and without a lair to go to.'

Chapter 9

The Day of the Deputies

The words which came closest to turning the tide for the strikers, and gave the government its most heart-stopping moments, were read out by Merrick Spanton, the NCB personnel director, at a meeting with members of the executive of Nacods, the pit deputies union, on 15 August. 'When mineworkers are going through pickets,' he told them, 'then in the Board's view there can be no good reason why officials should not go as well.' Those who were unwilling to be bussed into their pits, if necessary under police escort, he added, would no longer be paid. This had already happened in North Yorkshire, where the area director, Michael Eaton, who would soon take a much more central part, had stopped the pay of officials who declined to supervise the first modest wave of returning miners. But it was a different thing to translate it unilaterally into national policy. The outcome, as one senior minister said afterwards, was 'an unbelievable mess'.

Given the central role played by Nacods in the coalmining industry – by law, no underground work can be performed except in the presence of one of its members – Spanton's statement was bound to provoke a reaction. Up till then, any deputy faced with an intimidatory picket line, or even behaviour that he regarded as an affront to his dignity, thought he was free, under guidelines agreed after a series of violent encounters during the 1972 stoppage, to return home, telephone the colliery manager to explain his sitution, and continue to draw full wages. In the event 17,000 angry Nacods men voted 82.5 per cent in favour of strike action. By the last week of October they were within twenty-four hours of achieving what Scargill and the NUM had signally failed to pull off – bringing all the pits in Britain to a halt.

The Board had some logic on its side. The guidelines had been agreed to meet clear-cut situations like 1972 and 1974, when the whole industry was shut down and there was no virtue in setting overseer fathers at odds, as often happened, with their face-worker sons. In 1984 things were very different. Many miners and deputies had been at work virtually from the outset. Now, in the late summer, there were signs of a trickle-back, however modest, in almost every coalfield. The numbers were often small – 154 in Scotland during August, sixteen in the North-East, eleven in South Yorkshire, nine in Doncaster, 292 in North Derbyshire – but Hobart House was now committed, as a matter of policy, to boost them wherever the opportunity offered. There was little sense, though, in setting up armoured bus convoys and massive police escorts to get a handful of colliers to the pithead, if there were then no supervisors and safety men to take them underground. As Spanton said: 'If pits are to be kept at work or got back to work we have got to expect our employees to tolerate a great deal of abuse and intimidation on occasion to get there.' For him and his industrial relations director, Ned Smith, this was a straightforward and self-evident matter of dispute management. But at the same time it was a fairly drastic departure from the industry's customary practices. It should have been implemented with finesse. It was not.

The Board had prepared the ground with singular lack of care. Neither of the union's two most senior officers was present for the announcement. They had both sent apologies for absence because they were on holiday – Peter McNestry, the general secretary, in Scotland and Ken Sampey, the president, at Lake Garda in Italy. There was no written version of the new directive available to hand round for detailed discussion, and the Nacods vice-president, Glyn Jones, had to wait around afterwards for even the sketchiest of formal confirmations. Peter Walker, on information provided by Ian MacGregor, who was not at the meeting, jumped the gun and announced publicly that the new rules had not only been communicated but approved – a statement for which he later apologised, but which caused great ill-feeling at the time. When Sampey returned from Italy, he found that McNestry, recalled at short notice, had already demanded a reconvened meeting to sort things out. When it took place, on 30 August, both men complained bitterly that the deputies were being made 'piggy-in-the-middle'.

It was an apt phrase. Pressure on his members was rapidly building up from both sides. The Spanton directive was embodied in a telex sent out to the NCB's twelve area head-quarters, and within a month more than 3,000 Nacods men were off the payroll. At the same time the NUM, recognising the importance of the part the deputies might play in the larger dispute, had started to lobby Nacods for closer cooperation. On the very evening of the Spanton announcement, Scargill telephoned Glyn Jones on his return to South Wales. Characteristically blunt, he asked whether the pit foremen would now refuse to work with or supervise strikebreaking miners – specifically those who had arrived under police escort, or in privately owned buses or in cars driven at high speed through picket lines. Two days later, Jones was closeted with Peter Heathfield and the NUM president in the quaint little Doncaster terrace house which serves as Nacods head office.

The government and the Board would have been much more nervous had they known of this encounter. But they were slow to appreciate the perils of the minefield Spanton had created. Nacods, in its 74-year existence, has always been the most moderate of unions, never expected to create a moment of trouble. But the statutory duties imposed on its members, mainly under the Mines and Quarries Act 1954, give it absolute power to shut down the industry should it so

163

decide. In particular these men, with their intensive and regularly updated training in first aid, gas detection and emergency procedures, are responsible for all safety matters underground. No pit manager (even those who themselves hold similar qualifications) can order workers below in the absence of the deputy who has their particular 'district' under his charge.

Though widely dismissed as weak sisters, free-riders and bosses' men by the rank-and-file miners – an attitude which militated against their enrolment as full NUM allies and added considerable overtones of tension at the Doncaster discussions – the deputies had in recent years become a substantial, independent and far from compliant force in the industry. They had long shed their self-deprecatory view of themselves as the 'National Association of Can-carriers, Obedient Dopes and Suckers' and now fully shared the NUM's anxiety about the pit closure programme. Indeed, back in April, more than 50 per cent had supported a strike call of their own, which failed only because their rules require a two-thirds majority for any wholesale withdrawal of labour. As the dispute dragged on, with all its attendant unpleasantness and uncertainty, there was also a growing feeling that the Board was taking their loyalty for granted. A whole series of pin-prick problems had been brewing up, and the 42-year-old McNestry, in particular, who had only just been projected into national office – previously he was just branch secretary at Kellingley – was determined to do something about it. As the NCB soon discovered, he and the older, more experienced Sampey, with his pork-pie hat and pipe, made an unexpectedly formidable team.

The pay withdrawal issue festered quietly for several weeks, while the number of Nacods men laid off slowly increased. The mood was not helped by some over-enthusiastic interpretation of the new rules by local and regional managers. Wage packets were stopped, in several cases, without any real inquiry into the circumstances in which men failed to report for duty. It did not always need a mass picket in the road; often a credible threat was enough. Sampey cited a vivid example from Hickleton, in South

Yorkshire, where deputies arriving for work were told by the gate-watchers: 'There may be only two of us now, but there'll be 200 when you come off shift.' Feeling grew that the policy changes, however justifiable, were often being inconsistently and aggressively applied. As one senior Board member ruefully admitted: 'Some of our managers don't know the difference between scratching and tearing out a handful of skin.'

Such aggravations, gradually accumulating into a critical mass, finally blew up in a big way when the TUC met at Brighton in early September. Publicly Nacods – unlike the colliery managers' union, BACM, which stood aloof – endorsed the pledge of 'moral, financial and industrial' support for the NUM. Behind the scenes Scargill stepped up his efforts to woo the deputies. The executive, having already decided to call a special conference on the Spanton ultimatum, now put to the NUM leadership a proposal that in areas where strike action had been constitutionally declared – as in Yorkshire and Scotland – 'Nacods officials will not supervise any workmen drifting back against their union policy'. In return they sought assurances that pickets would now allow deputies to go into collieries to carry out statutory safety examinations. This was becoming urgent as a steadily growing number of coal-faces faced the risk of flooding, fire and general collapse. On the whole the foremen, like the managers, accepted the Board's contention that these were a genuine danger to the industry, in contrast to the more cynical miners, many of whom argued that crumbling pits merely increased the pressure for a quick settlement. In the end it proved impossible to get any solid and lasting agreement.

The safety question was also inflaming relations between Nacods and the Board at this time, particularly in Scotland. Unlike his colleagues in other regions, Albert Wheeler, the hawkish area director, forbade his pit managers, members of BACM, to undertake emergency maintenance work when other unions refused. His justification for this decision was that managers had their own work to do, but the results could be catastrophic. At Polkemmet, at the end of July 1984, the NUM withdrew safety cover after a trivial dispute.

165

Wheeler promptly ordered the pumps and fans controlling underground gas and water to be turned off, and after eight days of flooding, at the rate of 1.8m. gallons a day, the Board announced that the pit was in mortal danger. Several important Scottish collieries, including Polkemmet and Frances, failed to survive the strike and may never open again.

The immediate crisis, however, concerned Seafield, a big, relatively modern complex in Fife. The deputies were fighting to contain the build-up of both gas and water. Although the NUM were prepared to let some safety men and winding engineers in to help them, these were only available for one out of the two daily shifts. When a few strikebreakers started to drift back to work, even this cooperation was progressively withdrawn. The management retaliated by ordering everyone to come to the surface and switching off all power. Hearing this news, McNestry was furious. From the Brighton conference centre where the TUC was in progress, he telephoned Hobart House to tell Ned Smith that his men had been risking their skins in increasingly dangerous conditions to preserve the Board's assets and that, if their efforts were spurned in this way, they would unhesitatingly exercise their prerogative of switching off power throughout the nation's coalfields – including the area of Notts. Quiet but urgent words went out at this point, and the immediate Seafield crisis was averted. But the Nacods executive, deeply disturbed by all these developments, decided to call a special delegate conference in Doncaster to hammer out a new and more aggressive strategy.

When the executive met the following Tuesday to frame the agenda, they were faced with a plethora of potential issues – almost all of which, it was agreed, related either to the MacGregor closure programme or to the way in which the resulting strike had been handled. It shrewdly grouped a number of grievances – including the highly emotive 'Hammond Case', in which the Board had tried to limit its obligations to compensate officials injured when an unusually large section of roof had fallen in – and in the end defined three issues on which the members were invited to vote.

Strike action was 'unanimously and strongly' recommended in opposition to the Board's cutback in capacity, its attitude to conciliation procedures, and the 'guidelines' of 15 August, and unanimously backed by the delegates the very next day, 12 September.

The NCB at this point remained relatively relaxed: no union with a 66 per cent strike requirement, let alone the notoriously moderate Nacods, had ever brought it off. Mac-Gregor claimed on television that, contrary to what the deputies were saying, they had actually agreed the revised guidelines; and although this was at once denounced by McNestry it was then repeated, even more damagingly, by Walker.

Worse was to come. MacGregor had always been impressed by the success of President Reagan, when in 1981 he fired all the US air controllers during a strike and replaced them with outsiders and effectively destroyed their once-powerful union. He now detected an opportunity to do the same for Nacods which is, after all, an odd and anachronistic survival for which there are parallels virtually nowhere else in the world mining industry. He had come to believe that there were enough managers, trainees and qualified office staff in the industry to take over the deputies' function. Late one night, again in front of the TV cameras, he rashly put this belief into public words. It had been a bad evening. Returning to his Scottish retreat in Kintyre for the weekend, he had been pursued by the BBC's Newsnight team. With great reluctance he agreed to be interviewed at Heathrow airport. The west-bound traffic on the M4 moved at a crawl. When he arrived at the airport he could not find either the room or the crew. When the questions were at last put he was impatient and fuming. After a series of routine items on the progress of the dispute, he was asked about the deputies' threat. He replied, 'We've got plenty of guys with the certificates to do this job.' As one of the NCB directors later said: 'It was a disastrous mistake. He could not have touched a rawer nerve.'

As the ballot date approached, in the last week of September, alarm bells started to ring. Both sides realised that the determining vote would come in the Midlands area, which had voted 75 per cent against any kind of action back in April. Fearing a substantial reversal of this, the Board's South Notts area director, Harold Taylor, wrote a slightly desperate letter on 25 September affirming that there were 'no bounds to my admiration and appreciation' for the men who braved violence and intimidation to continue working, and appealing: 'Let us not destroy what we have achieved.' One of the men who received that letter, George Bell, a deputy at Calverton, near Nottingham, succinctly summed up the typical response. In April, like the majority of his colleagues, he had come out against a strike; now 'the Board's attitude towards the officials had changed everything.' When the votes were counted, in the rather unlikely presence of the bishop of Durham, on Friday, 29 September, the result was a landslide – 82.5 per cent overall for a strike, and a full 75 per cent among Bell and his fellow-Midlanders. The bishop summed up the significance of the result. In recognition of Nacods's new-found strength of purpose and to the delight of the hundred Kellingley delegates patiently lobbying the meeting, he said: 'I think the union concerned is out to use what power it has to get this strike settled as quickly as possible.'

Senior Board officials had been pretty unanimous over the original decision to seek more commitment from the deputies. It was endorsed at the highest level, by both MacGregor and Cowan. But there was growing unhappiness as the weeks went by about its implementation. In the third week of September, just before the date fixed for the ballot, the NCB's reports from the coalfields started to suggest that, contrary to all earlier expectations, a strike majority was now a real risk. This was the time when MacGregor himself was coming under mounting attack – the bishop of Durham, in his enthronement address, had already branded him 'an elderly, imported American'. That same day, at the Liberal assembly in Bournemouth, David Steel had called on Mrs Thatcher to fire him as an essential prerequisite for resolving the miners' dispute. Now, under pressure to initiate some evasive action, the Coal Board chairman asked Ned Smith to set up an urgent meeting. But McNestry, conscious of his steadily strengthening position, deliberately stalled, for five crucial days. When the talks finally started, on Wednesday 26 September, the voting was almost complete.

By now panic had set in, at least in the government ranks (the Board was still unconvinced that the threat was truly serious). The search for conciliation was on. But, as became painfully clear, the three-part structure of the ballot paper left very little room for manoeuvre. The detailed, practical questions could be quickly dealt with, and as far as the disputed guidelines were concerned there was an unconditional offer that they should be withdrawn. But it was too late to touch the central point – No. 1 on the voting paper – that the colliery supervisors had now aligned themselves alongside the striking miners in opposition to the closure programme. Suddenly the little-known Nacods men found themselves in the spotlight – seen by the government as a dangerous threat, and by large sections of the left and the trade union movement as a possible key to unlock the dispute.

There was, however, one very important difference between the attitudes of Nacods and those professed by the NUM. Both disliked pit closures, but the deputies fell well short of supporting the miners' total rejection. Their criticism focused more narrowly on the Board's long-established Colliery Review Procedure, the supposedly 'consultative' arrangements which in theory ensured agreement by all parties to any particular shutdown. Just as strongly as Scargill and his executive, Sampey, McNestry and their colleagues felt the process had degenerated into a rubber-stamp exercise, where the Board made its proposals and then effectively acted as judge, jury, appeal court and hangman in its own cause. But at least they recognised the possibility of reform. If acceptable improvements could be agreed, there might just be a basis for compromise.

The officially recognised manufacturers of compromise in the area of British industrial relations are to be found at the Advisory, Conciliation and Arbitration Service, first set up by the Wilson government in 1974. Under its present chair-

169

man, Pat Lowry, the former labour relations director at British Leyland, Acas has established a solid peacemaking record: in 1983 it resolved 77 per cent of the 1,621 cases handled by its national and regional offices. It had played little part so far in the coalmining confrontation, mainly because 'compromise' was a word not in Arthur Scargill's vocabulary. But McNestry had already had a secret meeting with the Service's chief conciliation officer, Dennis Boyd, in Doncaster. Now, with the ballot safely in the bag, he stated publicly that he wanted Lowry involved.

By the time of the first Nacods–Acas meeting the following Saturday, the Board had already started to move. McNestry had made it clear that his union wanted to see a binding – and genuinely independent – review body to replace the old discredited procedure. MacGregor now wrote in confidence to him, saying he was prepared to give 'full weight' to the findings of such a body, but he could not grant the fully binding commitment that the deputies were seeking. This set the stage for some of the most intense and critical negotiations in the course of the dispute.

Scargill, though always sceptical, recognised that a militant Nacods might still offer an outside chance of quick, decisive victory. He allowed himself to be nudged into the Acas talks at this point in order to stay close to the action. The government, and to some extent the Board, on the other hand, saw a clear threat of defeat or a much more prolonged and difficult period of strife. By further contrast, Norman Willis and the TUC Seven, who had been groping unsuccessfully for some means of exerting their influence on events, suddenly saw that the Nacods threat, skilfully exploited, could give them at last sufficient leverage to resolve the entire miners' dispute.

On 17 October, after yet another round of inconclusive talks had collapsed, Nacods gave notice that an indefinite strike would be called from 6 am on 25 October, with the likelihood that all safety cover would be withdrawn by the end of the following fortnight. Although MacGregor's reaction was to proclaim 'It is not going to happen', it concentrated the government's mind – especially after impassioned speeches from the two Nacods leaders had brought their initially reluctant Nottingham members round to express full support.

The Nacods move also brought a significant absentee back on stage. Ned Smith, the NCB's long-time personnel director, with his flowing mane of hair and barely concealed doubts about his chairman's diplomatic skills, had been notably missing from the most recent round of talks. In an oddly phrased statement dated 9 October he was said to have been 'suspended because of ill-health'. Faced with a barrage of inquiries, relays of spokesmen were briefed to explain that it referred only to the state of his back, which he had put out some weeks before, and not to any divisions over policy matters. Despite widespread scepticism, the explanation was literally true: Smith had strained his spine shifting some ladders. But it was only bad enough to keep him at home for a couple of days. The real trouble was his simmering behind-the-scenes disagreement with MacGregor over the conduct of the dispute, which was at last coming to the boil. On 19 October, though no formal announcement was ever made, he resigned, cleared his desk, and retired to his home in Chestfield, Kent, with the hope of playing a little golf. He was nominally captain of the local club that year, but thanks to the miners had managed to play only nine holes in that exalted role. Before he could add to the meagre total, though, Peter Walker, who had his own misgivings about the MacGregor strategy, took matters firmly in hand and insisted that he be recalled.

Smith was a classic product of the British coal industry: miner father, who had been blacklisted in Northumberland and migrated to Kent; cousins still at the coal-face, and indeed on strike in 1984–5; educated at the Black Hut school, in the yard of Kent's long-defunct Chislett colliery; first job as a face-measurer; and then a fast-stream management trainee with the NCB. He had initially got on well with his new chairman. When they attended a weekend school for clerical staff together, Smith told colleagues the American had 'charmed them off the trees'. MacGregor called him 'Smiddie' and went out of his way to endorse his handling of labour relations. In return, Smith promised: 'As long as I get my fat salary you will get my advice, and it will be the best advice you can get.' But there was always a proviso – if disagreements ever became really irreconcilable, he would go. That was the point, in Smith's view, that had now been reached.

The central issue, the necessity to close heavily lossmaking pits, was not in dispute between them; nor, to start with, was MacGregor's attitude to the unions, which Smith often tended to characterise as 'innocent' rather than antipathetic. But there were increasingly sharp differences over some of the day-to-day tactics. Smith questioned the deliberately heavy-handed use of armoured buses to get miners to work. He doubted the value of the Board's expensive advertising, which he thought more appropriate to the south-east suburbs than the northern pit villages. He disliked the tone of Mac-Gregor's personal letters to the miners (and intervened directly at one point to excise a reference to 'Scargill', without even the courtesy of a 'Mr', as the only begetter of the strike); he resented the interference of outside directors and advisers whom he regarded as ignorant about the industry. In addition he became volubly critical, as the autumn wore on, of the government's growing involvement in the peace talks, to a point where MacGregor told him: 'Smiddie, your advice is offensive to me.'

The incident that did most to sour relations between the two men, however, concerned something quite different: the question of who could best counter Arthur Scargill's masterly television performances. MacGregor, as he himself came to recognise, was just not in the same league. By late July, after the comprehensive collapse of yet another negotiating round, Smith, with his detailed grasp of the dispute and its background, was putting himself forward as a far stronger contender. 'I can beat him at his own game,' he repeatedly assured the NCB chairman. In the end, after long and tortuous negotiations, the miners' leader agreed to debate with him on ITN's Channel Four news. The date was fixed for 22 August.

The occasion was treated very seriously, not least by the

172

government. Giles Shaw, then coal minister, phoned Smith several times to brief him with detailed political points and titbits of information. But on the very morning of the encounter, MacGregor changed his mind. 'The show's off,' he told Stuart Purvis, the television editor involved. 'Smiddie's a technician. He's not a Board member, and he can't represent the Board.' At 4 pm, after a day of agonised pleas, he remained adamant. Smith, having nothing better to do, decided to take an early train home.

That was when the farce really began. A team of heavyweights from Independent Television News, headed by the editor-in-chief, David Nicholas, arrived at Hobart House to explain some of the facts of media life. Not only was there a fifteen-man outside broadcast unit expensively installed at a community centre in Selby, poised to record Scargill's end of the debate, but cancellation of the programme, which had been widely promoted over the weekend, would itself be seen as a major news event. MacGregor belatedly relented and urgent orders were sent out to find Ned Smith. When a frantic underling finally reached his wife, Irene, she tersely replied: 'Southern Region don't even know where their trains are. How do you expect me to?' He finally reached Whitstable, late, at 6.30 pm and rang MacGregor to be told that a studio had been booked in Maidstone for 7 pm and a helicopter ordered to get him there. Wearily he explained: 'Chairman, if Concorde landed on my lawn this minute, there's no way I could be in Maidstone by 7.'

In the end, after half-an-hour's impassioned persuasion, MacGregor finally agreed to appear himself. But even when the title music started, the TV men were still not completely sure he would be there. In the end he was, with no rehearsal and the aid of a set of hastily prepared and barely legible cue-cards. Scargill, by general consent, emerged as usual an easy winner. Smith, with a pint of bitter in his hand, disconsolately watched the whole shambles from his golf-club bar. From that evening, as he recognised, his Coal Board days were numbered. There was no great wrench in October when MacGregor again rejected his advice – this time on how to settle the Nacods problem – and he decided to call it a day.

Walker's summons, however, meant that he still had that one important job to do. It was a shrewd move. As McNestry later confirmed, Smith was by this time one of the few men in the upper echelons of Hobart House that he and his colleagues could trust. MacGregor was only persuaded to agree to talks at all – and to bring back Smith to lead them – after a Monday morning meeting with Peter Walker, David Hunt and Michael Eaton, newly appointed as the Board's communications chief. Breakfasting with McNestry the previous week (they had met, as many leading participants did during the strike, at an early morning TV broadcast), Hunt had been impressed with the seeming narrowness of the gap between the two sides. 'It's all a matter of trust,' McNestry had told him. Eaton had come to the same conclusion, preparing some of the ground with McNestry and Sampey, both of whom he knew well. The three men now urged MacGregor to see that a Nacods strike was a disastrous prospect and at the same time avoidable. This was the very message which Smith had vainly tried to bring home to his chairman at the end of the previous week. Now, under ministerial pressure, MacGregor relented. Talks would go ahead.

When Smith finally rejoined the Acas group on 23 October, time was running out fast. The threatened strike was only thirty-six hours away, and the deputies had shown no signs whatever of wavering. It is a tribute to his negotiating skills that, before the end of that very afternoon, the basis of an agreement had been found. Nacods was happy. The government, once it heard, could hardly believe its good luck. Scargill, who had never put much faith in his temporary allies anyway, shrugged it off angrily as a predictable setback. But the peacemaking group, led by the TUC's new general secretary, Norman Willis, who had seen McNestry as their best hope for a comprehensive settlement, were disappointed.

A deal swiftly crystallised. A draft document was produced, in the most conciliatory terms, which on inspection proved as overwhelmingly attractive to McNestry and his colleagues as it was unappealing and infuriating to the miners.

It unreservedly confirmed the withdrawal of Spanton's 15 August directive and restored back-pay in full to those who had been laid off as a result of its provisions. It guaranteed there would be no interference with the deputies' long-standing closed-shop arrangements, despite the imminence of new, tough legislation on that prickly subject. It studiously avoided any use of the dangerous word 'uneconomic' (though it did make clear that the Board's future plans would reflect 'both market and production opportunities'). It tidied up a variety of contentious legal questions, including the complicated Hammond Case, which had been inching its way through the courts for years. It promised that the 6 March closure proposals would be 'reconsidered . . . in the light of the loss of output which has occurred as a result of the dispute and the changes in the needs of the market'. The Board would also 'revise the objectives for the individual areas', and more specifically undertake to keep open the five 'named pits' – Polmaise, Herrington, Bullcliffe Wood, Cortonwood and Snowdown – which had first surfaced as a separate issue as part of the NUM's July demands. The only important reservation was that this was not an open-ended commitment. In time, it was proposed, the five would be 'considered in common with all other pits under a modified review procedure'.

Here was the key item. The existing procedure, under which 200–300 pits and individual faces had been abandoned in the past, had fallen increasingly into discredit. Now the Board agreed to re-examine the whole set-up in the light of extensive demands for improvement which Nacods had already debated, agreed and tabled. These covered: earlier warning when a new closure came under consideration; more time and better facilities, like access to detailed accounts, if union officials wished to prepare a case for opposition; enough notice of the final decision for national officers to consult their members – a stipulation that had not always been honoured in the past; and in case of irreconcilable disagreement 'appeal to an independent body'.

The Smith draft rehearsed all four of these requests, but only on the fourth did it incorporate any definite pledge. It

175

accepted that, as a final court of appeal, a new, independent review body would be established 'and full weight given to its findings'. This was only the barest shell of an idea, though potentially a very important one. On crucial questions like membership, appointment of chairman, detailed terms of reference, legal status, and the range of matters that would be open to inquiry (would they, for instance, include the social costs involved in depriving a whole community, with all its homes, schools, shops, transport facilities, traditions and job prospects, of its livelihood and reason for existence?), there was silence. But the deputies, for all that, patently found it an extremely tempting option.

Sensing that events were slipping away, Willis himself took a hand. First he tried to persuade an extremely reluctant Scargill that if the deputies were going to settle, the NUM should, even at the eleventh hour, get involved in shaping the terms. Then he tried to get a postponement of the final agreement in order to make room for these wider talks. Far into the night, in one of Acas's elegantly furnished first-floor rooms overlooking St James's Square, he tried to persuade McNestry to stay his hand. If the strike could only be postponed, rather than called off, he argued, the NUM might still be persuaded to settle themselves. Lowry, normally the most equable of men, was furious at this heavy-handed intervention. The agency's function, he argued, was to speed settlements. Yet here, where he had an employer and a union eager to shake hands, the TUC was using all its influence to derail the deal. But Smith, back at the Rubens Hotel where he had set up his temporary base for the talks, remained confident. Chatting cheerfully to some of the Nacods wives, who were also staying there, he broke off occasionally to phone McNestry and encourage him to stick to his guns.

It was 1 am on the 24th when the exhausted Nacods man called it a night. McNestry had said nothing to encourage the TUC team, but agreed to sleep on their proposals. Time, however, was running out. Later the same morning Willis met Scargill at the TUC, and was given a denunciatory gloss on the deputies' draft agreement, which made it clear that the NUM did not in any way regard it as a basis of a deal of their own. This conversation then broadened into a tense three-sided encounter as the top men in the NUM, the TUC and Nacods met round a Congress House table. Scargill, by this time, was furious, first that the deputies had accepted 'reconsideration' of the 6 March proposals, not outright 'withdrawal', second that the five named collieries would only be 'considered with all other pits', not completely reprieved. These were even worse terms, he insisted, than had been offered to the NUM on 8 July. McNestry and Sampey were unrepentant. They affirmed that in their opinion their claims had now been met. They told the miners' leaders that, in their judgement, the draft terms, as offered, could well 'prove useful' as a basis for resolving the miners' problems. They did however undertake to pass on the NUM leaders' views to their own executive, which was due to meet later that afternoon at Congress House.

It was a difficult meeting. Even at this late stage, the prospect of resolving both disputes in one blow, if it meant only postponing the settlement, still had strong attractions. But in the end Scargill's own attitude was the decisive factor: it was too dismissive. As one member of the Nacods executive put it later: 'If Arthur had been saying, "Well yes you're 70 per cent there but we want to make some changes," then there could well have been a majority for holding out. As it was, he had rubbished it from top to bottom.' In the event the ten-man Nacods leadership voted overwhelmingly to call off their strike. The mood was moderately euphoric. As Jimmy O'Connor, the union's Scottish area secretary, said: 'If you look at it in depth, what Nacods has achieved is exactly what Arthur Scargill is wanting to achieve, although perhaps not in the same words.'

The dark warnings from an assortment of critics, led by Scargill himself, that the agreement might not be worth the paper it was written on, were dismissed as sour grapes and lack of faith. The deal, as offered, was judged more than good enough to preclude any strike that depended on the moderate Nottingham deputies for support. Some potential weaknesses were noted even at the time: the fact that it was only an outline proposal, that its detailed implementation would depend on the agreement of other unions, including the NUM, and, most importantly, that it did not cover closures that the NCB could blame on damage caused by the strike itself. Later these were to loom large, bringing bitter complaints from McNestry that he had been 'dishonourably and insultingly' treated by the Board. But that was all for the future. From the government's point of view, on that warm October evening, the darkest hour had passed. With Nacods no longer a threat, the ultimate outcome, however long it might take and however much it might cost to achieve, would never again be in serious doubt.

Chapter 10

Tension in the Executive Suite

David Hunt, the forty-four-year-old Tory MP for West Wirral, was sitting quietly in Conservative Central Office on 11 September when the telephone rang. His task, as party vice-chairman, was to sift through the applications of some 1,000 would-be by-election candidates, weed out the more obvious rightwing fanatics before they had the chance to do something embarrassing, and reduce the list to a more manageable 400 or so. But the call from 10 Downing Street demanded a rapid switch of focus. Would he be interested in taking over the vacant junior ministerial job of energy department under-secretary in charge of coal? Yes, of course, Prime Minister. When would you like me to take up my duties? Short pause to consult watch. 'In 20 minutes time.'

The following morning he attended his first session of Peter Walker's daily coal committee. To his slight surprise there was quite a cheerful atmosphere, with even a restrained scattering of smiles. Several miners, he was told, had chosen that morning to return to work. But he found it hard to show great enthusiasm when he found that the number, however welcome, was only seven – leaving rather more than 130,000 NUM members still solidly on strike. Elsewhere, he soon discovered, there was precious little cause for celebration.

179

The Nacods dispute was still sputtering dangerously along, with its leaders that very morning calling for a ballot, with a strong recommendation to add the deputies' potentially crippling weight to the strike. MacGregor, after a series of publicity gaffes, had just allowed himself to be photographed fleeing from reporters and trying to hide his face behind a crumpled plastic bag – an incident which, when shown endlessly on television, reduced Downing Street to near-despair. Yet another round of negotiations was breaking down in acrimonious stalemate. Scargill, at Brighton, whatever the ultimate value of his achievement, had won a resounding affirmation of support from most of the major union leaders. The second national dock strike, though patchy and only very partially effective, was still far from resolution. In total, there was little to lift a new coal minister's heart.

He was not greatly reassured, either, by his first encounter with the senior membership of the Board. What was the overall strategy of the dispute, he kept asking, and received vague, often inconsistent answers. In fact, as quickly became apparent, morale at Hobart House was now at rock-bottom, and the sense of drift, suspicion and general discontent was all-pervading. Hunt, as the newcomer, saw immediately that, whatever course events might take, this destructive tension had to be resolved.

To understand how badly things had slipped, it is necessary to go back to MacGregor's original appointment. His arrival in September 1983 had generated a certain amount of critical trepidation. Norman Siddall, the retiring chairman, had openly opposed the government's choice on the grounds that it was both unnecessarily provocative to the unions and a slight on the record of the Board's existing managers. But by no means all the senior staff shared this view. They were fully convinced of the need to close lossmaking pits, they wanted to get on with a number of long-postponed decisions, like shrinking the number of Board areas from twelve to eight, and their soundings with acquaintances at British Steel led them to believe that MacGregor was 'a manager's manager'. Several were positively looking forward to the sweep of a new broom.

As things turned out, they had badly misjudged their man. MacGregor had accepted virtually all the main criticisms set out in the Monopoly and Mergers Commission report, and proposed to treat it, as he told them, as his 'bible' – not only in its calls for more commercial practices, linkage of investment with profit, and elimination of high-cost pits, but also in its astringent attitude to organisation and staff. At least two aspects of the NCB's traditional structure proved particularly alien to the new chairman's free-market instincts and North American business experience. He disliked the committee system, going back to the ideas of Herbert Morrison, when he drew up Labour's postwar nationalisation programme, under which important decisions were always hammered out collectively by the whole group of department heads, officials and specialists who would be involved in their implementation. He instinctively rejected the defence that, though cumbersome, this always ensured that everyone knew what they were doing. At the same time, he brought with him a belief that the upper tier of NCB managers, at both local and national level, were far too close to the unions. The set-up, he was convinced, was far too cosy and incestuous, and had to be dismantled as a first step to reform. He immediately set about the task, reducing the number and influence of full-time Board members, bringing in a number of part-time outsiders with no direct coal industry experience, and setting up his own operational unit, the Office of Chairman and Chief Executive, to take over all significant responsibility – both day-by-day running and longer-term policy mak-ing – for the industry's affairs.

The changes were spectacular, both in terms of individual careers and in the whole way things were done. Out went John Mills, the abrasive but highly regarded joint deputy chairman, who had brilliantly marshalled the Board's evidence to the Monopolies and Mergers Commission and the inquiry that gave the go-ahead for the Selby super-pit. Out went Philip Weekes, the South Wales area director, whose long-standing Board membership was suddenly not renewed. In came a group of MacGregor's friends and associates: David Donne, chairman of Dalgety, the international pro-

duce and agricultural group; David Newbigging, newly retired head of Jardine Matheson, the Hong Kong traders; and
Colin Barker (ex-finance director of International Telephone
and Telegraph) and Sir Melvyn Rosser (partner with the
accountants Deloitte, Haskins and Sells), who had both sat
also on the board of British Steel. Up went Jimmy Cowan,
once Scottish area director, now deputy chairman and chief
executive, and henceforth the only man, apart from Mac-
Gregor himself, who was in a position to know everything
that was going on. With Dr Anne Parsonage, the chairman's
personal assistant, and David Brandrick, the Board secretary, these were the sole occupants of 'The Office of
Chairman and Chief Executive'.

To everyone brought up in the far more open and collective
tradition of Lord Robens, Sir Derek Ezra and Norman
Siddall, this was an unprecedented and far from welcome
concentration of central power. It manifested itself, too, not
only in philosophic but in physical terms. On his first day,
the new boss had the drinks cabinet removed, cancelled the
regular weekly order for fresh flowers on the television set,
moved in his personal desk-top computer, threw out the
Henry Moore lithographs in favour of some industrial land-
scapes he had brought from British Steel and a Jak cartoon
portraying himself as 'the third coal-sack on the left' and,
more importantly, issued instructions that henceforth there
would be no separate office for the chairman – instead he
and Cowan would share a joint executive suite from which
all significant decisions would flow.

Cowan was less than universally admired. In Scotland,
where he had built up a strong working relationship with
Mick McGahey, he had acquired a reputation for closing pits
with minimum fuss. But his manner was often cold and
offhand and he was notorious for his unwillingness to commit
himself to any final decision. Unease at the tightness and
composition of MacGregor's inner circle was not limited to
its official members: it was sharply increased when it became
known that it had expanded to include at least three rather
shadowy outsiders: Gordon Reece, popularly held responsible for making some subtle amendments to Mrs Thatcher's

182

public image; Tim Bell, formerly with Saatchi and Saatchi, the Tory party's main advertising agency, and now the head of his own advertising firm; and above all the enigmatic and controversial David Hart.

Hart, a somewhat bizarre figure who had dabbled variously in novels, farming, property development and the cinema in the course of his short but not unspectacular career, decided quite early on to write himself a ringside ticket for the miners' strike. His ancestors, rich Polish Jews in the seventeenth century, were driven out, reduced to penury and painfully rebuilt their fortunes. His father, a merchant banker and director of Bodley Head, the publishers, sent him to Eton. After a short flirtation with films (notably one about Robert Maxwell's Buckinghamshire election campaign) he managed to make £1m. in the early 1970s property boom, lose the lot, go bankrupt, and then win his discharge, all in the space of about eighteen months. From time to time he had contributed articles to *The Times*, with a provocative, rightwing, libertarian flavour (the most memorable welcomed the rise in unemployment as a stage in emancipating the working class from wage-slavery), and at the start of the NUM dispute he got himself commissioned to travel round the picket lines to talk to the strikers and the men who were insisting on their right to work.

It was when he visited Shirebrook, in Derbyshire, and saw some of the early violence in that divided village, that he came to the conclusion that propelled him into the struggle: he decided that the intimidation of working pitmen and their families was not only systemic, intense and intolerable, but that it was also the direct responsibility of Arthur Scargill, who had so conspicuously refused to halt or even condemn such actions. He became a catalyst for the emerging groups set up to defend the right to work (as described in chapter 4), and he also made a determined and successful effort to get close to Ian MacGregor. He started with the advantage that his brother, Tim Hart, had briefly shared an office with the Coal Board chairman when they were both connected with the Lazard Frères banking business in New York. To this he added his own detailed, and at that time quite unusual, knowledge of what the working miners were up to, and a considerable measure of charm and personality. MacGregor affectionately called him 'Stalin' because of his firm, unqualified conviction that the NUM must be defeated at all costs; and soon, although few NCB people knew exactly who he was, his balding, moustachioed figure, climbing the stairs to the chairman's private office, became a familiar, though by no means universally welcome, sight to the Hobart House staff. And something of a thorn in the flesh to Whitehall as well. Once he rang Peter Walker from his West End hotel suite to say MacGregor had asked him to be his official publicity adviser and could he offer the energy secretary any ideas? Although it was well known that Hart had at least intermittent access to Mrs Thatcher, Walker was irritated enough to tell him he had plenty of ideas, and that in any case he did not think the strike could usefully be dealt with from Claridge's.

There were two main strands of worry at this stage over MacGregor's performance – apart from the fact, increasingly obvious to the Cabinet, that he was far more suited to reshaping businesses than to running strikes, which was the task that had devolved upon him. First, his accessibility – and susceptibility – to unofficial advice was proving a serious flaw. If Hart, Reece and Bell, in their capacity as image-moulders and attitude formers, had been scoring a series of successes, it would have been a different matter: but instead the NCB chairman, by his gruffness of manner, his patent unhappiness in front of the television cameras (BBC teams were undecided as to what they found more amazing – this aversion to bright lights, which made it appear he was always being interviewed in a disused coal-cellar, or the presence of Hart, just off-camera, waving a selection of cue-cards, most of which were then misread or ignored) and the erratic inconsistency of his responses, tended on numerous occasions to make the very worst of the Board's case. But the obverse of this was almost equally damaging: that in listening to his private entourage, he was ignoring or overriding recommendations of those actually appointed and paid to offer the benefit of their knowledge and experience. This applied not only to the Board's long-serving and widely respected head of information, Geoff Kirk, but to a whole layer of long-established professionals, like Ned Smith, the personnel director, who were only intermittently consulted, and then often overruled, on important aspects of the dispute.

The essence of the criticism was succinctly conveyed, though well after the event, by David Paterson, the thoughtful and well-informed president of the British Association of Colliery Management, which represents most of the top echelon executives in the industry, including many at the Hobart House headquarters. Addressing the delegates at BACM's May 1985 conference, he focused on the part played by the Office of Chairman and Chief Executive. 'The organisational structure' he recalled in quietly cutting words, 'was deficient in terms of its communicative ability.' Decisions were made which it appears were not transmitted down the line' and the 'handling of the dispute was in many ways inept'. The situation reached its lowest ebb, in his view, with the mishandling of relations with Nacods, the deputies' union. This could have been easily avoided, Paterson argued, had there not been 'a failure on the part of the Office of Chief Executive to ensure that a common policy was carried out in all areas during the earlier months of the dispute', and this was seriously exacerbated by 'the public posturings' of the Board.

The decision by Nacods, on 19 October, to call the first strike in its previously moderate history was almost certainly the low point in MacGregor's first year at the NCB helm. He had confidently assured ministers like Walker and Hunt that it would never happen, and then been proved wrong. Cabinet spokesmen were heard musing aloud that the Prime Minister could not 'ditch the general in the middle of the battle'. Even while the deputies were making up their minds how to vote in the ballot, he managed to alienate yet more of them with another of his disastrous television appearances. But whoever was, in the last analysis, responsible, the awkward reality was that in the battle for the hearts and minds of NCB employees at all levels, MacGregor was fast becoming a liability. Mrs Thatcher was alerted to the problem on a flying

185

trip to Yorkshire that week, when a crowd of Tory workers, many of them from mining centres like Hemsworth, pleaded with her to find someone who could match Scargill in front of the TV cameras. MacGregor appears to have realised it himself: in a meeting with Walker he agreed that something would have to be done to take him out of the publicity firing line.

The name of Michael Eaton first surfaced, in a series of urgent conversations, during the fraught days of mid-October. Nothing was going right for the Board. Bold predictions at the Tory party conference about the inevitability of success barely survived the chaos of the IRA bomb at the Metropole Hotel, Brighton. Another fruitless round of conciliation talks had just broken down. A thousand angry miners and their wives had besieged the police station at Grimethorpe, near Doncaster, in protest over arrests for 'coal picking', and the chairman of the South Yorkshire Police Authority had intemperately accused senior officers of 'acting like Nazi stormtroopers'. The time had come, it was universally felt, to find some new, credible and persuasive voice to counter the repetitive but often effective Scargill tirades. It was Eaton's rich Yorkshire baritone that won MacGregor's vote, and which answered the telephone on Thursday, 18 October when the harassed chairman rang to ask if he would take on the job of his 'personal assistant and temporary head of communications'.

Eaton, at fifty, was in charge of North Yorkshire – both the youngest and the longest-serving of the Board's twelve area directors. He was a shrewd choice, with qualities and qualifications fitting him to speak for the industry at all levels, but at the same time with a refreshing degree of independence. He first went down a coalmine at sixteen, and at various times in his early days belonged to both Nacods and the NUM (with whom he was once, unhappily, called out on strike) before graduating to mine engineering. As an engineer, he says self-deprecatingly, he was never better than average. But with his direct, conversational style he was always able to talk to miners in their own language and was 'good at dealing with people'. The Board soon picked him out as a high-flyer, and sent him off to California for a stint at Stanford Business School. Marriage, to his attractive wife Pauline, brought links to her family's prosperous building business, which now employs their two sons. Eaton, though the grandson of a collier and the son of an electrician, was well able to hold his own in the more rarefied world of competitive markets and investment finance.

He also knew the principal union leaders – thanks to the pervasive Yorkshire connection – at least as well as anyone at Hobart House. Ken Sampey had been the Nacods delegate when Eaton was manager at Yorkshire Main. McNestry, whom he rang personally on the first evening to explain his appointment, had been branch secretary at Kellingley, the biggest pit in Eaton's area. Even more important, he had known Arthur Scargill for over twelve years, and had argued, negotiated and sat on committees with him almost throughout that period. 'We worked together and we got on all right,' he was quick to tell reporters. 'We were joint chairmen of the Yorkshire miners' welfare, and that was what we were both devoted to – the care of miners.'

It was a rather less affable encounter with the miners' leader, however, that encapsulated the real flavour of their relationship. It concerned a pit closure which Eaton thought essential and to which Scargill was resolutely opposed. The NCB's new rising star was unlikely to forget the March morning in 1979 when the other man, by sheer persistence and negotiating skill, had had him literally stopped in his tracks.

Walton colliery, near Wakefield, had been losing money for years, and the only feasible way to keep it open would have meant spending £5m. to open up new faces, which in turn would have given access to only 1.5m. tonnes of new reserves – a derisive return for the work and cash involved. But as the minutes of a 1977 review meeting tersely and characteristically record: 'Mr Scargill said the NUM would oppose any closure other than one for coal exhaustion.' The conflict rambled on for eighteen months, finally going to national appeal, but in the end the Board's decision was upheld. Eaton, confident that the issue was closed, arranged to visit the pit himself on 27 March to break the news. A few days before, Scargill had jauntily told him: 'You'll not close Walton,' to which Eaton replied crisply: 'Yes, I bloody well will.'

Everything, as far as Eaton was concerned, was all over bar the issue of the press release. But he had underestimated his opponent. He set out on the appropriate morning, having allowed plenty of time to make the eight-mile journey to Walton in his NCB Ford Granada. Halfway there he was overtaken by a police car and signalled to pull over. When he wound down the window to find what offence he had committed, he was told instead: 'It's an urgent message. Could you please ring the Doncaster press office.' When he did so, it was to hear, in blank disbelief, from a junior secretary who was the only person available, that 'You're not to close Walton, you're to open a new face.' Scargill, in a whirlwind campaign, had mobilised the then NUM president, Joe Gormley, and the energy secretary, Tony Benn, to pressurise the current NCB chairman, Derek Ezra, and bring about a complete volte-face. It was only small comfort that six months and £5m. losses later the mine had to close as completely unsafe and Eaton was able to force Scargill to admit he had been wrong. But it was a salutary lesson in the dangers of underrating the man's powers of manoeuvre.

Eaton's combination of personality and experience made him everybody's favourite choice for the job of redefining and improving the projection of the Board's point of view. Mrs Thatcher herself had approved when his name was one of three brought up by her press secretary, Bernard Ingham, as they flew back together from York in the Prime Minister's private Hawker Siddeley 125, and he was able to remind her that she had met and liked him three years earlier at the opening of the Selby super-pit complex. Cowan recommended him. MacGregor personally made the telephone call inviting him down to London. David Hunt, after seeing his first television appearance, told Peter Walker: 'This looks like just the kind of guy we have been waiting for.' To the coal minister, who had grown increasingly concerned as the days passed about Hobart House's ineptitude and unsureness of touch, he came over 'like a breath of fresh air'. The energy secretary agreed and assigned Hunt, as a matter of urgency, to get close to the new man. As they consolidated their acquaintance – with a series of private dinners, often with their two wives in attendance – it became clear that Eaton fully shared the government's unease, and was eager to start reversing the long catalogue of errors committed by his senior colleagues.

Yet such was the extent of the neurosis in the upper reaches of the NCB hierarchy that his enthusiasm and attractive presence were almost their own undoing. MacGregor himself, initially, was unperturbed by the wave of favourable publicity that greeted Eaton's appointment – the long, welcoming interview on BBC Radio's World at One, that first weekend, and the massive headlines about 'Mr Fixit' in Monday's popular press. But the chairman's tranquillity did not extend to the chief executive. On the Tuesday, new talks were due to start in an attempt to defuse the increasingly threatening Nacods situation, and virtually every comment had assumed that Eaton would automatically take part. Instead, Cowan put his foot down. With less than two hours to go before the negotiators convened at Acas's offices in St James's Square, he issued a personal ultimatum: either the new 'spokesman' was dropped from the team or he himself would boycott the meeting and fly to Luxemburg for an international coal conference. In vain did Eaton point out that he could hardly be expected to give the world a favourable account of the meeting if he was not there. An uncomfortable MacGregor ruled in favour of Cowan, as the senior man, and 'Mr Fixit' made his debut kicking his heels futilely in the nearby Stafford Hotel while the crucial discussions went on without him.

But far worse was to come. The following weekend, Sunday, 28 October, the miners suffered their worst single propaganda blow of the strike. Thanks to some detective work by *Sunday Times* reporters it was established that Arthur Scargill, acting through the NUM's chief executive Roger Windsor, had made direct contact with the Libyan leader, Colonel Gaddafi, in search of funds to bolster the union's haemorrhaging finances. In the same year that Woman Police

189

Constable Yvonne Fletcher had been shot by Libyan fanatics in the centre of London (to be precise, outside the People's Bureau, just next door to the Acas offices) this willingness to deal with the backer of international terrorism was potentially – and indeed, as things turned out, actually – an extremely damaging misjudgement, calculated to induce a rapid and widespread erosion of support. But instead of this dominating the headlines, as the government profoundly and quite understandably hoped, the Board, in a further masterly display of incompetence, almost succeeded in driving it off the front pages and the main radio and television news bulletins in favour of further news about its own self-destructive internal divisions.

The revelation of the Libyan Connection, which later won its principal author, Jon Swain, the British Press Award as the 1984 Reporter of the Year, was a classic example of investigative journalism. Swain, who for several years had been *The Sunday Times*'s Paris correspondent, was rung up in London one Friday by an acquaintance working for France's largest trade union organisation, the Communist-run Confédération Générale de Travail (CGT). His information, which he passed on when Swain reached Paris by the first plane next morning, Saturday, 20 October, was that nine days earlier the two NUM men, Scargill and Windsor, had turned up at CGT headquarters in Montreuil for a long unpublicised meeting with an apparently important Libyan named Salim Ibrahim. Nothing, at that stage, was known about Ibrahim except that he was unfamiliar to the CGT staff, but within hours several intriguing points had been established: that Scargill had flown from Manchester for the encounter using an assumed name, 'Mr Smith'; that senior NUM officials either did not know he was in France, or had no ready explanation for his presence there; and above all that the French security services had a substantial file on the Libyan, whom they knew as 'Gaddafi's bagman'. He was a trusted confidant whose responsibilities included negotiating and arranging payment for the various groups and causes who enjoyed the erratic colonel's mercurial support, including a clutch of terrorist movements like the Italian Red Brigade and the Provisional IRA.

Over the weekend more details emerged. Ibrahim had stayed at the Paris Hilton from 7 to 9 October. The telex from Rome booking his room had stated that he would be arriving from Tripoli, that the bill would be paid by the Bangladesh Embassy and that he should be accorded VIP treatment, which meant he was not required to fill out a normal registration card with passport numbers and the like. During his stay he made two international telephone calls: one to Libya and the other to a number in South Yorkshire. This, as it turned out, was the home of Mumtaz Abbasi, an expatriate Pakistani who ostensibly kept a small Doncaster grocery shop.

Local retailing, however, accounted for only a very small part of Abbasi's colourful activities. In 1980 he had been arrested in Karachi, accused of plotting with a Libyan diplomat to blow up a Shi'ite mosque, and sentenced to twenty-five years' imprisonment. The next year a Pakistani airliner was hijacked to the Afghan capital, Kabul, by a Libyan-backed terrorist group, Al-Zulfikar, dedicated to the ousting of Pakistan's President Zia, and Abbasi, along with fifty-three other political prisoners, was released as part of the ensuing deal. Since then he has described himself as European representative for Al-Zulfikar, and from his Doncaster base (he holds a British passport) simultaneously built up links with a wide variety of other fringe political groups, Trotskyite, Irish, Sikh independence and so forth. On 13 October, five days after the Paris meeting between Scargill, Windsor and Ibrahim, which he had also attended, he was garrulously boasting, at a session of the Pakistan People's party held in Peterborough, that he had been in contact with the NUM for over a year and had now arranged for substantial Libyan funds to be made available to them. 'They won't have any financial problems any more,' he said. 'They won't forget me for the rest of their life.' He even mused aloud that their gratitude might extend one day to sponsoring him as Labour MP for a coalmining constituency.

191

None of this meant much to his Peterborough audience, and it certainly had no wider currency. But on Monday, 22 October, events took on a more urgent and practical turn. It promised to be an extremely significant week for the NUM, with plenty of work for Roger Windsor, who would normally be responsible for all the union's administrative affairs. Not only was the threatened Nacods strike due to start that Thursday, with a tense round of Acas talks simultaneously preoccupying the senior members of the executive, but after non-payment of the £200,000 contempt of court fine, the High Court was set to sequester the union's funds and put all its day-to-day operations at risk. Instead of staying to deal with this, though, Windsor booked himself on to the evening Lufthansa flight from Manchester to Frankfurt, and promptly disappeared. Intensive inquiries failed to locate him at any likely or unlikely hotel. His secretary claimed to know no more than that he was expected back in Sheffield on Thursday.

In fact, as it later transpired, Windsor had merely stopped off to meet Abbasi, who had already travelled to West Germany the previous Friday, so that the two men could pick up another set of tickets, paid for in Libyan currency, and fly on together to Tripoli, where Ibrahim and, as things worked out, Gaddafi himself were waiting to extend the warmest of welcomes. As Libya's official JANA news agency reported that Friday: 'Yesterday evening, the leader of the revolution received an envoy representing the British National Union of Mineworkers and inquired about the state of British miners who have been on strike for over 18 months now. The leader expressed sympathy with the striking workers who suffer from abuse and exploitation at the hand of the exploiting ruling class in Britain. He also conveyed . . . solidarity with the striking miners' struggle to gain their legitimate rights and their rights in productions.'

On its own that might have been dismissed as the usual windy rhetoric. Indeed one or two sentences got into that Saturday's British newspapers without attracting any particular attention or comment. But *The Sunday Times* was able to show, with chapter and verse, that a great deal more was involved. Swain and other reporters were at Frankfurt when Windsor and Abbasi returned there on Friday evening, via Libyan Airlines flight LN172. They watched the two men in animated conversation – reading accounts of the previous day's sequestration proceedings, making a series of telephone calls, discussing the high price of various anti-telephone bugging devices that happened to be on display in the airport lounge – and then accompanied them back to Manchester, where they left in a shared taxi before splitting up and taking trains to their respective homes.

Attempts by *Sunday Times* reporters to obtain some explanation for Windsor's activities produced an explosive compendium of denials, protests, contradictions and refusals to comment. Windsor threatened to call the police. Scargill walked thirty yards in silence, accompanied by McGahey, who then instructed a bodyguard: 'Throw this man off the road.' Ibrahim, reached in Tripoli, at first disclaimed any trip to Paris or knowledge of Windsor, Scargill or Abbasi, but then, when pressed about the agenda of the 8 October meeting, volunteered: 'Why don't you contact Scargill and Windsor? They'll definitely tell you.' And Abbasi, after claiming to have no connection with the NUM's business beyond a general sympathy to their cause, gradually retreated as he realised the strength of the evidence that had been accumulated – yes, perhaps Windsor had been the man he shared a taxi with leaving Manchester airport the previous evening; well, maybe they had met at Frankfurt, but 'completely by accident checking the Manchester flights'; only when told they had been watched getting off the Libyan jet together and meeting a Libyan People's Bureau official did he finally admit that he 'may' have met Windsor on the Tripoli–Frankfurt plane.

Publication on Sunday, 28 October, saw a further flurry of explanations and dismissals. Scargill, in an abrasive radio interview, insisted that he had been in Paris on 8 October only to talk about miners' welfare; that he knew nothing about Abbasi; and that if he met any Libyans on that occasion he did not know their names. The CGT, with its own reasons for disclaiming too close a relationship with Colonel Gaddafi,

193

pretended that no Scargill–Ibrahim encounter had occurred under its roof. The Bangladeshis indignantly rejected any suggestion that they had paid any bills (though they had). All these claims were progressively shown to be false; and in a fine example of belated irony, when Salim Ibrahim turned up in the Bangladeshi capital, Dacca, in January 1985, seeking to present his credentials as the newly appointed head of the Libyan People's Bureau there, he was quietly shown the *Sunday Times* cuttings about himself and expelled as a potential and unwanted spy.

Closer to home where it mattered, the *Sunday Times* revelations had an electrifying effect. Seeking support from Moscow, or Peking, or Eastern Europe, or well-established Communist organisations around the world, was generally regarded as within the rules of the game, as Scargill himself implicitly recognised when he insisted on drawing a somewhat spurious distinction between help from 'Libyan trade unionists' and from the Libyan government, to which they are in practice wholly subservient. This cut little ice with Britain's mainstream Labour leaders, however. As Neil Kinnock roundly stated: 'By any measure of political, civil, trade union or human rights, the Gaddafi regime is vile. Any offers from them would be an insult to everything the British labour movement stands for.' Norman Willis, the TUC general secretary, was if anything even more forthright: he demanded a categorical assurance from the miners' leadership that no backing would be either sought or accepted from the 'hideous tyranny' in Tripoli, and totally condemned the manoeuvres which had 'created the impression that the NUM is prepared to consort with a government which is heavily implicated in terrorist campaigns outside its own borders'. From within the NUM's own executive, Ted McKay, from the small North Wales area, expressed repugnance and alarm that his union was dealing with any government so closely connected with 'murders, bloodshed and brutality over the years'.

From the Board's point of view, the Libya story was like coming up with the treble chance: it did more to discredit

Scargill and Windsor than all the arguments over picket-line violence and the responsibility for intimidating working miners. But the first response produced far more in the way of embarrassment than jubilation. It was bad enough that a major conversation between Eaton and David Frost, featured on the TV-am breakfast show the very morning that the *Sunday Times* revelations appeared on the nation's breakfast tables, went out with no mention at all of the new development. This was not Eaton's fault; the interview had been recorded on the Saturday. But it looked fairly unprofessional. Far worse was to follow, however, with the general shambles that ensued within twenty-four hours of the publication of this 'scoop of the year'.

After the contretemps with Cowan the previous week, Eaton was busy re-establishing his slightly tarnished status as the Board's approved authoritative voice. To this end, a whole series of interviews and occasions for meeting the media had been arranged. Keith Harper, the labour editor of the *Guardian*, was already in his blue-carpeted first-floor office, chatting about the general progress of the dispute. John Richards, industrial correspondent of the *Daily Telegraph*, was waiting downstairs. Lynda Lee Potter, columnist of the *Daily Mail*, was due at 1 pm to gather material for a full-scale profile. Alex MacDonald, London editor of the *Birmingham Post* and secretary of the industrial correspondents' group, had just finished ringing round all his national newspaper colleagues to confirm last-minute arrangements for a lunch with Eaton, to be held the following day at the Clarence pub in Whitehall. In the middle of this, however, MacGregor arrived back from Boston, Massachusetts, where he had spent the weekend seeing his grandchildren, and decided that the first priority must be to extract maximum capital from the Scargill–Gaddafi revelations, or as Nell Myers, the NUM's press officer, acidly called them, 'The *Sunday Times*'s Le Carré number'.

The chairman's decision on the best way to achieve this result was for the Board itself to remain entirely silent on all aspects of the strike, and to allow Libya a clear run on the front pages. To this end, all NCB briefings, by Eaton or anyone else inclined to talk to the press, would be cancelled forthwith and until further notice, and Geoff Kirk, the Board's long-standing and widely respected information head, was summoned to translate this fiat into immediate action.

Kirk, who was drowned in a boating accident off the Isle of Skye while this book was being written, was justifiably regarded as one of the Hobart House old school. Quiet spoken and silver-haired, he had worked for the Board almost as long as it existed. He joined the staff in 1949, served five chairmen, and had looked after the communications function for over a quarter of a century. Like tens of thousands of miners, who are forbidden by law to smoke underground, he always preferred snuff to cigarettes, and over the years he had built up an unrivalled reputation among journalists for both the honesty of his opinions and the depth of his knowledge concerning the industry he served. But this stood him in poor stead with the new MacGregor regime. There had already been a series of clashes. On advertising, which had always been a Kirk responsibility, it was made clear that advice from outsiders like Tim Bell of Saatchi and Saatchi was more highly regarded; and to underscore the point he was required, at the shortest possible notice, to switch the Board's press advertising account from CM Partnership, who had handled it for years, to Lowe Howard Spink, which Bell some months afterwards joined as Chairman.

Similarly, there were endless rows over the best way to counter Scargill's well-established skill in front of a television camera. During one set of abortive negotiations, the Board spent hours debating who should best confront the miners' leader on the BBC's Newsnight programme. The first suggestion was Ned Smith, the personnel director, who had by far the best grip on the detail of the talks. But MacGregor, who thought Smith a 'romantic' and far too sympathetic to the pitmen, vetoed the idea. He was not, however, after several bruising experiences, ready to expose himself alone again to the Scargill rhetoric. Perhaps, it was suggested, in Kirk's increasingly exasperated presence, MacGregor and Cowan should *both* go along to beard the dragon. This finally broke Kirk's patience, and he heard himself wryly asking his chairman if it was really necessary 'to put up two Scotsmen to deal with one Yorkshireman'. It was not the best atmosphere for fruitful cooperation and enlightened understanding.

Kirk was one of those who most warmly welcomed Eaton's arrival, so he was doubly appalled at being called in, halfway through Monday morning, and abruptly told to cancel all appointments. But what about all the people already in the building, or jumping into taxis to keep their engagements? Did MacGregor seriously want to abandon all those? MacGregor seriously did. So at the tail of Harper's interview, Kirk walked in, looking breathless and perturbed, and the *Guardian* man, sensing that something was wrong, brought the questions politely but swiftly to a close. By the time he got back to his newspaper and checked around, it was clear that relays of NCB press officers were busily engaged in making Eaton incommunicado. Unilaterally rescinding the industrial correspondents' lunch produced some particularly robust language, and after comparing notes, most Fleet Street papers decided that the 'gagging' of Eaton – not the iniquity of the NUM's North African adventures – was the real story of the day. 'How we managed to get Colonel Gaddafi off the front pages I'll never know,' said one plaintive NCB executive. 'At last we had an item deeply offensive to the moderates and the middle-left in the NUM, and we let Arthur get off the hook.' It was a view widely echoed in Whitehall, where ministers and senior civil servants were aghast at the way such an opportunity had been mishandled. And there was still more fall-out to come.

Kirk himself had done nothing to encourage the idea that Eaton was being deliberately silenced. Following MacGregor's instructions he had told his staff to blame everything on 'the sensational developments of the weekend' – in other words the Libya bombshell. But tempers were far too frayed for rational explanations. As soon as Tuesday's headlines had been digested, Kirk was summoned by a furious Cowan and told to take 'indefinite. leave'. By the evening he had cleared his desk and gone.

After twenty-five years he was far too well known to disappear quietly, and his abrupt departure brought forth another fat crop of adverse and critical comment. Alan Wilson, general secretary of BACM, the pit managers' union, demanded an urgent meeting with MacGregor – partly to discuss Kirk's future, as one of his longest-established members, but also to highlight what he characterised as 'a lack of confidence' in the Office of Chairman and Chief Executive. The sober and judicious *Financial Times* accused the NCB of discarding 'its best public relations asset'. Bernard Ingham, Mrs Thatcher's chief press officer and certainly no sympathiser with the soft line, rang Kirk personally to express horror at his cavalier treatment. At a press conference on 31 October, which probably marked the absolute low point of the Board's always edgy relations with Fleet Street, MacGregor threatened to walk out when reporters refused to discuss the scheduled agenda, which was the breakdown of yet another round of Acas peace talks, and insisted on concentrating their questions entirely on Kirk's dismissal.

In the end, though, it was this episode, with all its errors and abrasions, that brought all the simmering Hobart House tensions to the boil, and made it possible to make a fresh and ultimately successful start on defusing the dispute. From a chapter of accidents, a new battle order and a more coherent strategy gradually emerged. Eaton, with his reputation surprisingly unimpaired despite the tumultuous events of his first fortnight in the spotlight, found himself invested with new authority, and the backing of powerful allies at the department of energy. He himself dates the Board's recovery from the very next day, 1 November, when he chaired a reconvened version of the previous night's disastrous press conference, with the principal members of the negotiating team – MacGregor, Cowan, Ned Smith, and the deputy personnel director, Kevan Hunt – to stand with him and present a genuinely united front for the first time in many weeks. Discussion of intra-board dissensions was politely but firmly barred, and for once the questioning focused firmly on the real issues of the dispute.

It was behind the scenes, though, that the really significant changes were taking place. Eaton, who was now sitting down regularly to discuss tactics with the coal minister, David Hunt, gave it as his firm opinion, on the strength of more than a decade of across-the-table experience, that Scargill, for all his professed eagerness to bargain, would never in fact accept a negotiated compromise. It was from these sessions that the two-pronged strategy emerged which in the end brought the strike to an end. There would be no more substantive talks with the NUM without a guarantee, in advance, that economic closures would head the agenda. In the meantime, there would at last be a concerted and sustained effort to persuade as many miners as possible to give up the struggle and return to work. The long final phase was about to begin.

Chapter 11

Back to Work with Mr Moses

On 1 November, the strike was still to all intents and purposes solid, with the exception of Nottingham, Leicester, South Derbyshire and one or two isolated pits like Agecroft and Point of Ayr where the majority of men had never at any stage joined the dispute. Scotland had 366 back, mostly at the big Lothian colliery, Bilston Glen, and there was a tiny handful of mavericks in every coalfield except totally strikebound South Wales. But the numbers had remained virtually static throughout the autumn, and there was much scepticism, both in Whitehall and the higher reaches of the Board, that even the most determined and systematic back-to-work campaign would have any real effect. Even if it did, many argued, it could never substitute for a negotiated settlement or resolve anything on its own.

One man, however, profoundly disagreed. As early as June, Ken Moses, the tough, independent and imaginative area director in North Derbyshire, had made up his mind that Scargill's urge to win and total refusal to countenance economic arguments for pit closures ruled out any kind of conventional agreement. He knew his man – he had been Michael Eaton's chief mining engineer in North Yorkshire at the time of the confrontation over the closing of Walton

– and he was convinced that there would be no end to his resistance until he faced an irreversible collapse of support. But analysis, on its own, would have meant little. Moses's great contribution, which has already won him important promotion and quite probably put him in line to become a future chairman of the Coal Board, was to show, in the most practical way, how that collapse could be engineered.

The chosen test-bed for his experiment was Shirebrook, a large and normally profitable pit (one of the NCB's Top Ten) which employs 1,920 men largely concentrated in the sprawling village of the same name which straggles across the Nottingham–Derbyshire border. North Derbyshire, always seen as a halfway house between militant South Yorkshire and the moderate Midlands, had, characteristically, split fifty-fifty when it originally voted on whether to join the strike. Despite this, and Shirebrook's own vote which came down 1,049 to 587 against, support once the dispute started had been close to 100 per cent. Only a tiny handful, led by a member of the National Working Miners' Committee, Roland Taylor, a surface engineer who was one of the first to win a High Court injunction blocking union disciplinary action, had defied the majority and remained on the active payroll. Around midsummer, when pictures of the violent encounters at Orgreave started to fill the television screens, Moses decided it was time to see if the 'Nottinghamshire attitudes' he had detected among some of his men were strong enough for the numbers to be increased.

The approach was meticulously prepared. Bill Steel, the Shirebrook pit manager, stuck a large-scale Ordnance Survey map on his office wall, and used nearly 2,000 red pins to mark the home of every Shirebrook employee. Many, congregated in the central village, were regarded at this stage as unreachable, but others, as with most miners in an age of cars and frequent job transfers, lived a considerable distance away and would not come under the immediate scrutiny of striking neighbours. These were pinpointed, and sorted into more detailed categories. Were they married or single, and how large were their family commitments? Did they normally work a lot of overtime, so that now they might be facing larger than usual financial problems? Were they active in union affairs? What were their known attitudes, for or against the strike?

Armed with such information, plus names, addresses and telephone numbers, managers then started systematically calling or visiting those judged most likely to return. There were 120 in the first batch. Often Moses wrote a personal letter first, paving the way. Always there was a guarantee that their jobs would be safe if they ran into any trouble from the NUM. And gradually, with extreme caution, and much fear of the consequences, some faint signs of interest started to show. The orange pins, used to mark those who had received letters, gave way, in ones and twos, to green pins, indicating those who were ready to risk the rigours of return.

The next step was to lay on the transport. Moses bought six buses, had them wrapped in protective mesh, and set up a network of secret, frequently changed pick-up points where any miner prepared to face the pickets could begin his potentially hazardous journey to work. Starting in the small hours, drivers with protective helmets picked up their apprehensive passengers, threaded their way through the Derbyshire and Nottinghamshire lanes – many of the early recruits lived in and around Mansfield – and then raced, under heavy police escort, the last three hundred yards to the pit gates. A thin scattering of blue pins now showed men who had rejoined the strength.

Progress in the early stages was painfully slow, and punctuated by bitter violence. By the end of July, roughly 100 men had succumbed to Moses's persuasions. Two of them, Bob Larby and Adrian Walters, lived in Shirebrook itself, in a street, Recreation Drive, which was promptly renamed 'Scab Alley'. Seventeen of Walters's windows had been smashed and both their homes, heavily fortified against threats of arson and bleach bombs, regularly besieged by men (and women) throwing bricks, milk bottles and on one occasion the Walters' dustbin. Equally regularly the police, many of them seconded from London, moved in to clear the road, making little distinction between rock-throwers and legitimate passers-by. At weekends patrols were attacked, panda cars smashed, and the police station, right opposite the miners' welfare club, frequently stoned. One of the men from the Met commented unjokingly: 'This village is the Belfast of England.'

That was part of the price the Moses recipe entailed, and for a long time it looked disproportionately high for the results achieved. In August he started preparing the groundwork to repeat the exercise at other pits in his area, like Markham and Whitwell. But the overall totals only inched forward – 518 on 6 August, 810 on 3 September, 963 on 1 October, and 1,242 on 2 November. Even these figures (which have to be set against a total area workforce of 10,500) were flattered by the inclusion of at least 200 workers at Bolsover, which to all intents and purposes counts as a Nottinghamshire pit and produced at least some coal throughout the dispute.

It was only in the first full week of November that the dam finally broke. More than a thousand men surged back, Shirebrook itself approached the crucial halfway mark, clusters of blue pins penetrated to the very heart of the embattled village and the Moses method was comprehensively vindicated. Already it had been adopted as the standard blueprint for any area willing to give the drift-back policy a try, and now it became the countrywide norm.

Police involvement was an essential prerequisite, not an optional extra. Any effective back-to-work drive meant the breaching of picket lines, and emotions inevitably ran high, particularly the first time a mining community saw its precious solidarity under threat. When Paul Wilkinson, a young North-East miner, volunteered to be bussed into work at Easington on 20 August, the whole village erupted. Nothing much could be done the first day, a Monday, as blue-uniformed officers surrounded him in a tight wedge formation and rushed him into the pityard. On Tuesday a large barricade had been built overnight across the entrance from drums and scrap metal, but Wilkinson never appeared: men from his former pit, East Hetton, were trying to persuade him to change his mind. The pit manager agreed there would be 'nothing sneaky': the man would go in through the front gate or not at all. Then on Friday the news spread that he had been smuggled in through the pithead baths, and there was a near-riot. Eggs filled with paint were lobbed at the police, cars overturned, office windows bombarded, fire-extinguishers turned on stave-carrying reinforcements, and the management, according to eye-witnesses, was looking shell-shocked, with lumps of masonry and broken steel chain laying all over the yard.

That scene repeated itself, with minor variations, for more than two months while Wilkinson, with massive police escort, ran his lonely gauntlet. Occasionally there was a small flash of humour: the day after MacGregor's most memorable TV appearance every picket paraded with a plastic bag on his head. But in general the mood was of dour, frustrated anger as Easington endured a police presence that came close to permanent occupation – all, as one villager put it, 'for one bloody man'.

To start with, it was almost invariably with one man that the break began. Area directors, once committed to encouraging the drift-back, tried in all sorts of ways to persuade waverers to form themselves into mutual-support groups. Letters were sent out, advertisements posted, secure telephone numbers arranged so that frightened men could make the first approach and be put in touch with others in a similar frame of mind. Partly the object was to make it easier to defy the majority; partly it was to divert criticism from those, like the National Council for Civil Liberties, who attacked as 'disproportionate' the resources applied to preserving one single person's right to work. In most cases, though, there was in the end no choice. Such were the social and intimidatory pressures against breaking ranks that it was only the lone individual, driven to the end of his tether by hardship, family responsibilities or overwhelming distaste for the way the strike was being run, who was prepared to take the plunge.

The police themselves recognised nothing disproportionate about their arrangements: they made available what they had calculated was necessary to do an inherently difficult and adversarial job. Techniques varied slightly from area to area, but the underlying thinking remained fairly standard. As the South Yorkshire deputy chief constable, Tony Clement, later explained, there was a routine link-up with the NCB. When a colliery manager knew he had men ready to be brought in to his pit, he would contact the divisional police commander. 'We'd say yes, or can you leave it because we've got something on elsewhere.' Then, once the date was agreed, 'they'd say there's going to be x number going back, and we'd gear ourselves up for it.' Detailed strategy was then thrashed out with the pit-commander, a middle-rank officer who had been detailed from the beginning of the strike to familiarise himself with the geography, personalities and relevant peculiarities of that particular colliery.

The basic policy on the day was always to get there first and take the ground. 'We didn't want to arrive at a pit and have to battle our way in. We always wanted to be in position when they arrived so we were in control of the pit yard. Then, if there's going to be any fighting it's them fighting to get in rather than us fighting our way through. We'd start moving our men anything after 1 am or 2 am, and get them on the road certainly by 3 am.' They were rarely caught out – partly because they were tipped off, by volunteer and on occasion paid informants inside the NUM, more importantly through the efforts of police spotters scattered through the district in unmarked cars who became expert in predicting the pickets' intentions and detecting any feints made to put them off the scent. 'It didn't take long before you could spot a miner's car a mile off, because it usually had four men in and was a P-registration or something like that.' Also, the strikers were rarely prepared to make a sufficiently early start. 'If the shift was 7 am, they wouldn't get there till six or half-past, but our men would have been there since three, ready to control anything that happened.'

When the November back-to-work drive began, there were just thirty-seven men on the NCB books in South Yorkshire. Ten collieries described themselves as technically open, but that had more to do with bravado than anything resembling coal production. On 24 October the number swelled to eleven, and police battled with a crowd of 3,000 at the gates of Yorkshire Main, reporting two arrests and no injuries. On 6 November, Silverwood opened for a day, with two strikers arrested, but shut again when the lone returnee got cold feet. Then, two days later, the storm started to break in earnest. Three more local pits opened their gates for the first time to admit strikebreakers and their police escort convoys. And one of them, almost unbelievably, was rock-rigid, totally committed Cortonwood, where eight long months before it had all begun.

The first reaction was of stunned, uncomprehending shock. The violence was delayed for twenty-four hours while the impact of the news sunk in. But when it came, in dense fog just before dawn on the morning of Friday, 9 November, it matched the very worst. Three thousand pickets and 1,000 police raged through the darkened streets of Brampton Bierlow and fought each other to a standstill under the blue and yellow National Coal Board sign that marks the entrance to Cortonwood's main pityard.

Brampton village, whose population barely touches 3,500, is home for the largest proportion of the 820 miners who normally work at Cortonwood. Its strike, like the rest of South Yorkshire, had started on 6 March, a week earlier than the rest of the country. Once propelled into the front line, the Cortonwood men had come to see themselves as the strike's natural standard-bearers. Their operational headquarters, on the first floor of the Brampton miners' social club, and their makeshift picket-hut, with its defiant sign, The Alamo, appeared on television screens and front pages as symbols of unbreakable resolve. Week after week they dispatched delegations, demonstration parties and car-loads of flying pickets to stiffen morale among strikers in other less united communities. But at home, in the shack with the battered leather armchairs, the chip-butty pan, the scrawled slogans and the cast-off TV set, they kept barely a token force. Even the police thought it unnecessary to pay more than an occasional call to keep more than a weather eye open.

Peace lasted, unbroken, through the spring, summer and most of the autumn of 1984. Just occasionally there was a faint hint of division – a rumour, quickly denied, that seventeen Cortonwood men had been seen at one of 'Silver Birch's' secret meetings; another, that the clerical employees at the pit were still hankering for a formal ballot; even reports that Jack Wake, the branch secretary, had been heard regretting a lack of democracy in some of the national executive's decisions. But nobody suspected, even when the NCB began to step up its pre-Christmas campaign, that at Cortonwood, of all places, there would be a serious rift in the ranks. When it came, it was greeted at first with disbelief, then with fury. The eruption took two days to build to its climax and it was almost a week before the village returned to a state of shocked and suspicious peace.

The first solitary strikebreaker was a young man of twenty-three, married, with two small children. His normal job was driving one of the colliery's underground trains. Typical of those tempted, whether by frustration or financial hardship, to risk breaching the picket lines, he had worked only a short time at the pit and lived well away from the main village community. Originally he had agreed to go in with a mate, but at the last minute his companion backed out. He was picked up at his home, three miles from Brampton, in the Barnsley district of Hoyland Nether, in the small hours of Thursday morning, 8 November. At 7.30 am, with an escort estimated at some sixty police vehicles, he was driven at high speed through the colliery gates.

The pickets, though their numbers had swollen to fifty after extensive reports of a nationwide return to work – the NCB claimed 2,236 'new faces' that week – were left flatfooted. It was a full hour later, when the news spread and some 700 people had gathered, that the first serious clashes began. Milk bottles and stones were thrown, police horses were unloaded from transporters to break up the crowds, and the old age pensioners waking in the bungalow estate that overlooks the pit workings had their first sight of officers with riot shields and protective helmets chasing suspects through their allotments and gardens. Deep hoofprints in the pocket-handkerchief lawns showed where the horses had passed. Two policemen were injured, three arrests made, and later that morning angry miners and wives shouted abuse outside the main local police station. That was not in Brampton, which lacks such an amenity, but in Wath-upon-Dearne, a mile down the road, where the NCB has its South Yorkshire area offices. In the shops and pubs there was lively discussion of the events. On a Barnsley–Mexborough bus passing the colliery at lunchtime, a woman told her friend that someone had gone back to work. 'Good luck to him' was the answer. And then, thoughtfully: 'But they'll crucify him.'

The lone worker, now with a much smaller escort, drove out of the pit just before midday. It was pouring with rain, but through the streaming van windows it was possible for him to see a new addition to the placards and graffiti adorning The Alamo. A crude stuffed dummy was hanging from a gallows labelled 'This is for scabs'. But there was no attempt to bar his passage or to follow him home. Maybe the trouble was over.

The calm was deceptive. That evening Arthur Scargill held a massive rally in Sheffield City Hall, some fifteen miles away, and a standing-room-only crowd of more than 5,000 mainly young miners greeted him with a sustained crescendo of adulation which could be heard twenty streets away. Dismissing any possibility of failure, the NUM leader roared out his familiar challenge to the government and the Coal Board. Victory was assured, he asserted, and when it was achieved there would be no forgiveness for a 'defeated' Mrs Thatcher or a 'defeated' Ian MacGregor. Above all, there would be no forgiveness for those who had 'scabbed'. For them, he predicted, there could be only one fate: they would become lepers, shunned as an embarrassment by the employers who were currently welcoming them back, and outcasts in their own communities. It was heady stuff, and his audience was still buzzing with the rhetoric as it poured out, just short of 11 pm, to pick up the cars parked thickly in all the roads around. An unmistakable scent of menace hung in the air.

In the small hours of the following morning, over 3,000 assembled outside Cortonwood's perimeter fence, intent to stop any repetition of the previous day's back-to-work exercise. They came from all over south and west Yorkshire. Many had been at Scargill's meeting. But, although they started to gather in significant numbers as early as 4 am, they had already been outsmarted in their primary objective. This time the working miner, still on his own, was brought in at 3.30 am when there were only thirteen token pickets on the gate. To pass them, though, he had been provided with an escort of at least 1,000 police.

As new waves of pickets and protesters arrived they refused to believe, or chose to ignore, assurances that they had missed their target. Milling around in the early morning fog both sides put the worst interpretation on every movement; at 6 am tempers frayed to breaking point. The police were headed by Chief Superintendent John Nesbitt of the South Yorkshire force. He was a former miner, made redundant in an earlier closure period, and also, coincidentally, the man who had earlier arrested Scargill at Orgreave. The police say that it was a hail of stones and ball-bearings, fired from large catapults, that provoked them into mass retaliation. Miners claim that it was only when police horses and men in riot gear were seen breaking through the murk that any serious missiles were thrown.

Within minutes, all hell had broken loose. Three lamp standards, a length of wall and a concrete bus shelter were demolished to provide one store of instant weapons; a hijacked milk float produced another. As the bottles flew a river of milk ran down the gutters and the street was a carpet of broken glass. A portable site cabin was torched and set rolling down the hill towards the advancing police, until it was rammed into the roadside by a police Range Rover. Another followed, and two official vehicles, with their anti-picket mesh windows, crashed in an effort to intercept it. A senior officer was heard shouting: 'Some clown is firing an air-gun', though this was later denied by the miners. One of the police horses, however, had its protective eye-visor shattered in a hail of rocks (though the animal itself was unhurt).

The struggle waxed and wavered for at least three hours.

209

Gradually the disciplined and heavily equipped police established the upper hand. Using dogs as well as horses, and driving their vans like sheep dogs to break up the pickets into smaller, more manageable groups, they started to force them away from the colliery and into the narrow streets of Brampton, which were soon littered with half-bricks, rubble and heaps of burning material. When the head of the local infant school arrived at 8.10 am she found her playground being used as a redoubt, from which bricks, torn out of the wall of the Methodist chapel opposite, were showering on to the police massed outside. The flaming huts, still smouldering, were now safely behind police lines and it was the regular local fire brigade that finally arrived to extinguish them. In the final tally, thirteen police and a number of pickets had been seriously injured, but only four men were arrested. Chief Superintendent Nesbitt said it had been the worst day of the dispute so far, and Mick Carter, Cortonwood's NUM delegate, reflected acidly that it would have been far cheaper all round if the NCB had kept the man at home and put him on full pay for the remainder of the strike.

The NCB was committed to a policy of getting men back to work wherever possible, the police to providing the necessary protection for this to happen, and the strikers to defying them by any means in their power. By Monday morning four men were ready to run the gauntlet into Cortonwood, and the resulting convulsion, though it did for the moment clear the air and force everyone concerned to stand back and take stock, left a lastingly bitter taste.

Again the escort convoy roared through the pit gates at 3 am. But this time, in a change of tactics, the police had to deal, not with pickets, but with an organised group of 150 demonstrators – some of them, at least, suspected of being not miners but unemployed youths from the vicinity (where, even when the local pits are in full production, one in four is without work). At the height of the renewed clashes a petrol bomb was thrown at one of the police Land Rovers, exploding in a Belfast-style flare that lit up the night sky. Soon afterwards a whole crate of home-made Molotov cocktails – petrol-filled milk bottles – was found in an alleyway. Police

and rioters played a grim hide-and-seek through the back-
entries and tiny gardens while barricades were set on fire
behind what had once been the village Co-op store (now
long abandoned) and the heavy roller from the village cricket
ground was manhandled on to the highway and propelled
towards the advancing police. It was 6 am before the dozens
of specially strengthened Transit vans that had been riding
herd round the back streets were released from duty, so that
the Police Support Units, brought in that night from as far
away as Norwich and Canterbury, could fall into them and
get some belated sleep.

Peter Wright, the chief constable of South Yorkshire, who
had spent most of the night trying to contain similar outbreaks
not only at Cortonwood but at more than fifteen other pits
and mining communities in the area, hotly denied at a press
conference in Sheffield the next day that the police were to
blame for inflaming the situation. Answering accusations
from Arthur Scargill he said: 'There is a lot of anger, frustration and all the other emotions that come along with a
strike going on for this length of time, and it is in the interests
of the NUM to focus that anger and frustration on the police
. . . We will continue to get this type of ridiculous accusation.
But we are not manufacturing these events.'

Such incidents, manufactured or otherwise, multiplied in
every coalfield as the NCB stepped up efforts to turn the
trickle into a flood. Statements firmly ruled out any scope
for new negotiations while the miners refused to discuss pit
economics; tempting opportunities were offered for debt-
ridden and by now deeply impoverished families to restore
their own financial state. Some 180,000 copies of the Board's
publication *Coal News* were sent out – one to each NUM
member's home – drawing attention to the fact that up to
£650 would be available as a 'Christmas bonus pay packet'
to anyone who worked four full weeks before the annual
shutdown. When Scargill denounced this as 'bribery' and
'blackmail', Hobart House answered that it would be just an
accumulation of normal wages, unpaid allowances, long-
service entitlements and holiday pay, and followed it up with
personal letters from many managers pointing out that, for

211

those who made up their minds quickly, there was in fact around £1,400 waiting to be earned, and that much of it would be tax-free. By the time the implied deadline ran out, on 19 November, just under 10,000 additional men had decided, for whatever reason, to throw in their hands, and the number of collieries wholly stopped had fallen precipitously from ninety-three to forty-seven. After that, to no one's particular surprise, it proved possible to move the finishing tape by a few more days, and in the final scramble, according to the Board, another 5,000 defied the pickets and raced under the wire.

All the statistics were scornfully questioned by the NUM and subjected to intense analysis as to just what they did or did not include. In one of his more pointed remarks, Scargill told a cheering audience: 'Every time the canteen cat walks in twice the Board counts it as two men back at work.' Stung by such accusations, Ken Moses called in the leading City accountants Thomson McClintock to verify that his returns were not padded. But although NUM spokesmen took every opportunity to cast doubt on the extent of the drift-back, they also showed a marked reluctance to release detailed figures of their own. On the one occasion they did so, on 16 November, the results were inconclusive. At that point the Board claimed 59,000 at work and the union almost 10,000 fewer, at 49,235. But as the miners had always claimed there were many more men on strike in Nottingham than the Board was willing to admit, the discrepancy was smaller than it seemed; and in any case, whichever version came closer to the truth, there could be no dispute that even the first half of November had seen a significant abandonment of the strike, and that the process had some way to go.

Just how significant, however, remained for all parties a matter of considerable dispute. Michael Eaton, now established as the Board's principal public voice, became so enthusiastic on the day the NUM published its breakdown that he predicted a total collapse of the dispute by Christmas, with more than half the workforce voluntarily back at the coal-face. Within forty-eight hours, though, he was energetically distancing himself from this rash view, after it had been pointed out that, despite the impressive numbers, barely a handful of the 'new faces' had actually been able yet to go underground, let alone produce any coal, and that the 7,000 additional returnees he had been anticipating for the following week were now unlikely to materialise.

Opinions were changing fast, too, on the other side. At the start of the November campaign, the general view was that morale would hold. Tony Benn appeared on a picket line at Arkwright, one of Moses's pits in North Derbyshire, eloquently expounding the case for holding firm to five men who had been tempted to give up. Dennis Murphy, the NUM area president in Northumberland, successfully persuaded twelve of the twenty-seven men being bussed into Whittle colliery that they should turn round and go home. As the days passed though, and especially after the defections at Cortonwood, faith faded in the power of appeals to brotherly unity. The first sixteen went back in South Wales, where the sole local member of the National Working Miners' Committee, Tony Hollman, at Cynheidre, had earlier been forced to accept total defeat. Murphy's earlier success at Whittle was rudely reversed as 133 miners out of the 700 work-roll decided that enough was enough. John Cunningham, the well-respected branch secretary at Ellington, also in Northumberland, told a meeting of 500 strikers at Ashington that the current NUM leadership 'did not know the meaning of democracy and was hell-bent on destruction', left the hall without a single shout of 'scab', and two days later led 107 of his members back to their pit (past a picket including his twenty-nine-year-old son, who swore he would never speak to his father again). So concerned was the Northumberland NUM executive by such dramatic defections that it offered to counter the Board's financial incentives with a £100 bonus of its own for every miner who remained on strike – a gesture which would have cost nearly £500,000 and required the sale of their Newcastle-upon-Tyne headquarters.

As the erosion spread, and those still striking recognised their lack of power to slow it down, there was a sharp escalation in frustrated violence. Assaults on those seen as 'scabs' reached a new pitch of frenzy, with the two most memorably vicious acts perpetrated in the course of the dispute.

The first took place at Airedale, near Castleford, in West Yorkshire, where a working miner, Michael Fletcher, was chased into his own home by a masked gang waving baseball bats, and savagely beaten for more than five minutes in his living room while his pregnant wife and two young children huddled upstairs listening to his screams. The second, even more horrifying, was in South Wales, where two strikers dropped a concrete block from a motorway bridge on to the car carrying a working miner, David Williams, to Merthyr Vale colliery, and killed outright his taxi-driver, David Wilkie. They later stood trial for murder and were sentenced to twenty years. Even the miners' president, who till then had resolutely refused to utter any condemnation of picket-related violence, was moved on that occasion to dissociate the union from the acts leading to Wilkie's death and expressed his 'deep shock' at the tragedy. It was an emotion almost universally shared, and police all over the country noted from that day a dramatic sobering-up on both sides of the picket line.

On 30 November, the day Wilkie was killed, the surge had already spent itself. With the last of the immediate monetary incentives exhausted, the back-to-work totals, which had dominated the headlines and led the news bulletins since October, fell back to levels barely greater than those recorded in the late summer and vanished on to the inside pages. Scargill cheered up the audience during one of his December speeches by recommending those members who had succumbed to temptation to collect the Christmas bonus, pay off their debts and return to the strike in the New Year. Those who did, he said, should not be rejected as traitors but welcomed as lost lambs. Some members of the government, despite public expressions of confidence that the return to work would resume and redouble after the holidays, secretly worried that there might be something in what he said. But most of his own members took a more realistic view. They knew that the men who were back cleaning the safety lamps and rebuilding the vandalised surface installations had crossed the Rubicon and were lost to the strike for good. They could only take comfort in the words of Jack Pattinson, the NUM branch president at Rossington, near Doncaster, who said prophetically around this time: 'We'll not always be skint, but they'll always be scabs.'

Chapter 12

How They Kept the Lights On

At 4.50 pm on Tuesday, 6 November, the red warning card went up on the controls at the Portsmouth offices of the Southern Electricity Board, indicating that the supply system was rapidly nearing the limits of its capacity and that major load-shedding might shortly be required. That was the closest Britain got to significant power cuts in the whole course of the strike, and in fact it never happened. Four record surges of demand in January 1985 failed to produce a single flicker of the nation's lights, and General Winter, whose prospective aid had buoyed up the miners for ten miserable months, turned out to be a broken reed.

It was a remarkable achievement, compounded of foresight, luck, careful preparation, and a virtuoso performance by the people who ran the Central Electricity Generating Board,* with its Scottish equivalent, the South Scotland Electricity Board, and organised distribution of the substantial amounts of coal that the NCB continued to mine. There

* The CEGB is responsible only for England and Wales. The rest of the United Kingdom is supplied by the South of Scotland Electricity Board, the North of Scotland Hydro-Electric Board and the Northern Ireland Electricity Service, which all performed with similar diligence and efficiency.

216

were many crucial elements – the decision by Nottingham-shire and the other Midland coal-producers to keep working, the massive coal stocks, totalling around 55m. tonnes, which had been built up at both pitheads and power stations, the super-efficiency of the oil-fired generators, many of which had been virtually mothballed for a decade, the robustness of the nuclear stations when called on to run close to their limits, and the ability of the road transport industry to replace rail at the shortest possible notice and on a truly massive scale. But none of this would have worked without a great deal of high-class and dedicated management, and it was no surprise to find several of the key names – Sir Walter Marshall, chairman of the CEGB, Frank Ledger, his director of operations, and Malcolm Edwards, the Coal Board's marketing director – figuring prominently in the first post-strike honours list.

Britain has fifty-five coal-fired power stations, representing some 53 per cent of total generating capacity, with sixteen oil-burning plants (23 per cent) and thirteen nuclear stations (14 per cent) making up the bulk of the difference. But for cost reasons, in recent years the normal pattern has been to rely on coal for close to 80 per cent of actual electricity production, with nuclear power plugging away steadily on base-load and reserving the almost prohibitively expensive oil contribution for occasional peaks and emergencies. The trick during the strike was to reverse this and run oil and nuclear power for all they were worth, regardless of price, so that they could contribute to their full limit, and indeed beyond – several of the huge 660-megawatt sets, like those at Littlebrook and the Isle of Grain, ran for months at a full 10 per cent or more above their theoretical maximum and astonished everyone in the industry, including their original manufacturers, GEC. Together with a modest amount of hydro-electricity they provided roughly 50 per cent of the power needed to run the factories and kitchen stoves.

However, that still left 50 per cent to be found elsewhere, and that could only come, one way or another, from coal. The fundamental importance of Nott's decision to keep working was that, once solidly established, it filled a full three-fifths of the gap. The remaining 20 per cent, though still formidable and highly vulnerable to picketing, industrial accident or a sudden unexpected surge of demand, was just about sustainable, and with flair and dedication at all levels it was duly sustained.

There were many hairy moments. One typical mixture of serendipity and sang-froid was brought into play at Cannock, in the West Midlands, where efforts were being made to release some of the 14m. tonnes of valuable open-cast coal piling up around the country because of a TGWU blockade. Though this had been nationally agreed as a gesture of support for the miners it was frequently possible to do a deal, particularly when the local authorities could be persuaded that the growing mountains of the stuff were becoming a public danger. As the NCB's Cannock negotiator remembers: 'All the bigwigs were standing sceptically around while our thermal testing showed not even a sniff of a heating problem. Then we sent in a digger, and suddenly there was a cloud of steam. We fell down on our knees and knew the Lord was on our side.'

Throughout Mrs Thatcher's period of government there was steady pressure on the CEGB to build up stocks and to keep even heavily uneconomic oil-burning capacity in working order. This was sharply stepped up during Nigel Lawson's tenure at the department of energy, giving rise to frequent rows over responsibility for paying the bills. It was one of these which precipitated the departure of the then Board chairman, Glyn England, in 1982, and although there was a general understanding at the CEGB's headquarters about what was happening – 'Nobody mentioned Scargill but there wasn't much doubt as to why we were doing all this,' as one senior official there remarked – there is little evidence of detailed tactical planning until the strike was actually under way. One clue to this is that many bits of equipment vital to the running of the big oil-fired plants were out on loan elsewhere when the first flying pickets went into action on 12 March 1984. These included even some of the huge 150-tonne steel shafts whose function is to revolve at 600 rpm at the heart of the turbines. So little are stations like

Pembroke normally in use that it is common practice to help out other people when their plant is being maintained. As a result they had to be smuggled back, under tarpaulins, before any electricity production could begin. Given that this involved using a huge sixty-wheel transporter truck, travelling with full police escort at not more than 12 mph, it offered a standing invitation for an NUM ambush, but everything passed off without incident and Pembroke was able to make its contribution, moving up smartly from No. 72 to No. 28 in the CEGB's revised merit order list.

This was the core of the Board's battle plan, once it was clear that the strike was going to be a long-haul affair. In normal times the electricity industry operates its power stations to minimise the unit cost of supplying consumers. It arranges its power stations in ascending order of marginal costs and then gradually brings them into use according to the level of demand, first nuclear and hydro-electric, then coal, and oil only as a last resort. In crisis conditions, though, this goes out of the window and the overriding objective becomes to maintain supply – particularly when the government is determined, as it was, that its opponents must not be allowed the satisfaction of seeing a single 60-watt bulb go out. That was why no voltage reductions or supply restrictions were imposed, although they would have been a useful way of stretching out the coal reserves. Instead the Board invested its very best brainpower, under the direction of Frank Ledger, into writing a computer programme, codenamed Endurance, whose purpose was to switch the whole emphasis of its operation from cost efficiency to coal-stock preservation.

In broad terms this incorporated four central strands of thought. Nuclear and hydro-electric, which always provided the first level of base-load, would continue to do so, but with all stops pulled and the minimum possible down-time for routine maintenance. The great arc of coal-fired stations in the Trent Valley and the Midlands, stretching from West Burton and Cottam in the east to Rugely A and B in the west, should be kept going full out and fed with every tonne of fresh output that the working areas could provide. The mighty but still almost mint-condition oil stations on the south coast and along the Thames Valley – Fawley, Isle of Grain, Littlebrook and Kingsnorth – should be run to the limit, and if necessary even into the ground. And the big northern and Scottish coal plants, deep in the most strikebound regions, like Drax, Ferrybridge, Blyth and Longannet, should sit quietly ticking over through the summer, ready to commit their remaining stocks when the winter really started to bite.

That proved, in the event, a pretty accurate anticipation of events; but it needed much more than a computer programme to make it work. Imagination and ingenuity had to be on call twenty-four hours a day, and there were plenty of individual feats in all departments, from oil-burner technology to industrial relations. This last was especially important. The leaders of the two main power supply unions, Eric Hammond and John Lyons, made it clear from the start that they would not use their leverage to win the NUM's struggle for them, but that by no means meant that they were ready to be pushed around. Lyons, for instance, sought an interview with Sir Walter Marshall, early in the autumn, to make it clear that his members would never cooperate in the use of troops to move coal from picketed pityards. Also they had to work inside the power stations with men from the TGWU and the General, Municipal and Boilermakers, many of whom were a lot more sympathetic to the miners' cause, and there was continual debate over the proper response to picketing and the use of 'blacked' supplies.

On balance, the CEGB's response to such problems was refreshingly mature. At Littlebrook, for example, the management astonished an NUM picket group – and earned itself much staff good will – when one day early on it invited them to come in to the canteen and use the public address system to put over their message, instead of taking uncomfortable pot-luck outside the gates. And at Didcot and West Thurrock, where there were regular water-testing deliveries of freshly mined coal, there was no attempt to overrule or discipline workers who refused to handle them. As a result there was far less resistance than anticipated to the use of abnormal amounts of oil in what were previously all-coal or coal-and-oil stations, and that was vastly more important.

Thanks to a series of technical modifications made during the strike, it became possible to use oil to produce up to one-third of the electricity in coal-fired stations like Blyth in Northumberland and Aberthaw in South Wales and thus give an effective 50 per cent boost to their otherwise unreplenishable stocks. There was never any serious bar to that sort of innovation: the limits came only with much more ambitious propositions, like the Board's plan to run an oil pipeline from the River Ouse to Drax in North Yorkshire, which was, understandably, blacked by the TGWU for the duration.

New pipelines, in any case, were rather pie-in-the-sky. Far more central was the wholesale use of lorries, which quickly took on the nature and magnitude of a military operation. The large, modern, cost-effective pit is routinely connected with its main customers by a round-the-clock 'merry-go-round' train service, moving 1,100 tonnes a trip. To match this, with trucks carrying an average of 22 tonnes a time, means putting a fleet of fifty vehicles on the road, and for many of the North Nottingham mines, each capable of raising 1m. tonnes a year, there was a 100 per cent turnround to the new style of transport. 'You were talking about one lorry setting off from pit to power station every 5.5 minutes, 24 hours a day five days a week,' explained one of the NCB men involved.

The number of trains never dropped to zero, despite all the best efforts of the railwaymen. There were always independently minded people around, like the Midlands signalman who rang Peter Walker at home to say he normally shared shifts with a Communist, but would happily turn a blind eye when he was on his own, so that the coal committee could liaise with British Rail on the rescheduling of shipments. With help like that, it was usually possible to get seventy or more trainloads a week past the pickets, but that was a far cry from the 565 which regularly serviced the central coalfields before the dispute. The difference was made up with no fewer than 800,000 lorry journeys, keeping the lifeline open, not only to power stations but to tomato growers, steam engine rallies and industrial users.

It was just as important, in the eyes of Walker and Edwards, to stop any major coal-using factory from going on short time as it was to make sure that the domestic television never flickered. So the Midlands were 'like a Klondyke for hauliers'. They came down in hundreds from Scotland, and in dozens and scores from Cornwall, Wales and the South-East – though very few, for some reason, from unemployment-stricken Tyne and Wear – and they camped in the lay-bys, sleeping in their cabs, picked up their often four-figure weekly wage packets, and used their CB radios intensively to avoid pickets and keep out of trouble. Many corners were cut to get the job done. Weighing the load at both ends, which is prudently and often legally required in the haulage business, was one of the first things to go. The NCB reckoned it had no time for such niceties, painted a 'Plimsoll Line' round the inside of each truck roughly 10 per cent below the police overloading limit, and filled it up to there.

There were few complaints: but householders and villagers along the new coal routes were a lot less forgiving. Oxfordshire County Council submitted a formal compensation claim to the CEGB for damage to country roads caused by the 600 coal and oil lorries a day thundering into Didcot from the Midlands, and between 1 January and 19 February 1985 there were five serious or fatal accidents on this route: a driver half-drowned when his 20-tonne truck skidded through a parapet over the Thames on the A415, a young pharmacist and two others were killed in separate crashes involving moving or stationary fuel-carriers north of Banbury on the A41.

Coal did not only move on the highways. Tiny ports all over Britain, many of them barely discernible on a walking-scale Ordnance Survey map, suddenly found themselves the destination for an armada of exotic flag-carriers. Only Polish coal, carried in Russian ships and benefiting from a long-standing mutual arrangement between British and Soviet dockers, had no difficulty landing; bigger vessels, especially those from the United States, could neither find suitable berths here nor be sure of not falling foul of the TGWU. Standard practice, therefore, was to land in Rotterdam and reload into small coasters, which then set off to find a dock or jetty so remote that the miners and their allies had never heard of it. Flixborough, in Lincolnshire, was by these standards an international entrepôt centre.

The unexpected beneficiaries here were places like Glasson on the Lune estuary down river from Lancaster, or Howendyke on the Yorkshire Ouse, or Barton-on-Humber, with its almost impenetrable Barrow Clay Pits Wharf, which was busy throughout, handling up to four West German colliers at a time. A survey of such minute specks on the landscape, taken in August 1984, showed that between them they were registering over 1,000 more arrivals than they had seen a year before, and that the newcomers were as large and as frequent as the vicissitudes of tide and general accessibility allowed. Only the most passionate pleas to the trade unionists of Holland, Belgium and West Germany even momentarily slowed this trade down, and as soon as the pressure came off it resumed.

Seaborne coal, however, was of infinitely less importance than oil. Even with Notts fully operational, it would have been impossible for the government to succeed if the miners had found any way to block the North Sea pipelines and the regular arrival of the tankers. With the National Union of Seamen firmly committed to support the NUM, there was always a potential problem with imports, and to avoid that there was a heavy reliance on Russian vessels, many of them loading initially in the Dutch Antilles. At one stage, their presence nearly triggered a very tricky incident. One of the Soviet tankers, it was complained, had failed to pay harbour dues on some previous visit, and the Admiralty Court, which looks after such matters, ordered its peremptory arrest. This was doubly embarrassing, as not only was it about to discharge its contents at Kingsnorth, the biggest of the Thamesside power stations, but behind it was a queue of similar vessels each urgently anxious to unload and get on

223

its way. As Kingsnorth is crucial, both in its own right and as a transmission point for the two almost equally substantial installations at Isle of Grain, the arrest could have created a most damaging bottleneck. While the CEGB made a desperate Saturday morning application to the court to get the arrest lifted, preparations were set on foot to buy the boat outright if necessary and to take over its obligations, just to get it out of the way. Fortunately for the taxpayers, the lawyers found a way out in the nick of time.

Such alarms apart, though, the multi-faceted 'endurance' exercise was an outstanding success. Despite year-long efforts by City stockbrokers, energy consultants, aerial survey companies, leftwing academics, scientific journalists and business analysts to prove otherwise, the stocks never came within even touching distance of the danger mark. Arthur Scargill, at one point, had himself flown over several of the northern power stations and told his next audience that the coalyards there looked 'a lot like my hairstyle: thick on the outside but not much in the middle'. It was rather better as a joke than a piece of observation, and even the onset of winter made it less rather than more accurate as the weeks went by.

At the end of the third week in February 1985, a glass of early morning champagne was served to the members of Peter Walker's daily coal committee. For the first time since the dispute started more than 1m. tonnes of coal had been safely delivered to customers within a period of seven days. Just over 590,000 of that came from the Midlands, including Notts, but there was also 246,960 tonnes from Western region (Lancashire, Staffordshire and the like), 64,470 tonnes from the North-East, 64,370 tonnes from Yorkshire, and even 15,240 tonnes from dour and determined South Wales. To all intents and purposes, the champagne-drinkers concluded, their part of the affair was effectively complete.

Chapter 13

Endgame

Fred Lilley normally earns his living as a process server and inquiry agent in the Nottinghamshire mining town of Mansfield. But Monday, 1 October 1984, was not a routine day. It involved, in rapid succession, a train journey to King's Cross, a tense wait in the Law Courts while some tricky paperwork was prepared, a breakneck car dash to London's Battersea heliport, a 200-mile helicopter flight to Blackpool, a quick reconnaissance trying to penetrate the tight security round the Winter Garden, where the Labour party conference was in session, a ploy with a *Daily Express* photographer's borrowed visiting card to get past the doorman, and a £50 note passed to a helpful steward so that he could track down his quarry in the crowded hall. Just before 4 pm, which he had been told was his absolute deadline, he moved into place beside Arthur Scargill, who was sitting conveniently in one of the aisle seats, and delivered what was probably the most damaging writ ever received by a British trade union leader. The NUM's autumn troubles, and the long chain of events that would ultimately bring the strike to its untidy and inconclusive end, had been punctually set in train.

Four o'clock was important. Robert Taylor and Ken Foulstone, the two Manton miners on whose behalf the writ had been issued, had evaded 1,000 pickets that morning and gone back to work, armed with Mr Justice Nicholls's judgement that the whole dispute must be treated as unofficial, having been illegally called. But as long as Scargill and his executive publicly rejected this decision, even wavering strikers would remain in doubt. Foulstone and Taylor, campaigning for a mass abandonment of the dispute, wanted matters resolved as fast as possible, which meant, in practice, arraigning the miners' president for contempt of court. Under the vagaries of the law, though, the machinery had to be started that afternoon, otherwise proceedings would be postponed for several weeks. Thanks to Lilley, they had just got in under the wire.

Once started, the legal machinery ground inexorably forward. The union was fined £200,000 and ordered to purge its contempt by accepting that the strike had been unconstitutionally declared. It refused (as did Scargill himself, who had been personally fined £2,000; but that was paid by an anonymous benefactor and ceased to be part of the action) and on 25 October, after granting a postponement for reconsideration, Mr Justice Nicholls ordered sequestration of all the NUM's assets. When this produced only defiant non-cooperation, and the revelation that most of the money had been deliberately squirrelled away abroad, the court's response was to put all NUM finances under the control of an officially appointed receiver. That, at last, brought Scargill, Heathfield and McGahey into court, but their appeal failed. From 1 December, they effectively lost all control over the union's affairs; and although in practice this did not prove an absolutely crippling handicap, it seriously and progressively limited any genuine freedom of manoeuvre.

Legal problems, however, were only part of the darkening picture. Scargill had a minor personal triumph at the Labour conference – and acutely embarrassed the party leader, Neil Kinnock – by winning heavy support for a motion blaming all strike-related violence on the police. But after that very little went right. The back-to-work movement gathered momentum. The backing from other unions, so fulsomely promised at Brighton, had almost wholly failed to material-ise. Nacods, who had looked like a promising ally, allowed themselves to be written out of the script, and yet another semantic bout with the Coal Board had ended on 31 October when it proved impossible to bridge the gulf between pit closures decided 'in line with the principles of the Plan for Coal' and those agreed 'in line with the broad strategy of the Plan for Coal'. The Libyan affair continued to reverberate, alienating sympathy both at home and abroad – especially among the Italians, with their deep-seated hatred of the Gaddafi regime – which was a serious matter with 75 per cent of the miners' financial support now coming from foreign unions.

Hardship and privation in the pit villages, despite miracles of improvisation, particularly by the women's support groups which flourished everywhere and played an immensely im-portant part in keeping up flagging morale, was reaching levels impossible to ignore. Deaths of men and boys trapped trying to dig coal out of abandoned waste-heaps were now well into double figures, even before the winter properly started; while the prospect of power cuts and fuel shortages, on which so much hope had been placed, receded further with every new set of confident Whitehall forecasts. As early as 9 November, Jack Eccles, the General and Municipal workers' North-West regional secretary, who also happened to be the current TUC chairman, so far forgot himself as to say, in a radio interview: 'My personal view is that with the strike dragging on for so long, a 100 per cent victory is no longer possible. How much longer the suffering must continue before it is realised by striking miners that the objectives of their principal officers cannot be reached, I don't know.' He was promptly hauled over the coals by the general secretary, Norman Willis, but only because he feared that the expression of such thoughts threatened to damage the movement's already fragile unity and to jeopardise any role it might have as honest broker. With Eccles's underlying sentiment there was little disagreement, and it was now that Willis, with extreme patience and caution, started to explore

227

for some way in which the whole bitter, intractable mess could be not too damagingly resolved.

A necessary first step though was to establish his own credentials. After many years in Len Murray's shadow, Willis was little known outside the TUC bureaucracy, and despite his well-upholstered girth he was often regarded as rather a lightweight. He comprehensively invalidated that view with one bold and powerful speech. At Aberavon, in the heart of the totally strikebound Welsh coalfield, he forthrightly condemned the violent excesses that had been committed on the picket lines, and was rewarded with a screaming chorus of boos and catcalls, and the dangling of a noose over his head. But that evening he also won recognition that a man of real substance had projected himself on to the national stage.

Even before Eccles's rash interjection, the TUC inner cabinet had been made well aware of the strike's poor chances. John Monks, Congress's head of industrial relations, had frankly summarised them in a confidential report presented on 7 November, where he pointed out that union efforts to block the vital oil supplies had had 'little discernible effect', that there was little early likelihood of 'crucial fuel shortages at the generating stations' and that, in the absence of any further talks scheduled between the main parties, 'prospects for an early settlement of the dispute are remote'. If the TUC was not happy about the situation, it was clearly implied, it would have to devise some way of getting more effectively into the act.

Willis took the best part of a month to prepare his move, working in secrecy so deep that the details here are being given for the first time. As 1984 neared its end and the strike entered its tenth month, the general perception was that the TUC had largely gone to sleep on the subject. On 5 December there were two major speeches, from opposite ends of the political spectrum, both taking them to task for their lassitude. Leon Brittan, the home secretary, in an attack so vehement that it caused John Prescott, the shadow employment minister, to walk out, said that all union support should be withdrawn from the miners unless they showed themselves prepared to obey the law. Meanwhile, Mick McGahey, at a rally in Alloa, Central Scotland, complained that Congress had still failed to deliver on its two-month-old Brighton promises.

Even while they were speaking, Willis and another six of the TUC's top leaders were deep in discussion at the department of energy, urgently seeking some formula to settle the dispute with Peter Walker, Tom King the employment secretary, and a gaggle of their senior civil servants. This meeting, which has never even been reported to the TUC general council, was the first of three – two before Christmas and one far into the New Year – where the energy secretary held lengthy, detailed talks with 'The TUC Seven', Willis, David Basnett, Ray Buckton, Moss Evans, Bill Keys, Jack Eccles and Gerry Russell. It took place in the minister's light, airy office overlooking the Thames, where the relevance of the decorations, which include a sombre painting of a Durham pit village and a Calman cartoon depicting Walker as an unashamed 'wet', was not lost on the visitors. Conversation started fairly coolly, but then developed into what all the participants prepared to discuss the occasion describe as a 'friendly' encounter.

Walker, who himself has never talked about it, began with a lucid description of the government's point of view. Scargill, he said, had embarked on a war he could not win. With coal stocks still high, and the oil-burning stations in first-class order, there was no longer any doubt that the winter would pass without power cuts. The Cabinet was by no means totally inflexible: it remained eager for an 'honourable settlement', if one could be obtained. But it would not in any circumstances countenance a deal that Scargill could present as a victory. The impression conveyed to at least one of those present was that the government would quite like an early settlement, mainly to staunch the strike's growing drain on the economy, but while the NUM refused any real concession on the closure question it saw no reason to sue for peace. The union leader who formed that opinion wrote in his diary later that night: 'Not a very productive meeting, but at least it has opened the door.'

What the TUC Seven had brought to the secret meeting were the first glimmerings of an idea. After months of what one of the team called Scargill's 'scholastic point-scoring' over Plan for Coal – did it or did it not make any reference to the closure of pits on economic grounds? – it had occurred to them that the much-quoted but little-read plan might itself contain the seeds of a workable compromise. Certainly by this time they were under pressure from an increasingly desperate NUM to do something, and most of the stated demands were either unattractive or unattainable. On the solidarity front, they were being asked to mount all-out industrial action to reverse the courts' 'most vicious threat in our history to the freedom and independence of British trade unions', while financially the request was that they should shoulder the whole of the NUM's operational burden. Specifically the suggestion was that they should take a lease on some of the union's Sheffield property so that it could 'function normally' despite the efforts of the receiver, and at the same time contract to make up the salaries of any staff that he elected to dismiss, and to provide funds for day-to-day operation – all of which efforts to maintain an 'NUM-in-exile', they were advised, would put them too in contempt of court.

The proposed alternative, sketched to Walker on 5 December and formally put to him a week later, built on the fact that Plan for Coal, even in its most recent 1977 version, was very vague about prospects for after 1985. That seemed to provide a legitimate opportunity for making a fresh start. The main proposal embodied in the four-part TUC scenario was that all the strikers should go back to work while the plan was rewritten to 'include among other things market and output prospects as well as employment and community strategy' – a formulation which would have greatly expanded the context in which closures had previously been discussed. Meanwhile both sides should guarantee no victimisation and the Board agree not to proceed with its 6 March programme, and keep the five named pits in operation until it was possible to determine their future under the new arrangements. To Willis the great attraction was that this could be presented not as an outright victory for anyone, but as a mutually accepted gesture to ensure the future of the industry.

After the unreported 5 December session, the first decision to be made by Willis's liaison group was how to proceed. They believed that Walker had not closed the door on their approach, and they had Scargill's assurance that he would not oppose fresh talks. But should they go public, or remain in the shadows? Keys, leader of SOGAT 82 and an experienced negotiator, favoured continuing in private, as did Willis himself; but in the end the majority, swayed by Basnett's urging that they must be seen to act, voted to announce that the next Walker meeting (which was the first as far as the rest of the world knew) had been set for 14 December. The atmosphere there was again serious and businesslike, but taking place as it did in the full glare of publicity, it was unsurprising that there should have been a perceptible hardening in Walker's stance. He welcomed the TUC's initiative, but thought it necessary to remind them of one unpalatable fact. Throughout all the 'many hours and days of negotiation' the NUM, he said, had consistently adhered to one basic proposition, that there could be no pit closures on uneconomic grounds. 'This was a view which had been unacceptable in the past, even under Labour governments, and it was unacceptable now and would be in the future.' With no sign of a change of heart from the miners' leaders, even the faintest hope of peace by Christmas evaporated into smoke.

Ironically, it was Christmas, more than any other single factor, which did most to weaken morale in the communities sustained by Britain's 174 remaining coalmines. Not because it was a dismal flop, with hungry children grizzling for a Santa Claus who would never come. Quite the reverse. It had been so carefully prepared, worked so hard for and looked forward to for so long that it could hardly fail to be an enormous, heart-warming success. The trouble was, once it was over there was nothing – just the certainty of ever-tightening hardship and ultimate surrender. The realists had known this for weeks, if not months. At St John's colliery in mid-

Glamorgan, the thirty-three-year-old lodge secretary, Ian Isaacs, had made his own clear-eyed assessment as the funds diminished and the effectiveness of the pickets, never overwhelming, steadily ebbed away. A Militant supporter, who had written his diploma thesis at Ruskin College, Oxford, on the fabled radicalism of his home town, Maesteg, his whole philosophy revolved round a belief in the power of the well-organised worker, but he had looked at the signs this time and drawn his own conclusions. 'The strike was all done on a haphazard basis. We should have billeted our men in towns where power workers live and really worked at getting to know them and convincing them. We reached the stage where we didn't even have the money to travel to see the power station people. By November we were logistically beaten.'

Such doubts were well hidden, and not for public consumption. But by the time the last candle had been blown out and the last beautifully wrapped toy distributed (130,000 of them from the French trade unions alone) they had become almost common currency. The miners' traditional spirit of communal self-reliance, strongly reinforced for the past nine months by shared detestation of the police, the DHSS and the London-based news media, had performed wonders in sustaining life and morale for so long. Now, inexorably, it started to run out of steam.

In places like Dawdon, County Durham, Christmas did not creep up unawares. It was planned from the early autumn, when the miners' wives making up the Dawdon women's support group first decided that every striker's 'bairn' should have at least a present and a party. They raised £2,000 in the end with bingo, raffles and a sponsored fancy-dress walk. The police on local picket duty clubbed together to put in £70. Five hundred free turkey dinners were laid on at the welfare club, and £27 laid aside to give every grown-up a small glass of wine. Parties were everywhere – tramps costume for the children (so no tactless non-striker's infant could show off in a new dress), school parties, wives' parties, NUM official parties, and the Christmas Eve disco at the welfare.

There were similar scenes throughout the coalfields. In Maesteg there was £100 from Australia, so every small child could have a £1 coin. At Cortonwood, the gallows outside the 'Alamo' picket-hut with its crudely stuffed dummy and the label 'This is for scabs' had been replaced by a tinselled Christmas tree and a large cheerful sign offering seasonal greetings to all who passed. The branch secretary at Bold, outside Liverpool, made a special trip to Cook's to cash the 20,000 deutschmarks – £5,100 worth – collected by sympathisers in Stuttgart. Mrs Rose Tennant stayed till the last moment in the streets of North London collecting cash and donations before dashing back to Shirebrook with the £700 that she, her friends in the support group and an East London emergency delegation calling itself Send a Santa to Shirebrook had managed to get together. Countrywide such efforts raised a total of £294,000. But then it was all over, and brutal reality reasserted itself.

In fact it had never gone away. In Tonyrefail, in the Rhondda, one of the many villages whose own pit has long closed and whose men in normal times drive many miles each day to work, groups of striking miners stood outside the corrugated-iron welfare hall waiting for opening time. But although it was the day before Christmas Eve, there was no party arranged – instead the clumsily written notice pinned to the door read: '3.30 pm for veg parcels'. The day before it had been groceries, and the next day would produce a turkey, bought from cash donated by the relatively affluent and non-mining citizens of Swansea. And even the contents of such parcels needed to be watched. Ever since the previous May, when reliance on handouts began, wives at the St John's support group had been carefully logging values to make sure that the flour, beans, peas, soup, eggs, rice and teabags in each bag they distributed did not come to more than £3.40, after suggestions swept round the pit areas that social security payments might be docked if the figure rose above £4.

Some union officials, even at local level, remained fiercely determined to ignore such mundane considerations. As Richard Evans, the red-bearded branch treasurer at Tonyrefail

said, as he presided over the distribution of the veg. packs:
'This strike has gone beyond the industrial. Thanks to the
attitude of the police and judiciary it has become political.'
But his colleague in the next valley at Nantgarw, Noel
Stevens, was less sanguine: 'We have just got to sit it out and
make the best. There's nothing else we can do. It's out of
our hands. It's all up to our national executive and the
government.' In Dawdon, on the north-east coast, trapped
between Sunderland (male unemployment 26.3 per cent) and
Hartlepool (male unemployment 30.1 per cent), the late
December fog rolled in and shrouded the pit's 660,000-tonne
stockpile of power-station coal. As the security guards closed
ranks against predators, the village reconciled itself to buying
an evening's fuel supply at £1.25 a bag – a fifth of a wife's
supplementary benefit, if she was lucky enough to draw it –
and looked bleakly forward into 1985.

With the New Year, the small, tell-tale cracks began to
show. Chesterfield football club withdrew its concessionary
admission charge for striking miners (£1.20 instead of the
usual £2) on the grounds that more than half the men in
North Derbyshire were now back at work. The South Wales
NCB put up £700 to sponsor a Glamorgan striker, so that he
could join Mother Theresa in India and get himself off the
picket line. And at Nantgarw, two selectors resigned from
the local rugby club because their best winger had abandoned
the strike and they could not bring themselves to pick a scab.
    Indeed there were ominous stirrings all round the Welsh
valleys. In December the area had clearly emerged as the
last bastion of serious resistance, with twenty-one of the last
twenty-six pits still without a single miner signing on. But as
the months passed, the priorities of both leaders and rank
and file had progressively diverged from those expressed in
the gospel according to Scargill. In places like Merthyr Vale,
nestling under the grim shadow of Aberfan, there are virtually no jobs for a redundant man to go to. A warehouse
and factory built ten years ago by Hoover lies empty, in mint
condition, and defies all efforts, from the Welsh secretary

Nicholas Edwards down, to find an interested buyer. Bill King, the Merthyr branch secretary, had never argued that every pit job should be preserved regardless of cost, only that something should be done to start replacing the 4,000 jobs already lost in the district since 1979.

Such modest objectives, and the patent magnitude of the problems, attracted a level of local backing unmatched in any other coalfield. The Wales Congress for the Support of the Mining Communities, a diverse combination of Plaid Cymru, the Labour movement and the Welsh churches, used its considerable influence in helping to keep the strike solid, at a time when it was visibly eroding elsewhere, and in return won significantly enhanced authority within the union. It was ready with strong encouragement when the Welsh pitmen's leaders, now deeply doubtful about their national president's negotiating strategy, decided to initiate a search for some more promising alternative.

Their scepticism was not noticeably assuaged by the events of Monday, 6 January, when Scargill went to Birmingham to meet the union's fifty or so hard-core, broad-left activists who gathered once a fortnight throughout the strike to discuss progress and plans. The NCB had claimed a total of 700 'new faces' returning since New Year's Day, and MacGregor had made one of his now rare television appearances that very morning to predict a further surge. Everyone expected that the sole item on the agenda would be a searching examination of the options that still remained open. So Eric Clarke, the jovial Scottish area secretary who chaired these affairs, was somewhat astounded to have a thick wad of documents suddenly thrust into his hand, covering two items that had almost no direct connection with the day-to-day running of the strike. They were, however, dynamite. One, dressed up as a long-overdue tidying-up of voting structures, would have had the effect of abolishing the union's 41-year-old federal structure, ending the jealously guarded autonomy of the individual areas, and setting up 'a single national organisation to embrace all workers within the British coalmining industry'. The second, even more immediately disruptive, proposed the expulsion of Nottinghamshire, the second-largest

235

area and, with the exception of Yorkshire, the only net contributor to NUM funds, as punishment for its rule-changing effrontery in December.

Discussion of these moves more or less eclipsed the strike, both in Birmingham and at the NUM executive meeting that followed, except that the president took the opportunity to slip in a proposal that in future negotiations with the NCB should be conducted not, as hitherto, by just himself, McGahey and Heathfield, but by the whole executive. This was to pre-empt rumblings in the ranks, notably from Northumberland's Dennis Murphy, that no one outside the troika really knew what was going on; but in fact it turned out to be irrelevant. The Board showed no interest, and no talks within this wider forum ever took place.

The national executive met on 10 January, and despite the misgivings of many members, including McGahey, recommended the whole package to a special delegate conference on 29 January. The two Notts members, Ray Chadburn and Henry Richardson, abstained, but that did not help them when they returned to their home base. At a stormy meeting of the Notts area council, Richardson was stripped of his secretaryship, and the rule changes releasing the area from its obedience to Sheffield defiantly reaffirmed. A week later, in snowbound Mansfield, Chadburn apologised emotionally to his working members for telling them, nine months before, to 'get off their knees', but could only answer 'I can't, I can't!' when they called on him to forsake Scargill and throw in his lot with the rebels. Richardson, determined to fight his dismissal, was still receiving all official correspondence in his capacity as secretary-in-exile, bringing a forthright response from Roy Lynk: 'I don't care if Henry Richardson calls himself the Shah of Persia, I'm the general secretary of Notts.' The union was now clearly on course for a split from which it might never recover, and in case any NUM leader should underestimate the danger, South Derbyshire, which had also worked from the beginning, was agreeing that same day in Buxton to ballot its members on rule changes which would give them the same independence as the Nottingham men.

236

While South Wales sought some new way to break the negotiating deadlock – the best idea on offer at that time was an elaboration of the Nacods independent review body, actively being canvassed by Welsh church leaders – Scargill and the Yorkshire president, Jack Taylor, were trying to staunch the drift back to work that was now well established even in the strike's original heartland. At the county's biggest pit, Kellingley, where the branch delegate, Howard Wadsworth, had become so apprehensive about falling morale that he had written to every miner asking him if he now, belatedly, favoured a strike ballot, Scargill turned up on 19 January to rally the men and tell them that the dispute had reached 'crunch time'. Many in the crowd noticed that, almost for the first time since March, he did not once use the word 'victory'. Returnees in many places were now so numerous that it had become undiplomatic to utter the standard imprecations. 'You go on the picket line and shout,' said Albert Bowns, the pit delegate at Kiverton Park which the South Yorkshire police a month before had put at the top of their list for sustained defiance, 'but it's just going through the motions. It's very difficult for neighbours to call each other scabs.' That doubtful honour was now reserved for the seven who had gone back on 22 August.

The NCB, still unstreamlined after fifteen months of MacGregor, remained riddled with strange joint bodies where miners and management, whatever their macro-differences, continued to meet throughout the strike. At one of these, the Coal Industry Social Welfare Organisation (CISWOL), Peter Heathfield had the chance, on 16 January, to exchange a few words with Ned Smith on the possibility of setting up new 'talks about talks'. Both agreed to seek clearance from their respective principals, and tentatively wrote 21 January in their diaries.

There were people in both Whitehall and the Board at that time who would have been happy to leave the NUM, as one of them said, 'swinging in the wind'. Nevertheless MacGregor gave his approval, and the talks duly took place.

237

But ministers, not for the first time, were only belatedly and partially informed about what was happening, so the session was almost ready to start before anyone in government even knew it had been arranged. The lobby briefing that afternoon from Bernard Ingham, the Prime Minister's press secretary, was distinctly negative, stressing that before any real bargaining began there must be a clear guarantee from Scargill that this time he really would address the issue of uneconomic pits. When Heathfield bought an *Evening Standard*, shortly after leaving what he thought had been a useful encounter, he was astonished to read in large headlines that the talks had got nowhere. Smith was equally angry when he turned on his television to see his colleague Michael Eaton saying much the same.

In fact this particular initiative, which, as the ultra-cautious Smith–Heathfield minutes show, was only the most tentative and preliminary attempt at re-establishing contact, was dogged by disaster. Downing Street's unhappiness, already profound, was deepened further three days later when *The Times*, after an NUM executive meeting, reported that there was already 'a draft peace agreement'. MacGregor, made unequivocally aware of this feeling, now backtracked and argued that Smith and Heathfield had substantially exceeded their brief.

The main outcome of the débâcle was to promote the idea of a written promise from the NUM that it was prepared to help solve the problem of uneconomic capacity before there could be any more conciliation attempts. This had been first suggested in a letter from MacGregor to Stan Orme the previous November, but now, despite Smith's warning that the NUM was being asked to do something that had never been imposed on another union in the whole history of industrial relations, it became a central condition for further progress.

This was the signal for the TUC to get back into the act. Willis's Seven had not lost contact with the energy secretary, but they recognised that there were many difficulties in the way of a settlement, not all of them created by the government or the NCB. They did not like either the guarantee-in-advance or Scargill's flat veto on any wording that contained a synonym for 'uneconomic'. That, they believed, had scuppered their notion of rewriting the Plan for Coal, and they fared no better with a compromise they suggested based on the fact that the NUM had been happily operating the 1972 Colliery Review procedure for years, and that it contained a specific reference to closing pits when they no longer had a market for their coal. When the miners came back saying that although they had used the procedure they had never actually ratified it, one despairing member of the Seven exploded: 'Scargill would make a bloody good company lawyer, but he just isn't a negotiator.'

Willis was to some extent trapped. If he took too tough a line, as some of his prominent members advocated, he was in real danger of splitting his own seven-man negotiating team. He therefore rejected the strongly canvassed idea that the TUC should develop its best notion of an acceptable agreement, and then invite the NUM either to endorse it or go on alone, without any further promise of general union support. Instead he continued his behind-the-scenes explorations with MacGregor, but these bore little fruit. On 1 February he reported gloomily to the miners' executive that the Board 'appeared to feel their position was strengthening'.

The miners were not the only people worried by this. Nacods, seeing the return-to-work pressure inexorably building, feared that the demands being made on the NUM would undermine their own hard-won deal. On 24 January Peter McNestry had telephoned Peter Walker, telling him that the deputies would 'not stand idly by' if the government was simply intent on crushing the pit-workers. Although Walker assured him this was not the case, and that the Nacods agreement was 'sacrosanct', McNestry was not satisfied, and on 8 February, in a surprise move, a joint meeting of the Nacods and NUM executives called for a resumption of full negotiations without preconditions, a demand that was promptly rejected as offering nothing usefully new.

On 11 February, Willis resumed his own search for peace. By now he was regularly sleeping 'over the shop', in the flat above Congress House which is owned by the solicitors,

Robin Thompson & Co. With his trusted deputy Ken Graham, long recognised by Whitehall and others as a first-class 'fixer', he started a non-stop round of secret conclaves with MacGregor and Cowan, conducted in a series of flats and hotel rooms around Hobart House, and on 13 February had a document to show to Scargill and McNestry which he said embodied the Board's 'final' position. He warned them, however, that it contained 'difficult points', and indeed it did. There were three in particular. One asked the NUM to recognise that their interests were 'best served by the development of an economically sound industry'. The second laid down that any pit without further reserves 'which cannot be developed to provide the Board, in line with their responsibilities, with a satisfactory basis for continuing operations . . . will be closed'. And the third said bluntly that, at the end of whatever colliery review procedure might be agreed, the Board would make the final decision.

The NUM response was to reject the document out of hand, but McNestry thought he detected a double hint of opportunity. The formerly rock-like miners' executive seemed to be showing signs of restiveness and strain, and the NCB's words about pits being closed without further ado when their reserves ran down appeared to cut right across the Nacods assurances. In the early hours of Saturday, 16 February, he rang the NCB deputy chairman at home and, hearing a woman's voice, said cheerfully: 'Is that Mrs Cowan, because if it isn't I've got Jimmy by the balls.' His optimism was premature. Neither marital nor semantic leverage made any impact, and Cowan insisted that Willis had delivered the final offer.

McNestry's other observation, though, proved to have substance. The NUM was genuinely getting restive, and when Scargill proposed what amounted to a total rewrite of the NCB formula, his executive, unprecedentedly, knocked him back on point after point. Trevor Bell, leader of the coal industry clerical workers, did most of the talking, but he sensed he had the backing of at least the Yorkshire president, Jack Taylor, and the South Wales area secretary, George Rees. Both men had been warning the president that, failing a quick settlement, pressure to lead their increasingly desperate members back to work without an agreement would soon become irresistible. Bell insisted that they should concentrate only on the three key sticking points in attempting to amend the offer, and, against Scargill's wishes, the rest agreed.

Willis recognised a real swing of opinion, and immediately rang Cowan to build on this 'significant shift'. When they met the next day, Sunday, 17 February, he strongly advocated exploitation of the points the NUM now appeared to accept – the Board's duty to manage the industry efficiently and responsibility to decide a colliery's future, the modified Nacods review procedure, and the need to seek reconciliation and a restoration of relationships within the bitterly divided coalfields.

Cowan, once again, refused to budge, and when Willis reported back, after a wholly abortive four-hour talk, even Scargill seemed dismayed. He asked the TUC Seven to marshal whatever influence they had with the government to press for the three essential modifications which were now all the union sought. In response to a direct question from Ray Buckton, he confirmed that, if these changes were made, the NCB's amended document would form an integral part of a final agreement, struck and accepted in advance of any negotiations on other outstanding matters. Armed with that promise, the TUC men decided to go right to the top, in a last effort to persuade the government there was an alternative to seeking unconditional and humiliating surrender. After some discussion they resolved that they should ask to see the Prime Minister herself.

She agreed, and the meeting was set for the following morning, Monday, 18 February, just before she left for Washington. In its way it was a big breakthrough – Mrs Thatcher's first direct encounter with the TUC since her bitterly resented ban on union membership at the government's communications-monitoring centre in Cheltenham (GCHQ) and her first meeting, also, with its new general secretary. Initially there had been some official doubt about Willis, not least over the job that his wife Maureen had in Neil Kinnock's private office, but Walker, increasingly convinced of his ability even before the Aberavon 'noose' episode, had assured No. 10 that he was both completely trustworthy and fully in command of his team.

In their turn, the TUC group were much impressed by the Prime Minister's detailed grasp of her brief. Once she returned to the employment department under-secretary, Douglas Smith, to check an abstruse point in the Nacods agreement, but otherwise she showed a formidable and comprehensive grasp of the dispute – right down to the obscure and almost forgotten origins of the NCB's fifteen-year-old colliery review procedure. Nor was her interest confined to the business in hand: over coffee, before the talking started, she warmly inquired after David Basnett's son, tragically paralysed after a rugby accident, who they discovered was being treated in Stoke Mandeville hospital by the same consultant who was looking after Margaret Tebbit, one of the Brighton bomb victims.

At Mrs Thatcher's suggestion, Willis started the ball rolling. He repeated his judgement that there had been a 'significant shift', but explained that there was still real fear in the NUM that, by accepting in advance the Board's right to close any pit it deemed uneconomic, it would be abandoning all its long-established rights – and these were rights on which every other union, including Nacods, would also insist – to state a contrary case. He then lucidly rehearsed the objectionable points in the NCB document.

The Prime Minister said she appreciated the TUC's efforts to promote a settlement, but she insisted, as the internal minutes of the meeting show, that any agreement, whatever its contents, must be absolutely clear and unequivocal. 'It is not in anybody's interests to dodge the issues at the heart of the dispute. Unclear arguments contain the seeds of future disputes and the final settlement should be understandable to the miners and the public. Otherwise there could be belated accusations of bad faith.' But after that crisp exposition of her 'no fudge' philosophy, she showed interest in the view that the NUM had shifted its ground. 'The government,' she said, 'has great difficulty in judging the position of the NUM executive, particularly when NUM leaders make repeated public statements about the union's unchanged position.'

At this point Peter Walker stepped in, and after dealing with some problems connected with extending the Nacods agreement to include the NUM, he raised a crucial question. Did the NUM now agree that any fresh wording written into the NCB text would be part of a final deal and not just an agenda for further talks? Mrs Thatcher added: 'Yes, that is a very important point.' It was also precisely the point that Buckton had cleared with Scargill before they agreed to proceed to No. 10. Willis said he had no doubt that his colleagues would correct him if they disagreed, but he was personally sure that was the case. The rest of the Seven nodded their unanimous assent, and the substance of the business was complete. In fact things had proceeded so expeditiously that they finished well within the hour allotted, and for form's sake another round of coffee and biscuits was ordered to fill out the time.

With Mrs Thatcher in full accord, Walker and the Seven sat down that evening to thrash out the final details. The most important change was to modify the bald assertion that pits with inadequate reserves 'will be closed' to make it clear that any shutdown proposal, whatever its rationale, would go through the modified closure procedure which it was hoped to set up by 1 June 1985, and that if that date could not be met the old procedure would continue to apply. It fell far short of the NUM's hopes, as the TUC team recognised, but when they foregathered the following morning at the elegantly furnished Goring Hotel in Victoria, for their final base-touching session with MacGregor, they were in little doubt that they had gone as far as they could go.

Willis, however, thought it his duty to relay to the NCB people the objections he thought the NUM were bound to raise, and he did this at such relentless and repetitive length that even his colleagues grew restless. Finally MacGregor intervened and threw a buff envelope across the table, drawling: 'Mr Willis, I think you godda read this.' The letter inside was the definitive answer to Willis's pleadings, concluding

243

with the words 'having given careful consideration to your view, I wish to make it clear that this must now constitute our final wording'.

The bizarre, not to say farcical series of misunderstandings and muddled arrangements that followed made almost complete nonsense of the TUC efforts, and contributed largely to the strike's final, inconclusive outcome, the return-to-work-without-an-agreement which was now being more and more widely canvassed, particularly in South Wales. Willis himself had been appalled at the idea when he first heard it from Scargill a week earlier. In an impassioned denunciation, he argued, from all his own and his father's half-century of combined industrial relations experience, that such a course could only represent defeat, and be universally seen as defeat. It would not leave the NUM with a single negotiating leg to stand on when they tried to deal with outstanding isssues like the corrosive question of amnesty for the growing army of sacked strikers, and might well also jeopardise all the industry's existing structure of agreements and procedures. Scargill listened impassively, without committing himself, but Willis determined he would do everything he could to find a better way. Events, personalities and even the Congress House geography conspired against him.

The day of the MacGregor meeting, 19 February, Scargill and his twenty-six-man executive had spent the morning at TUC headquarters. The Seven taxied back from the Goring at lunchtime and Willis sat down to write them a careful progress report, having deputed Roy Jackson, head of the TUC education department, Assistant General Secretary to look after the miners' president, offer him a snack lunch, and warn him that the meeting they had already arranged for 2.30 that afternoon might be slightly delayed. Scargill, TUC leaders insist, accepted this without demur.

When the rest of the NUM executive turned up, on the dot of 2.30, they were told nothing of this. Scargill gave them the impression that he knew nothing of what had transpired that morning and was as much in the dark as they were about any new version of the Board's document. He suggested they might as well disperse for the afternoon, just so long as they left their telephone numbers. Grumpily they swept past reporters and returned to their hotels. David Hunt, the coal minister, was astonished to bump into Alex Eadie, one of the NUM-sponsored MPs and a regular executive attender, back at the Commons before 3.30. 'That was a short meeting, Alex,' he said. 'How did it go?' When Eadie told him nothing had happened, Hunt exhorted him to go back and find out what on earth was going on.

When Willis and his senior TUC officials turned up a few minutes late for the meeting, they were furious to find that Scargill had sent his people away. Protesting his innocence, the miners' leader insisted he was not trying to be unhelpful, but the damage was done. When the executive members straggled back, bad-tempered and irritable, they were in a far from ideal mood to consider a patently less than perfect deal on its objective merits. Nevertheless they listened in receptive silence, ranged round the horseshoe table in the TUC's fifth-floor general council meeting room, as Willis expounded the latest and final NCB offer. He did not read out MacGregor's covering letter, an omission for which he was later criticised by some NUM moderates, but he did convey its blunt message. Exhorting consideration of the proposals 'with very great care', he added: 'When we last met, the position was fixed. Since then changes have been made. But the executive should be aware that it is the clear judgement of the liaison committee that no further changes are achievable. That is the judgement of us all. We have been told that in writing by the NCB. The changes that have been made have been wrung out of those concerned after the TUC had made the case at the highest possible level. There is no higher to go.'

The first question, from Jack Taylor, the Yorkshire president, was whether he had understood correctly that the NUM would have no right to make further changes in a document which, after all, had been negotiated by intermediaries. That somewhat surprised Willis as Taylor had been present when just that point was thrashed out and agreed a week before, but he contented himself with saying, tactfully, that the NCB would be willing to provide 'clarification' of any points the

NUM desired (an offer that was never taken up). He admitted, in answer to further questioning, that the Board had held out no hope of an amnesty for sacked strikers, but observed that once the crucial wording on closures had been agreed, the way would be open for further negotiations on other matters. Then he and the Seven withdrew.

The storm signs, by then, were clearly in view. When Scargill, on his own, had been shown the final revision earlier in the afternoon, he had flicked quickly and contemptuously through it and told the TUC staff around that it was '100 per cent worse' than the earlier draft. Heathfield then read it more slowly, but he too pushed it away in disgust before reaching the end. Now the whole executive, moderates and radicals alike, took their cue from the leadership and dismissed the whole effort as a waste of time. Even the normally affable president of the Northumberland miners, Dennis Murphy, cuttingly dismissed Willis as 'a boy sent to do a man's job'. The contrary view of the Nacods executive, that important improvements had been made, was impatiently tossed aside, and the NUM's reconvened delegate conference, meeting the following morning, accepted Scargill's advice almost without debate and overwhelmingly rejected the deal.

The Willis initiative was over and the strike would go on – but not for long. The money was running out – even while deriding the TUC's mediation effort, the miners were pleading for cash to replace the £8m. funds frozen by the sequestrator in Luxemburg and Dublin, and top up the bulging but quite inadequate suitcases full of cash which leftwing unions at home and abroad were prepared to drop off at the Sheffield headquarters, or even occasionally Scargill's Barbican flat. But Willis consistently refused, on clear legal advice that such help would never be safe, either from the sequestrators or from Michael Arnold, who had been appointed the NUM's official receiver. Union support, such as it was, had also started to run increasingly thin. Even the faithful railwaymen had been writing to the TUC expressing concern at the threat to their jobs, as a direct result of the sacrifices they had made for the miners. As NUM officials talked darkly about the 'dishonourable men' who were letting them down, leading

TUC figures like Terry Duffy, of the engineers, saw even less point than before in letting the miners kid themselves that more industrial aid might be forthcoming.

Meanwhile, on 25 February, the Notts area council, after a 2:1 vote at the pits, finally decided to call off the overtime ban which they had loyally operated since it was first called in October 1983, a gesture which would add another 100,000 tonnes a week to the government's already adequate stockpile. For any striker nearing the end of his patience or his resources, there was no lack of writing on the wall.

The proliferating feeling of frustration and pointlessness now began to crystallise firmly round the notion that Willis had so passionately denounced to Scargill. The mass return to work, with its connotation of 'peace with honour' and 'heads held high' and 'living to fight another day' had a clear appeal, even if it left everything unresolved. First floated in public by Mick Costello, the industrial correspondent of the *Morning Star*, after a casual chat with some Yorkshire miners, it was taken up in a February radio interview by Dr Kim Howells, the forceful and imaginative spokesman for the South Wales NUM (who incurred Scargill's wrath and got himself temporarily suspended for his pains), and after that it took on a life of its own.

It was on Tuesday, 26 February that it came to full flower. Mardy, the last pit in the Rhondda, had been a symbol of iron-hard resistance for generations, ever since it won the name of 'Little Moscow' in the turbulent 1920s. That night 600 of the 700 strikers there packed into Ferndale Workingmen's Hall and Institute for perhaps the most significant single lodge meeting in the whole year-long agony of the strike. From behind the building's flaking four-storey façade came a message which quickly spread across the country. In the words of Arfon Evans, the thirty-six-year-old branch chairman: 'There was a clear recognition that Thatcher was not going to allow the kind of settlement we could sign and that the best way to stop the NUM being smashed was an orderly return to work.' Mardy had spoken, and the rest of Britain's battered coalfields could not be far behind.

Chapter 14

The Final Hours

A Scottish miner, soaking after six hours in the rain, and hoarse from shouting 'No surrender!', screamed out his own verdict as Arthur Scargill emerged from Congress House to announce, tight-lipped and white-faced, that the strike, after the narrowest of votes, was now effectively at an end. 'We've given you our hearts, we've given you our blood, we've given you everything, and then you sell us out. You're tarred and feathered with the rest of the scabby bastards.' His incoherent rage, as with the rest of the sodden crowd, was indiscriminately directed, but certainly more towards the ninety-eight faint-hearted or realistic delegates who had finally swung the decision than to the still defiant NUM president, who had just ringingly thanked them, from the bottom of his heart, for the part they had played in 'the greatest industrial struggle ever seen'. As he retreated again into the hall, many of the strangled, weeping voices assured him: 'Arthur, you've been betrayed.'

The delegate conference, on Sunday morning, 3 March 1985, had been called the previous Thursday, 28 February, after an inconclusive seven-hour meeting of the NUM executive and an endless series of fruitless telephone calls between Sheffield and Hobart House. Bleakly, Scargill told reporters:

'It appears that the NCB, at the insistence of the government, is not prepared to negotiate. It is a complete war of attrition and we shall have to take a decision in the best interests of our members.'

For the next forty-eight hours every miners' lodge and branch in the country, outside the working areas, was locked in debate as to how those best interests should be defined. Even while the executive was in session, the Board claimed that another 1,114 men had gone back – the highest Thursday total throughout the dispute – and that the proportion working was now 50.75 per cent. But there was no unanimity on what should be done. Kent and Yorkshire still favoured carrying on until there was a full negotiated settlement. South Wales, with only 1,500 men who had given up the strike, reaffirmed its leadership of the movement to return to work in dignity but without an agreement. 'We came out as one and we will go in as one,' the area president, Emlyn Williams, told a packed conference at Porthcawl. Durham leaders, backing his call for a 'coordinated, orderly return', couched their support in more openly emotional terms. 'It is unreasonable on humanitarian grounds,' they said, 'to call upon the membership to endure still further pain and sacrifice to themselves and families in loyalty to the union.'

But for some, as was widely recognised, the pain and sacrifice would inevitably go on. This applied especially to the 728 who had been fired by the NCB for strike-related offences. Emlyn Williams recognised the problem and said there could be 'no reconciliation' until the forty sacked Welsh miners got their jobs back, but stopped short of making this an absolute precondition. Scotland went further and voted that there should only be an organised 'march-back' on the basis of achieving a general amnesty for all its 180 miners dismissed and 'victimised' during the dispute. Given the hardline attitude of the local area management this was patently a non-starter – a fact rammed home in a Friday press statement, issued in Edinburgh, tersely pointing out that, with 50 per cent of the area workforce already cutting coal, there could be no question of the union 'leading' anyone anywhere.

That night, on a television programme celebrating the strike's approaching first anniversary, Scargill made his last, half-joking, half-desperate, bid for peace. Facing Michael Eaton, the Board's chief spokesman, in front of the cameras, he suddenly produced a copy of the once despised Nacods agreement, and offered to sign it on the spot. 'If Mr Eaton wants to negotiate, is he prepared to settle on television tonight the Nacods agreement in its entirety with the NUM? If so I'll accept it.' But Eaton, unfazed, turned him down. It was far too late, he told him. The Nacods document was now inseparable from the full eight-point TUC plan, 'and you know it full well'. After that, it was clearly either capitulation or a fight to the end; and with another 1,656 miners back that day, there was dwindling room for real choice.

When the Sunday conference finally convened, however, at the TUC headquarters in London's rain-swept Great Russell Street, the outcome, though widely forecast, was still far from certain. Among the four main options – continuing the strike, accepting the NCB's offer, or giving up, with or without an amnesty – the second was regarded as a non-starter but opinion between the others remained so finely balanced as to constitute near-stalemate.

At the start this was literally true. The executive was so divided after considering the reports from the individual coalfields that it could make no recommendation. That so angered the floor that they were sent back to try again. After a tense thirty-minute wait, delegates heard that they were now split exactly eleven:eleven and that the president, as usual, had declined to use his casting vote. The strike would therefore, for the moment, continue.

When the main debate started, eight main resolutions were down for discussion. The hardest line, as expected, came from Kent, demanding continuation of the dispute and re-asserting the 'right to negotiate freely' with the NCB. This, in the end, was resoundingly defeated, by 170 votes to 19, and Scotland's call for a return conditional on a general amnesty went down by a similar margin. Another four assorted motions, from Northumberland, Durham, Durham Mechanics and Scottish Craftsmen, having been withdrawn, that left the floor free for a run-off between Yorkshire and South Wales. Yorkshire held fast for carrying on until at least there was agreement to re-empoly the sacked 728 and to clarify the future of the five 'named pits'. But ultimately it was the clear-eyed realism of the Welsh motion that carried the day. Accepting that there was now 'a drift back of members to work in all areas' and that 'the Coal Board have no intentions whatsoever to have any discussions with the union unless they sign the document presented by the TUC to the union on Sunday, February 17', it called for the dispute to be brought to an end without an agreement. The national executive were asked to negotiate an amnesty, but this should not be made a prior condition of the strike coming to a dignified and honourable end. Against eloquent opposition from the president and many others, the proposal was carried by ninety-eight votes to ninety-one (the Scottish result being precisely the other way round) and the greatest industrial storm to engulf Britain this generation began slowly and messily to subside.

The 'march-back', devised to pre-empt the increasingly humiliating 'drift-back', was planned to take place on the Tuesday morning. In the meantime there was an opportunity to count the cost to the country and to take a first look at the future. First estimates by the City stockbrokers Simon and Coates set the overall cash figure at £3.25 billion – roughly £140 for every working citizen – which would have made it far and away the most expensive dispute the country has ever experienced. The miners, allowing in full measure for the more nebulous factors of retarded growth and lost exports, boosted the total to an even more heroic £7 billion. Both these, however, probably represent a substantial exaggeration: not burning heavily subsidised, monopoly-protected coal is not as expensive as it can be made to look. The conventionally accepted bill was mainly made up of six items. The four smaller ones – £180m.–£200m. for extra policing, £200m. for British Steel, £200m. in lost traffic to British Rail, and maybe £350m. in uncollected tax and additional social security payments – are more or less in the right area; but the two big ones are much more arguable.

251

The first is electricity, which having used up £3.5 billion of oil and gas, saved £1.5 billion by burning less coal, and run down its grossly excessive coal stocks by £0.7 billion, can be plausibly argued to have lost between £1.3 billion and £2 billion. But that only works if the price of oil is taken as independently fixed. When British oil, 80 per cent of whose cost goes in tax to the Treasury, is substituted for British coal, which normally benefits from about 30 per cent worth of direct and hidden support, the sums are much less clear-cut – especially if any allowance is attempted for the impact of such substantial extra demand on an otherwise weak world oil market, with its consequential and far from unimportant effect on the exchange level of sterling. It was only appropriate that the first financial reaction to the strike's end was a drop in the value of the £.

Similarly, there is an apparently simple calculation which offsets £2.2 billion in unpaid coalminers' wages, unincurred operating expenses and unmade investments against £3.3 billion in undug coal, and produces a cash drain of £1.1 billion. But that is purely the impact on the NCB. In terms of cost to the nation it has to be shaded to take account of losses a high-cost coal industry would almost certainly have recorded if it had operated full-blast through a year of worldwide energy glut. But that of course if the kind of sum that the uneconomic-pit argument was never seriously allowed to get to grips with.

To the individual miners who had stuck it out until near the end, there were no such comforting macro-economic adjustments: on average they and their families were looking at a sacrifice of about £9,000 and precious little to show for it. The pits they were going back to in many cases also showed savage scars. Thirty-eight of the industry's 490 working coal-faces had been lost in the course of the strike, thanks to flooding, fire, or geological collapse. Eighteen more were already giving 'serious cause for concern' even before the first full safety checks could be carried out, and another twenty-two 'salvage faces' where valuable machinery had not been recovered were now mainly beyond hope. Although it was accepted that the five bellwether pits, Cortonwood,

Bullcliffe Wood, Herrington, Polmaise and Snowdown, would all be temporarily reprieved, at least long enough for them to go through some modified form of review procedure, that procedure itself was far from agreed, and the prospects for them and many others were deeply uncertain.

That certainly applied to Mardy, the last remaining pit in the Rhondda, where the decision to march back in unity with heads held high was carried out with all the moving dignity that its proposers had intended. Where once there were fifty-four mines, working the whole length of the valley, there is now only one, and that, just before the strike started, had reluctantly agreed to a semi-merger with Tower, on the other side of the hill, which would eliminate 200 surface jobs and, as all the men recognise, probably presage Mardy's closure altogether. Notwithstanding, the 753-strong workforce, not one of whom had abandoned the strike even for a single day, formed up on the Tuesday morning to follow their colliery band and the massed lodge banners for the long, slow, solemn trudge back into work. As dozens of foreign cameramen and television crews had accurately anticipated, it was a distillation of all that should be encompassed in an honourable surrender. The footage went round the world.

Elsewhere, though, the stage management left much to be desired. Chaos was the operative word, and it came in every conceivable variety. There were the men sent home by iron-jawed managers because they were five minutes late, having waited too long for their procession to form. There were mass walk-outs, like the 300-strong shift at Merthyr Vale who refused to work alongside a strikebreaker. There were quarrels at the pit gate, as at Ashington and Bates, in Northumberland, when the men refused to acknowledge new shift times set in their absence. At Ackton Hall in Yorkshire men were brusquely told to stop parading around with their banners or they would not be paid. At Six Bells, Abertillery and at Penrikyber it was Nacods men who disrupted proceedings – once because over-eager men had been allowed to start work underground unsupervised, and again because they had been subject to hostile abuse.

But the real hazard, as it quickly transpired, was still picketing. The Kent miners, with their three heavily lossmaking pits, Tilmanstone, Snowdown and Betteshanger, and their well established reputation for hardline militancy, had rejected the majority decision to go back without settling the amnesty issue. They fully endorsed the view of their leader, Jack Collins, who had stood outside Congress House on the Sunday warning: 'The people that have decided to go back to work and leave men on the sidelines, to unload these men, are traitors to the trade union movement.' On Tuesday morning they fanned out across the country to turn the march-back into a mockery.

They were not altogether alone, either. The Scots and a sizeable minority of Yorkshire miners shared their distaste for unconditional surrender, and it was a line of young Doncaster pitmen, encouraged by Kentish visitors, who halted the president himself in his tracks. Scargill, with a Scots piper in attendance, set off to lead 1,000 men into Barrow colliery, near Barnsley, but turned round and smartly marched them back again once he had appreciated the situation, saying 'I never cross a picket line.' Exploiting this attitude, even more deeply engrained after twelve months on strike, Kent miners turned up almost everywhere. At Trelewis Drift in mid-Glamorgan they turned back 271 of the returning marchers, though they were less successful at Blaenserchan in Gwent, where all but fifteen of the lodge's 411 members decided to ignore them. In Yorkshire, where there was a much more intensive effort at disruption, Kentish activity prevented an orderly resumption at twelve pits, including Askern, Hinckley, Frickley, Prince of Wales and Markham Main.

The most spectacularly ridiculous incident was at Corton-wood, where it all began. On Monday, 4 March, a year to the day from their own fuse-igniting walkout, the whole village community – barring the 'scabs' whose numbers had now swollen to ninety-two – turned out to share a bright-red birthday cake donated for the occasion by Mrs Anne Scargill, and to rehearse the procession that would take the men back the following day to work out whatever might be left of their pit's problematical future (which will, as has now been decided, cease at the end of 1985). To general amazement, four more 'new faces' had elected to go back that morning, twenty-four hours ahead of the mass return, thus risking a lifetime's obloquy for the sake of a day's pay, and the police were out in their usual hundreds to see that the armoured bus would safely complete its final journey. What nobody anticipated, as they abandoned the battered old Alamo picket-hut (now newly embellished with the sign 'Come home to a real fire, burn MacGregor'), was that when they marched back in the morning it would be full of Kentish strangers. The parade started to assemble around 8 am, hung around for fifteen minutes outside the welfare club waiting for the brass band that never turned up, decided that someone had forgotten to pass on the order, formed up behind the magenta and white lodge banner lettered 'United We Stand, Divided We Fall' and walked in ragged file down the quarter-mile hill to the colliery gate, where the new picket was waiting belligerently. After twelve months, though, another day here or there hardly seemed to matter, so all but two, who slipped through the pit gate regardless, decided quite amicably to take their lunchtime sandwiches home, and try again to-morrow.

It was an anticlimactic end to an extraordinary year, but perhaps appropriate to an event which, as one of its most perceptive reporters summed it up, had always managed to be simultaneously farcical and momentous, cruel and noble. Farce, in this case, had the last word. But even as he watched on his television some of the more nonsensical final-day antics, the South Yorkshire assistant chief constable, Tony Clement, who had seen more than his share of the strike's momentous and cruel aspect, drew a more sombre con-clusion. Even at the peak of the violence at Orgreave, he reckoned, there had never been more than 4,000 Yorkshire pickets who were genuinely committed, 'out every day, active and positive in what they were trying to achieve'. But when he saw the pictures at the end, with the 41,000 strikers in the county who had stuck it to the bitter end all returning more or less together, he realised for the first time the magnitude of the forces that could have been involved. 'If that sort of number had been out on the ground, we should never have been able to handle it,' he reflected later. But this time, it was over. By the end of the week, the last picket had evaporated, and the British coalmining industry, bruised, bitter and a great deal poorer, was precariously back at work.

Chapter 15

Aftermath

Four months after the miners had marched back, Sir Geoffrey Howe, the foreign secretary, attacked Arthur Scargill in terms which left no doubt that although the strike might be over, the dispute between the government and the NUM leader was not. 'For the first time in British postwar history' Howe told a Tory meeting in mid-July, 'we have seen a major trade union leader openly in league with countries which threaten our security, openly taking his storm troopers abroad for training in how to subvert our democratic, legal and economic systems, and less openly, importuning some of the least democratic governments in the world for financial contributions to his campaign against the British people.'

It was, by any standards, a fierce series of accusations; coming from Howe, who has the reputation of an oratorical plodder, such denunciation was even more remarkable. Yet it was hardly surprising. For Scargill was intent to make it equally clear that he regarded the year-long stoppage as merely an episode in the great working-class struggle against capitalism. If others took the view that the miners had suffered a crushing defeat, they were wrong. He and McGahey and Heathfield issued a joint statement in March

257

which asserted the exact opposite. 'All our future struggles will be stronger as a result,' they declared. The strike had inspired 'hope, effort and solidarity not only in Britain but around the world'. So much for Howe's attack on the NUM's international connections.

Moreover, Scargill's bravado was not without basis. In early July, he had secured the support of the first post-strike NUM conference for 'all actions' of the union executive which had led the strike. The union had challenged 'the very heart of the capitalist system'. Let no-one talk to him about defeat or setbacks. His only criticism was for others: 'a weak, collaborationist or non-existent trade union movement' which had allowed the government to withstand the strike; the Notts, north Derbyshire and Leicestershire miners, who had given the government 'a lifeline' as it waged class war against the union; the TUC, which has failed to provide desperately needed cash; and the media which had played a role 'of which Goebbels would have been proud'.

There was no hint of self-criticism. Those who cited the failure to ballot the national membership themselves failed to recognise the wrongness of doing so when 80 per cent were on strike. 'You have written history', he told the conference, where grim-faced Notts delegates sat impassively while others applauded. 'The only way is to fight again with the same determination, the same pride.'

Neil Kinnock thought otherwise. He immediately issued a statement intended to limit the damage Scargill's implicit threat of renewed strike action might do to Labour's chances in the Brecon and Radnor by-election that same week. He had listened to the families who had suffered on the coalfields, said the Labour leader. They spoke from bitter experience. They would never forget the strike or its lessons. 'Indeed they live daily with the realities of its results and the extra power now held by the Board.'

In terms that had obviously been carefully weighed to distance his party from Scargill's unabated militancy without risking an open breach with the NUM leadership, Kinnock laid it as near the line as he could. The Coal Board had won, the striking miners had lost. The only course now open to miners was the return of a Labour government. Anything else was fantasy.

Other union leaders had also urged that the lessons of the strike be learned. But Scargill was able to prove as the Commons prepared for its long summer recess that whatever others said, he was still a force to be reckoned with. Evidence of this came quickly after Kinnock's statement. Labour lost the Brecon and Radnor by-election to the Liberals by a 2 per cent whisker and Scargill was immediately blamed.

When Kinnock had Scargill on the same platform at the Durham miners gala the following weekend, he tried again to put the NUM leader in his place as a militant whose cries for battle should be stifled in the interests of the Labour government Scargill maintained he wanted. But Kinnock was trapped once more. He was also committed to backing NUM unity against the threatened breakaway by Notts miners and others. This put him automatically in Scargill's camp on the major issue currently before the NUM and it was this which ensured Kinnock's continuing plight as Labour struggled once more to shake free from the consequences of a strike that had caused Kinnock's colleagues to dub 1984 'Labour's lost year'.

The more Scargill refused to acknowledge defeat and the more Labour became ensnared in the NUM's internecine warfare, the more the government realised that they had a target too good to ignore. Peter Walker was quickest off the mark. He followed Scargill's post-strike manoeuverings as closely as he had watched the strike strategy. Howe's attack on Scargill's known Soviet-bloc links during the strike and the Libyan connection picked up themes that had brought forth a stream of Walker criticism at the height of the strike.

Howe's condemnation of Scargill 'storm troopers' going abroad for training referred to another episode Walker had been quick to denounce and which *The Sunday Times* had investigated. This was the NUM executive's decision to send twenty competitively selected activists to a Moscow institute which specialised in ideological training. If Scargill had purposely schemed to provide the government with fresh post-strike ammunition, he could not have been more successful.

259

To cap it all, he then moved against Notts in a way Howe thought worthy of Lenin's concept of power by democratic centralism.

Again Walker had moved fast to analyse what Scargill meant by the rule changes adopted by the NUM conference. An analysis prepared for Walker deduced that, despite assertions to the contrary, power would flow out of the NUM's historic federal structure, in which the areas have separate legal identities, and into the national hierachy in Sheffield. It was this threat which fuelled the Notts revolt and threatened to ensnare Kinnock in the union's internal affairs. For Labour cannot remain indifferent to a successful breakaway from a national union with which its links are historically so close. The TUC leadership, however critical of Scargill's leadership, was even more directly involved. For Labour can only affiliate unions that belong to the TUC, and TUC policy has always been sternly anti-breakaways.

For both Labour and the TUC, the miners' strike had a prolonged fallout. Kinnock had feared it but hoped that his good offices, combined with the shock of the strike's collapse, might mitigate its effects. But, as the strike's progress throughout 1984 showed, neither organisation used its influence to prevent the strike becoming a struggle to the bitter end, with striking miners finally deserting in droves, the union's federal structure in tatters and the government in the strongest industrial position since Mrs Thatcher came to power.

Indeed, the 1984 autumn resolutions of support by the TUC and Labour conferences make sombre reading in the light of the strike's finale. The TUC general council received overwhelming support in September for a statement urging that the dispute be made more effective by not moving coal, coke or oil in place of coal across NUM picket lines. The Labour conference in October was even more fulsome, paying tribute to the miners' 'historic struggle' and alleging organised violence against miners, their picket lines and their communities by an unconstitutional, nationally controlled police force.

Only the power union leaders exposed both resolutions as meaningless while the NUM was itself split and power stations and transport workers ignored the strike. They were booed but they were proved right. Kinnock had hoped that a compromise could be reached to accommodate both the industry's economic position and the miners demand for job security. He accepted that pit closures had been going on for twenty-five years but, after initially declaring himself in favour of a national ballot, slipped into neutral gear when this was rejected, arguing that the NUM's internal workings were a matter for the union and not the party. In July 1985, he had to accept that they had become unavoidably a party issue, and that behind-the-scenes efforts at compromise had failed. His leadership was on the line.

For the Tories, however, the prospects of ongoing ructions within the NUM and Labour party offered unexpected opportunities. It had not been so when the strike ended. The enormity of what had happened was not then apparent. The government determined that there was to be no gloating or partisan celebration at Scargill's humiliation. The memory was still fresh of Mrs Thatcher's commitment to defeat 'the enemy within', an unscripted comment to a private party meeting which carried overtones of the Falklands war and appeared to link the striking miners with the Argentine enemy. As the strikers trickled back, the Downing Street line softened. 'I want, as a government, to give hope to the striking miners,' Mrs Thatcher told Sir Alistair Burnet in January. 'They have suffered terrible privations and they must be worried to death about their debts.'

Highly secret contacts between Downing Street and the TUC in late 1984 had ensured that the same message got through. The TUC was assured in particular that there would be no revenge legislation against the unions after a miners' return to work. When the possibility was raised later of legislation against strikes in essential industries, Mrs Thatcher quashed it. Winning the TUC over was an important part of Walker's endgame strategy. He used all his negotiating skills, including the memory of his shop steward father, to do so and both he and the Prime Minister developed a high regard for Norman Willis, the incoming TUC general secretary, as a man of courage and integrity. Walker's court-

261

ship of the TUC fitted in with a strategy that was intended from the outset of his appointment as energy secretary to divide Scargill from his rank and file and from the rest of the trade union movement. Walker began by reading everything he could about Scargill, going back as far as mattered in his development as Britain's foremost militant.

Walker's conclusion was that Scargill was a dedicated and astute marxist revolutionary whose ambitions would lead him to challenge any government which stood in his way. Walker also knew from his own experience as industry secretary and environment minister in Edward Heath's government that the miners were a special part of the industrial scene. Any dispute involving them would be fundamentally different; and any strike led by Scargill would be that much more difficult. The aim was to play it long while Scargill was forced to play it short.

It worked but it was a closer call than it appears in retrospect. Walker prepared with meticulous care. Coal stocks were moved to give the power stations maximum endurance. Wearing his cabinet hat as the government's most prominent Tory wet, Walker secured agreement for a financial package that would smooth the way for pit closures without compulsory redundancies and with unprecedented retirement inducements. All was staked on Scargill being unable to win a national strike ballot, which he would need to confront the government. Was the NUM not wedded to its rule book which required a national ballot before there could be a national strike? So ran the Walker thesis.

His first shock was the Cortonwood row, which caught him totally unprepared and gave him an insight into how the coal board's diffuse structure could become dangerously shortcircuited. His second was Scargill's success in spreading strike action on an area basis, backed up by pickets.

Scargill, however, made his own miscalculation, which was to prove more enduring. Having failed to close the Notts coalfield in the way pickets had South Wales, where only ten out of twenty-eight pits had voted to strike, he was left with the problem of how to answer calls for a national ballot to settle the strike issue one way or another. It was a question he never resolved. When Brian Walden cross-examined him at length about it on Weekend World in the first month of the strike, he foresook the union rulebook and invoked the tradition of never crossing a picket line. He either failed to realise or chose to ignore that Notts had long become part of that growing trade union movement that prefers the rule-book to folklore and will not be swayed by emotional appeals or mass intimidation.

'We were just throwing money at the Notts area, a lot of money, day in and day out, sending pickets and getting nowhere at all, not even getting to the pits,' a Selby union official recalled afterwards. Mrs Thatcher and Leon Brittan had ensured that police action to keep Notts that way had full government backing. With this line of defence secure, Walker's daily inter-departmental committee was able to make Whitehall history by organising resistance to Scargill in a way that allowed maximum flexibility and instant decision-making far removed from the usual Whitehall routine of lengthy preparations and paperwork.

Scargill's route to victory became increasingly perilous as the government's became, in terms of energy resources, ever more secure. At the end, the phasing of Scargill's campaign was clearly identifiable to Whitehall watchers. He began by attempting a national strike without a ballot, turned to the use of mass picketing which was never massed enough, then appealed for help to other unions and finally relied on foreign finance to keep the strike going.

It was at all times, however, considered a basically political clash by the government. Early on, senior cabinet ministers shared Walker's view, endorsed throughout by Mrs Thatcher, that the strike was of major constitutional import-ance. To defeat it, and here the Falklands parallel is justified, the cost was relegated to minor importance, even in the Treasury's eyes. Nigel Lawson believed that it was a good investment. Mrs Thatcher and Walker were convinced that there was no other option open to them but to fight with every resource they could muster.

In the end, that was not necessary. Emergency regulations and the use of troops were never envisaged. Nor was the removal of pithead stocks from strike-hit pits, although Walker would not have hesitated to use his legal powers to move them, had the need arose. He had been an instant enthusiast of the possibilities of moving coal by road and swept aside Whitehall calculations of what was possible, predicting accurately that the road haulage industry would run all the blockades thrown at them to win the coal trade while it was there.

There were, all the same, on the government's side, moments of internal danger and anxiety at unforseen twists in the drama. Walker's strategy depended crucially on other unions not joining in. To keep them out, the Thatcher–Walker policy was to stress constantly the deal on offer to the NUM and avoid a widening of the dispute. Suggestions by some Cabinet ministers for new Tory industrial relations laws to be employed against the NUM by the Coal and Steel Boards were thus ruled out. A well-trailed Treasury move to impose a 'Scargill surcharge' on electricity prices in mid-1984 was similarly knocked into limbo for fear of an adverse reaction from the all-important power unions. Other potential dangers to the grand design were not so easily despatched. The dock strikes were roundly cursed and the Nacods dispute even more acutely regretted. Inside Whitehall the dispute continues about those responsible for these mishaps.

The Coal Board also came under a more glaring light than hitherto. Some ministers thought the NCB hierarchy to be inherently unreliable because of industrial or political background. Ian MacGregor was seen as a man without enough natural allies to see him through a conflict for which he was not suited. Had Mrs Thatcher expected there to be a long drawn-out fight of the kind that ensued, she would not have appointed a elderly American Republican to lead the NCB, it was claimed in Whitehall when MacGregor began to come under attack as a presentational disaster. But this was not the view advanced by ministers in the early days of the strike. He was then described as a nimble adversary, more than able to stand up to Scargill. In the media battle, it was Scargill who was seen to have the bigger problem. MacGregor also impressed visitors in the first few months with his grasp of what was at stake and the determination needed for victory. 'We're in a poker game,' he said in May. 'As the game goes on, the pressure builds up on both sides. The first one that blinks loses. I don't intend to blink.'

MacGregor, for all his years, was also not lacking in personal courage. Asked about the danger he faced, he replied: 'At seventy-two it doesn't matter very much. The Mafia once had a contract out on me from the Teamsters.' He was adamant that he would end up on the winning side. 'We're fighting for the future of this country,' he said, as the picketing approached its zenith. 'In poker, there cannot be a draw, only a winner and loser. And I will not be the loser.'

The strains of bringing the strike to an end nevertheless uncovered tensions inside the government–Coal Board machine, as well as elsewhere. MacGregor's indifference to the propaganda skills which became increasingly important brought the Downing Street–Walker axis into the forefront against expectations. MacGregor's chief attribute in Mrs Thatcher's eyes was that he never panicked in the face of Scargill's militancy. Yet there was no shortage of suspicion around Whitehall at what the other part of the machine was up to. Private accusations that there was always a danger of someone else buckling under were constant. It was the government's good luck that Scargill was in even more desperate straights on his internal front and that, as the strike progressed, the odds lengthened almost daily against him.

Scargill's presentational problems were even more curious to those who recalled the Joe Gormley era. Nell Myers, Scargill's press officer and close confidant, went on record afterwards to defend the union's belligerent attitude to the media. 'The industrial correspondents, along with broadcasting technicians, are basically our enemies' frontline troops,' she wrote in the *Guardian* in June 1985. They were responsible for nothing less than 'a cyclone of vilification, distortion and untruth'. The fact that the government was equally suspicious of industrial correspondents and preferred dealing with Westminster lobby journalists only added to the irony.

The dispute pointed up the importance of mass communications as no other strike had ever done. Television excelled in bringing picket-line violence into the living room and police excesses were not spared. Scargill's insuperable problem was the highly visible fact that the lights were burning at Christmas nine months after the strike to put them out had started. Walker knew well before Christmas that he had enough capacity to keep the lights on for the rest of 1985. By then, there was no way Scargill could win.

In one of the more perceptive of post-strike analyses, John Lloyd, industrial editor of the *Financial Times*, wrote that 'the real strike had a politically revolutionary dimension intertwined and indissoluble from its quite real industrial objectives'. It was this threat that motivated the government most and which kept Kinnock as much at arms length from the NUM as the picket-line violence. Mrs Thatcher never came under serious political pressure to abate her resistance to Scargill. The polls showed throughout that most people rejected Scargill's interpretation of what was at stake.

Walker was left, in the end, musing what kind of deal the miners could have had under a leader of the Gormley mould, determined to secure the best pay and conditions possible within the overall constraints of a nationalised industry run on criteria laid down by the state. But Scargill had long abandoned the Gormley style of the art of the possible and gone for more ambitious targets. He had, at least, been consistent in his vision of what union leadership meant. In his celebrated interview with *New Left Review* in 1975, he said that another crisis situation of the kind the coal industry underwent in 1972 and 1974 might produce conditions that made a socialist revolution possible.

Such a revolution might be nearer in a number of western countries than many people thought, Scargill opined. The events of 1984-85 seemed to exclude Britain, at least, from that count.

Index

Index

Index

Maxwell, Robert, editor 158, 183
Megarry, Sir Robert 113, 114, 117
Merthyr Vale pit 214, 234, 253
Metropolitan Police 64, 65, 66, 203
Midlands: coalfields of 8, 65; and
  overtime ban 36; ballots in 56;
  pits stay open in 72; strike
  deemed unofficial in 119; TGWU
  members continue working in
  149; and Nacods action 168; and
  power station supplies 217, 219,
  222, 224 *and see* Scunthorpe
Mills, John, dep. chairman, NCB 181
'Miners' Ballot Fund' 123
Miner, The 32
Miners' Federation of Great
  Britain 1, 10, 20
Mines and Quarries Act (1974)
  163–4
Monckton Hall, closure of 34
Monks, John (TUC) 228
Monopolies and Mergers
  Commission 30, 33, 181
Moor Green, closure of 34
Moore, John (Treasury) 130
Morgan, Idwal, Barnsley cokeman
  154
MORI polls 3, 55, 78, 266
Morning Star, The 11, 247
Morrison, Herbert 181
Moses, Ken (N. Derbys NCB)
  200–3, 212, 213
Murphy, Dennis, pres.
  Northumberland NUM 213, 246
Murray, Len, gen. sec. TUC: and
  support for NUM 146, 147, 150,
  152 'new realism' of 147, 157;
  and Brighton Congress 145, 153,
  155, 157
Myers, Nell, NUM press officer 195,
  265

Nacods (National Association of
  Colliery Overmen Deputies and
  Shotfirers) 50, 127, 186, 187; and
  NCB directive on pickets (15

Aug.) 161–7; importance of in
  mining industry 161, 163–4;
  pledges support at Brighton 145,
  165; and safety of mines 165–6;
  strike threat of 138, 161–2,
  166–71, 174, 185, 189, 192, A12;
  meets Acas 170, 174; draft
  agreement of with NCB 174–8,
  227, 242, 243 (threatened) 239,
  240; calls off strike 177; and
  NCB's final offer 242, 243, 246;
  and Scargill's last bid 250; and
  return to work 253
National Coal Board (NCB): and
  background to strike 2, 8, 18, 19,
  22, 264; and Plan for Coal 5–6;
  and 1967 redundancies 8; and
  1972 strike threat 10–11, 12–13,
  and see Plan for Coal; and
  wage-settlement (1979) 22; and
  revised Coal Industry Act 23;
  and 1981 confrontation with NUM
  23–5; encouraged to
  overproduce 26; MacGregor's
  appointment to 3, 27–30; losses
  of 28–34, 39, 43; assets of 30;
  closure programme of 31–2,
  33–4, 37–8, 43 (and pay offer)
  34; and overtime ban 33, 36,
  56; closure announcement by
  (6 March) 40, 42, 49, 50,
  128, 132–3, 175, 206, 230; and
  Cortonwood closure 41–3; offers
  new redundancy terms 50–1,
  53–4; and start of strike 41–3,
  49, 51; and Employment acts 68;
  Doncaster HQ of surrounded 70;
  and ballot issue 78; export trade
  of 88, 139; largest employer at
  Orgreave 101; and support of
  working miners 119, 120, 162; in
  peace talks with NUM
  (April–July) 111, 127–8; daily
  reports of to Walker 129, 130–1;
  close to agreement 127, 135;
  'propaganda offensive' of 134–5;

Index

Index

clash with police at Hunterston 87; at Orgreave 67, 91, 93, 94–6, 98 (defeated by police) 67, 83, 88–9, 99–105; intimidation by 107–8, 109, 115–16, 202–3; judicial limitations on 119; at Immingham 138 at power stations 151, 220; new ruling on proposed (Aug. 1) 152, 155; and NCB directive to pit deputies 161–5; Hart talks to 183; and back to work drive 203–5, 213–14 (at Cortonwood, Nov.) 206–10; and death of taxi-driver 214; picket to join Mother Theresa 234; disrupt marchback to work 254–6; insufficient for success of strike 263; *and see* Jones, David

pit deputies *see* Nacods

Plan for Coal: (1950) 5–6; (1974) 13–14, 19, (Scargill's attachment to) 14, 19, 155; targets of not achieved 20, 31, 47; MacGregor to produce new 132–3; joint discussion of (July) 135–6, (and word 'beneficial') 136, 155; and collapse of post-TUC talks 159–60, 227, 239

Point of Ayr pit, N. Wales 146, 120

Poland, coal from 91, 96, 222

police: and 1972 strike 13 at *Stockport Messenger* siege 4; and Ridley plan 18; 'low pay rise' of 33; mobilisation of massive presence of 41, 59, 63 (in Notts) 58, 59–62, 63, 67–8 (and government policy) 130 (cost of) 251; and death of Jones 62; and start of strike 63–7; crowd control training of 66–7, 97–8; powers of generate disquiet 69–71; attacked at Sheffield 82; in clash at Hunterston 87; at Scunthorpe 94–5; fight pickets at Orgreave 67, 83, 88–9, 99–105

(huge presence of) 95, 98–9, 103 (and use of horses) 108, 109 (violence of) 104 (and arrest of Scargill) 101, 209; at TUC Brighton 145; and arrests of coal pickers 186 at Shirebrook 202–4; and back to work drive 204–6, 209–10 (and link up with NCB) 205; in battle at Cortonwood 201, 206, 207–11; and taxi driver's death 214; violence blamed on 211, 226, 260; and miners' Christmas funds 232; at Cortonwood march back 255; *and see* National Reporting Centre, Police Support Units

Police Federation conference (1984) 67

Police Review 67

Police Support Units (PSU's) 63, 66–7, 211

Polkemmet pit, W. Lothian 86, 87–8, 166

Polmaise pit, Scotland 38, 46, 135, 175, 177, 252–3

Port Talbot steel complex 84, 85, 88, 105

power stations 12, 16–17, 26, 157; remain largely picket free 84; 261 picketing of 72–3, 102, 150; supplied during strike 107, 158, 217–24, 228, 262

Prendergast, David, Notts. area agent 81, 114, 116

Prescott, John, MP 230

Prior, James, MP 22

Pye Hill pit 109, 112

Ratcliffe on Soar generating station 75, 107

Ravenscraig steel complex 84, 86–8

Reagan, Pres. Ronald 167

Reece, Gordon (NCB) 182, 184

Rees, George, S. Wales area sec. 240–1

Richards, John, correspondent 195

Index